How Spanish Grew

HOW
SPANISH
GREW

by

ROBERT K. SPAULDING

UNIVERSITY OF CALIFORNIA PRESS

BERKELEY AND LOS ANGELES

1967

University of California Press
Berkeley and Los Angeles

Cambridge University Press
London, England

Printed by offset in the United States of America

¿Si buscamos suauidad i dulçura? ella la tiene acompañada de gran ser, i magestad, conuiniente a pechos varoniles, i nada afeminados. ¿Si grauedad? tienela tan apazible, que no admite arrogancia, ni liuiandad. ... ¿Si modos de dezir? en ellos ninguna lengua le haze ventaja, tan proporcionados, i ajustados, que sin afectacion declaran, i contienen gran emphasis i significacion. ... ¿Si copia, i abundançia? alcançala tan grande, que no mendiga, como algunos piensan, sino antes como riquissima descriue, pinta, i enseña con variedad, i buen adorno de palabras, vna gran multitud de cosas, que en otras lenguas no se hallan.—Bernardo Aldrete, *Del origen y principio de la lengua castellana* (1606)

Preface

SYSTEMATIC *historical grammars of Spanish are few as yet, but even so I do not mean to offer hereinafter a substitute for the works of this kind which eminent scholars have provided. Rather is it my notion that in the pages following students of Spanish and those generally given to the acquisition of knowledge—and to them is this book addressed—may view in outline the evolution of the language of Spain in its sounds, its forms, its constructions, and its words, with consideration of their relation to the political and social history of the country whose speech they represent. Only a knowledge of Latin and Spanish is assumed, and nomenclature is reduced to the minimum.*

The direct ancestor of this volume was Walter von Wartburg's Evolution et structure de la langue française *(deuxième édition, The University of Chicago Press, 1934), which in its turn looks back to Otto Jespersen's* Growth and Structure of the English Language *(fourth edition, New York, D. Appleton and Company, 1923). Confessing to the same inspiration is William James Entwistle's* The Spanish Language, *together with Portuguese, Catalan and Basque (further described below), which is both broader and narrower than my treatment of the subject, and which I cannot fail to duplicate in part. His many pages devoted to the Spanish of America have made my invading that territory quite unnecessary.*

In the matter of illustrative quotation I have attempted a more generous documenting than was the intention of

Professor Wartburg. My sources are everywhere stated, but it is to Rufino José Cuervo and Ramón Menéndez Pidal that I am most indebted. For all that, there is a proportionate amount of material of my own collecting. In the desire to be of service to those interested in following out the evolution of Spanish I have listed my bibliographical sources more fully and definitely than my most immediate predecessor. On the other hand, the space devoted to Spanish stylistics, given the paucity of information on the subject, is regrettably small in comparison to the discussion in the Evolution et structure.

The organization of the existing data, qualified by my own first-hand gatherings, I may claim as my own. This becomes the truer, and the more difficult to accomplish, since the material in print is less abundant the nearer we come to the language of the modern period. Perhaps I should not be in any haste to make assertion of originality for the attempt to characterize each period, especially in its morphology, syntax, and vocabulary. There are few studies of this sort to lean upon, few essays, I say, viewing any epoch as a whole. The same is true of the traits of the dialects and of all and sundry deviations from the standard language.

It is intentional that monographs which are recorded in the works contained in the General Bibliography or elsewhere are not again and separately mentioned, unless of prime importance. Especially is this true of older and inaccessible studies. Intentional, too, is the occasional preference for Spanish translations of learned treatises, for these will not frighten off certain prospective readers, and those who choose to consult the translation must apprehend that there is also an original, just as they will appreciate that it is superfluous to list under Bibliography *titles which are already in the books that are included there.*

R. K. S.

Contents

CHAPTER   PAGE

1. The Indo-European Languages: Spanish Among Them 1

2. Pre-Roman Spain
   The Iberians and the Basques 5
   The Celts 11
   The Phoenicians and the Carthaginians . . . 13
   The Greeks 16

3. Roman Spain
   Spain in the Roman Empire 21
   The Latin Spoken in Spain 28
   The Chief Characteristics of Spoken Latin . . 33

4. Germanic Spain
   The Migrations; The Visigoths in Particular . 45
   The Germanic Element in Spanish 49

5. Arabic Spain
   The Appearance of the Arabs in the West; Their Ascendancy in Spain 53
   The Cultural Impulse 56

6. The Period of Old Spanish (to 1500)
   Toward the Rise of Castile 63
   The Spread of Castilian 68
   The Earliest Texts and Early Literary Texts . 71
   The Matter of Orthography 76
   Evolution of Sounds 82
   Evolution of Forms 100

CHAPTER   PAGE

6. The Period of Old Spanish (*Continued*)
    Evolution of Constructions   118
    Vocabulary   130

7. The Period of Spanish Ascendancy
    (1500–1700)
    The Growing Interest in Spanish, the National
        Language   135
    Style and Vocabulary   141
    Evolution of Sounds   153
    Evolution of Forms   166
    Evolution of Constructions   169
    The Position of Spanish in Europe   174

8. The Period of French Prestige (1700–1808)
    The Progress of Scholarship *a la francesa* . . .   187
    A Language Gallicized   191

9. The Modern Period (1808–   )
    Some Influential Grammatical Contributions .   197
    Evolution of Sounds, Forms, and Constructions   201
    The Orthographic Accent   207
    Vocabulary   209
    Slang   217
    Leonese   220
    Aragonese   225
    Andalusian   229
    Popular Spanish   236
    The Acoustic Impression of Castilian   243
Index   247

Abbreviations

C.L.	Classic Latin	[ĉ]	*ch* as in *church*
Eng.	English	[s]	*s* as in *so*
Fr.	French	[š]	*sh* as in *shoot*
Ger.	German	[ŝ]	*ts* as in *boots*
Gk.	Greek	[y]	*y* as in *yes*
Lat.	Latin	[ŷ]	*j* as in *Jones*
M.S.	Modern Spanish	[ž]	*z* as in *azure*
O.S.	Old Spanish	[ẑ]	*dz* as in *adze*
Sp.	Spanish	[x]	Castilian *jota*, as in *jabón*
V.L.	Vulgar Latin		
>	"develops into"	[i̯]	semi-consonantal *i*, as in *bien*
<	"develops from"		
*	means that a form is conjectured, but not documented	[u̯]	semi-consonantal *u*, as in *bueno*

The hook under a vowel (ę, ǫ) indicates open quality; the dot (ẹ, ọ) indicates close quality.

In citations roman numerals indicate the largest subdivision of a work: book or part if it is divided into books or parts, chapter, act, or poem; arabic numerals indicate the subdivision next in order.

General Bibliography

THE WORKS listed below are of such frequent reference throughout the pages following that hereafter they will be cited only in abbreviated form.

BELLO, A., and CUERVO, R. J. *Gramática de la lengua castellana,* décimonovena edición, Paris, Roger y Chernoviz, 1918.

BOURCIEZ, E. *Eléments de linguistique romane,* troisième édition révisée, Paris, Klincksieck, 1930.

ENTWISTLE, WILLIAM J. *The Spanish Language, together with Portuguese, Catalan and Basque,* London, Faber and Faber, n.d. [1936].

HANSSEN, F. *Gramática histórica de la lengua castellana,* Halle a.d. Saale, Max Niemeyer, 1913; Buenos Aires, El Ateneo, 1945.

LENZ, R. *La oración y sus partes,* tercera edición, Madrid, 1935.

MENÉNDEZ PIDAL, R. *Manual de gramática histórica española,* séptima edición, Madrid, 1944.

———. "Orígenes del español," Madrid, Hernando, 1926 (*Revista de filología española, Anejo I*).

MEYER-LÜBKE, W. *Introducción a la lingüística románica,* versión de la tercera edición alemana ... por Américo Castro, Madrid, 1926.

———. *Romanisches-Etymologisches Wörterbuch,* dritte vollständig neubearbeitete Auflage, Heidelberg, C. Winter, 1930–1935.

NAVARRO TOMÁS, T. *Compendio de ortología española,* Madrid, 1927.

———. *Manual de pronunciación española,* cuarta edición corregida y aumentada, Madrid, 1932.

NEBRIJA. *Gramática de la lengua castellana,* etc., edited ... by Ig. González-Llubera, Oxford University Press, 1926.

VALDÉS, JUAN DE. *Diálogo de la lengua,* prólogo de J. Moreno Villa, Madrid, Calleja, 1919.

Important works which have appeared since the publication of the original edition are:

GARCÍA DE DIEGO, V. *Manual de dialectología española,* Madrid, Instituto de Cultura Hispánica, 1946.

LAPESA, R. *Historia de la lengua española,* Madrid–Buenos Aires–Cádiz, Escelicer, n.d.

MAP O1

1

The Indo-European Languages: Spanish Among Them

AT SOME time in the remote past there was spoken at a point, or points, of what now constitutes Europe and Southwestern Asia a language from which, after many, many changes, have descended the principal tongues, ancient and modern, of those areas.[1] Possibly this very old language, usually known as primitive Indo-European or Indo-Germanic, arose along the eastern and southern shores of the Baltic Sea. Lithuanian, one of the speeches of the region, is believed to preserve with great fidelity the "phonetic system of the hypothetical Indo-European parent-speech." The Indo-European (or Indo-Germanic) "family" is the most important of all linguistic groups, comprising Sanskrit and many other languages, both dead and living, of India; Persian; Armenian; Greek; Albanian; the Balto-Slavic group (Lithuanian, Lettish, Russian, Polish, Bohemian-Czech, Serbian, Bulgarian, etc.); the Germanic group (Gothic, long since extinct; German; Scandinavian; English); Celtic; and the Italic group (Oscan, Umbrian, Latin). Latin has, in the respective parts of the Roman Empire, become Italian, French, Provençal, Catalan, Spanish, Portu-

---

[1] One of the earliest catalogues of the languages of the known world, among those with any scientific pretensions, was compiled at the beginning of the nineteenth century by a Spanish scholar, the Jesuit Lorenzo Hervás y Panduro, *Catálogo de las lenguas de las naciones conocidas* (Madrid, 6 vols., 1800–1805).

guese, Rhaeto-Romanic (spoken, and with no great uniformity, by a relatively small number of people in Alpine valleys in northeastern Italy and southeastern Switzerland), and Rumanian—but the speech of Rumania, the former Roman province of Dacia, has been greatly modified, particularly in its vocabulary, by the infiltration of Slavic and other elements.

Scholars are no longer so confident of their knowledge of the "primitive" Indo-European language as they were a scant century ago when one of them (Schleicher) made bold to compose and print a fable in what he thought gave a fair idea of it. Not so remote in time (hence more readily available and more abundant are the materials) is the basic tongue of the Romance languages, Latin. Here we can trace, often without gaps, the steps which lead from the spoken idiom of the days of the Roman Republic and Empire to present-day Spanish.

The population of Spain, including the Canary Islands, which now constitute two of its fifty provinces, and the Balearic Islands, is 24,583,096.[2] To be sure, of this figure over twenty per cent are Catalans, whose language perhaps should be grouped with the Provençal of southern France. Then, something less than half a million are Basques, of whose language more will be said in a subsequent chapter. The Galicians (two millions and above) in northwestern Spain, use a dialect which is as much Portuguese as Spanish. These three groups, Catalans, Basques, Galicians, employ Spanish as their official language, and to few of them is it totally unknown. Figures for the Central and South Amer-

---

[2] The figures in this paragraph are taken from the *World Almanac* for 1939.

ican countries warrant scrutiny, and they do not necessarily indicate the numbers of those who know Spanish, for particularly in Mexico, Guatemala, Peru, and Bolivia, the native races are often entirely ignorant of the language of their conquerors. The population of Mexico by the census of 1930, is sixteen millions and over, of which two millions speak no Spanish whatsoever. The population of Central America is a trifle over seven millions. The islands of the West Indies (Cuba, Puerto Rico, Santo Domingo) add seven millions more. South America (Argentina, Bolivia, Chile, Colombia, Ecuador, Paraguay, Peru, Uruguay, Venezuela) increase the total by nearly forty-four millions. Finally, the Philippine Islands add thirteen and a half millions, but only two-thirds of a million are held to speak Spanish. And the descendants of the Jews expelled from Spain in 1492, who spread principally to the southern and eastern shores of the Mediterranean Sea, have not been counted, nor have the inhabitants of various Spanish possessions on or off the coast of Africa, nor of the Spanish-speaking areas in the southwestern United States. Even thus, the figure rises to a minimum of eighty millions, higher than for any other Romance language, and followed at a considerable distance by French (sixty-two millions) and Italian (forty-one millions).

When we consider the role Spain has played in world colonization, Spain's specific contribution to the arts, to literature, and to religion, its speech—so worthy in its own right, and called by a modern Swedish scholar (F. Wulff) the most impressive in sound (*sonore*), the most harmonious, the most elegant, and the most expressive of the Neo-

~ 2 ~

Pre-Roman Spain

The Iberians and the Basques

Numerous are the traces of prehistoric man in the Iberian peninsula. In almost all parts of the country remains have been found in the form of dwellings, tombs, fortifications, implements and utensils, and manifestations of primitive art. Most impressive perhaps are the colored drawings of animals on the walls of the caves of Altamira, near Santander on the Bay of Biscay. These are usually held to be the finest of their age, the Upper Magdalenian period (i.e., the period representing the highest degree of civilization attained during the time of the earliest known human culture, namely, the Stone Age).

Herodotus (*History,* I, 163) uses, most vaguely, the term Iberia for the Spanish peninsula, and in time the country as a whole was so called, especially by the Greeks, but more strictly speaking the Iberians lived in the valley of the Ebro (Lat. *Iberus*), near its mouth, or around its headwaters. The Greek geographer Strabo, writing in the first century B.C., has left a good early account of the country in his *Geography (Book III)*. According to him, the chief Spanish peoples were, in the northwest, the Celtici and the Gallaeci; to their east the Astures; continuing eastward, the Cantabri, the Vascones or Basques, the Cerretani and the Indigetes who dwelt approximately in the province of Gerona; in

Valencia and southeastern Aragon, the Edetani or Sidetani; in Alicante and Murcia, the Contestani; in central and eastern Andalusia, the Turduli; in the west of Andalusia, the Turdetani, who by Roman times had forgotten their own language (Strabo, *Geography*, III, 2, 15); in central Portugal and a portion of Extremadura, the Lusitani; in the vicinity of Ciudad Real, the Oretani, whose name is recalled in the *Cordillera oretana*; in the region of Madrid, Toledo (their capital, according to Pliny), and part of Guadalajara, the Carpetani; the Vettones in western Spain between the Duero and the Guadiana; the Vaccaei in the north of Old Castile; the Celtiberi, in part of Aragon and in New Castile. There were other tribes with whose names Strabo is reluctant, he says, to fill his page, and we may safely follow his example.

In the view of some scholars the Ligurians preceded the Iberians (using the word in its broader sense of pre-Roman natives of Spain) in their occupancy of the peninsula.[1] The relation of the tribes above mentioned to the earliest Iberians, who probably came from northern Africa, is a matter of conjecture. Possibly, though this is a question long debated and still undecided, one of the most ancient groups is represented by the Basques of the present day, who may be descended from the Ligurians. The area now occupied by the Basques is the provinces of Vizcaya (= Biscay), Guipúzcoa, Alava, and also the northern portion of Navarre, forming roughly a semicircle having San Sebastián as its center. There are Basques also across the Pyrenees in France in the province of Basses-Pyrénées. In the last half century

---

[1] Cf. Adolfo Schulten, *Hispania*, Barcelona, 1920, pp. 101, 108–109.

the limits of their territory in Spain have shrunk, particularly to the south and east, Spanish being spoken very generally throughout Alava.

As has been suggested, the relation of Basque to Iberian, assuming that there was a speech to some degree common to the several ancient tribes, is uncertain, but the presence of Basque elements in widely separated place names leads to the suspicion of a connection between the two. Thus Elvira, the site of ruins near Granada, may contain the element *ili* or *iri,* one form of the Basque word meaning "town," and *berri,* meaning "new." The ancient designation of the place was Iliber(r)is. Iria Flavia (now called Padrón) in Galicia, and legendary as the landing place of the stone coffin bearing the body of Saint James, may embody the same word. Such similarities, however, are by no means conclusive, and the less so for Iria Flavia when one observes a Julia Iria in northern Italy.

Strabo (*Geography,* III, 1, 6) apprises us that the Turdetani or Turduli of the region of the Betis had an alphabet, and "ancient writings, poems, and metrical laws six thousand years old, as they say. The other Iberians are likewise furnished with an alphabet, although not of the same form, nor do they speak the same language."

The language of the Iberians, preserved in a few inscriptions, transcribed but not yet translated, was presumably still in existence at the end of the first century A.D., for Tacitus mentions a peasant of the province of Hispania Citerior (or Tarraconensis) who refused to betray his accomplices in crime, *voce magna sermone patrio frustra se interrogari clamavit* (*Annals,* IV, 45).

Words inherited by Spanish from pre-Roman times are not numerous. Most, if not all of them, have been questioned, and many of them, like *izquierdo* and *toca,* can be related to modern Basque terms. Among the words which are deemed to antedate the Romans are the family name *García; arroyo,* small stream, rivulet; *balsa,* pond; *baluz,* grain of gold; *carpio,* hill, appearing in proper names (cf. *Bernardo del Carpio*); *coscojo,* kermes berry; *manteca,* fat, lard; *minio,* cinnabar or red lead; *morón* (?), hummock; *muga,* boundary, limit; *nava,* plain surrounded by mountains (cf. *Navarra,* Navarre); *sapo,* toad; *urraca,* magpie; *vega,* fertile plain; and many words ending in *rro, rra: becerro,* calf; *bizarro,* gallant, spirited; *cachorro,* puppy, cub; *cencerro,* cowbell; *garra,* claw; *guijarro–a,* pebble; *pizarra,* slate; *zorra,* fox. But *catarro,* catarrh, is Greek. *Cigarro–a,* cigar, cicada < *cicada + rro–a;*[2] *tabarro,* horsefly < *tabanus + rro; zamarra,* sheep-skin jacket < Arabic. *Burro* is Latin. The etymology of *chorro,* jet; *cotorra,* magpie; *modorra,* drowsiness; *pachorra,* sluggishness; *panarra,* simpleton; *pitorro,* tube; *sarro,* incrustation, tartar; *tabarra,* bore; *tarro,* jar; *tunarra,* vagabondage, is dubious, but the extent of the suffix is obvious. *Sarna,* itch (*Est sicca scabies: hanc vulgus sarnam appellant,* says St. Isidore of Seville, *Etymologiae,* IV, 8, 6, writing in the sixth century of our era), may be either Celtic or Iberian-Basque. Proper names like *Iñigo* and *Javier,* formerly spelled *Xavier,* deriving respectively from the saints of Basque origin, St. Ignatius of Loyola, the founder of the Jesuit order, and St. Francis Xavier (Xavier is originally a place name, a town not far from Pamplona),

---

[2] Cigarro may derive from the Maya word *siqar.* Cf. Meyer-Lübke, *Wörterbuch,* no. 7950*b.*

are originally of Basque provenance. The most noteworthy
pre-Roman word which does not seem to be Basque is
páramo, meaning "bleak, desertlike tableland." There is
indeed an abundance of such terrain in Spain. This word
appears first[3] in an inscription of the second century A.D.
found in the city of León in 1862 upon the demolition of
a wall:

CERVOM ALTIFRON

TUM CORNUA

DICAT DIANAE

TULLIUS

QUOS VICIT IN PA

RAMI AEQUORE

VECTUS FEROCI

SONIPEDE[4]

The term is now found in place names mostly (*El páramo*
south of León, *La paramera de Molina* in eastern Guadalajara), even in South America, where the same topographical
feature occurs. Menéndez Pidal (*Manual,* § 4, 1) now considers *páramo* of Ligurian origin.

---

[3] It appears also in the minor geographer Julius Honorius. Cf. Schulten, *Hispania,* p. 30.

[4] "To Diana does Tully consecrate the horns of the long-faced[?] deer which
he took on the level of the tableland, borne on his swift horse" (*Corpus inscriptionum latinarum,* II, 2660).

BIBLIOGRAPHY

CASTRO, AMÉRICO. *Lengua, enseñanza y literatura*, Madrid, V. Suárez, 1924, pp. 9–28.

CASTRO GUISASOLA, F. *El enigma del vascuence ante las lenguas indoeuropeas*, Madrid, 1944.

GÓMEZ MORENO, MANUEL. "Sobre los iberos y su lengua," in *Homenaje ofrecido a Menéndez Pidal*, Madrid, Hernando, 1925, III, 475–499.

————. "De epigrafía ibérica," in *Revista de filología española*, IX (1922), 341–366.

HÜBNER, EMIL. *Monumenta linguae ibericae*, Berolini, Typis et Imprensis G. Reimeri, 1893.

MENÉNDEZ PIDAL, RAMÓN, "Sobre las vocales ibéricas ę y ǫ en los nombres toponímicos," in *Revista de filología española*, V (1918), 225–255.

————. "Sobre el substrato mediterráneo occidental," in *Zeitschrift für romanische Philologie*, LIX (1939), 189–206.

NAVARRO TOMÁS, T. "Rasgos esenciales de las vocales castellanas," in *Philological Quarterly*, XXI (1942), 8–16.

PHILIPON, E. *Les ibères*, Paris, Champion, 1909, pp. 1 ff.

SCHULTEN, A. "Ein keltiberischer Städtebund," in *Hermes*, L (1915), 247–260.

————. *Numantia, die Ergebnisse der Ausgrabungen*, 1905–1912, München, F. Bruckmann, 1914–1931, 4 vols.

The Celts

About 1000 B.C. the Celts are thought to have entered Spain by the eastern end of the Pyrenees. In the sixth century B.C. another and more consequential invasion, coming this time from southwestern France, spread Celtic tribes over most of the peninsula, where traces have been reported at such widely separated points as Coimbra in Portugal, Segorbe in the vicinity of Valencia, Cazlona near Linares, and Cártama near Málaga. Territory especially belonging to the Celts was the west (Galicia and Portugal), and the northeastern portion of the central plateau where numerous fortifications (*castros*) and fortified cities (*citanias*) have been unearthed. Strabo (*Geography,* III, 3, 5) assigns to the Celtici the area of Galicia, adding that a colony of Celts settled along the Guadiana; Pomponius Mela and Ptolemy also emphasize the Celticism of southwestern Spain. The Celtiberians (though whether the term indicates a fusion of the Celts with Iberians can properly be doubted)[5] dominated the area we now know as the province of Soria. The record of the Celtic advance southward appears in the word *briga,* eminence, fortification. This is found in a large number of place names, especially in the west and on the central plateau: *Abobrica* (Pliny, *Natural History,* IV, 34); *Arcobriga, Flaviobriga* (Pliny, IV, 34); *Juliobriga* in the north (Pliny, III, 4); *Segorbe* near Valencia < *Segobriga; Augustobriga* in Soria; *Coimbra* < *Conimbriga; Setúbal* in southern Portugal < *Cetobriga; Mirobriga* and *Nertobriga* in Andalusia (cf. Pliny, III, 4). In fact, the number and the antique savor

---

[5] Cf. Schulten, *Hispania,* p. 111, n. The term is first used by Livy (*History,* XXI, 57).

of towns so named leads Pérez Galdós humorously to invent
a "Ficóbriga" (*Marianela*, II). But not all these settlements
were necessarily named by the Celts, for the Romans probably applied the term to many of their own municipalities.

Such Celtic words as Spanish possesses were presumably
carried into Spain by the Romans, who had previously met
them in Gaul. Among the most ancient, so old that the
Romans themselves hardly knew them to be borrowings,
are *abedul*, birchtree; *aloya*, lark (dialectal in Alava and
Burgos); *bragas*, breeches; *caballo*(?), horse; *camisa*, shirt;
carro, cart; *cerveza*, beer; *sayo*(?), smock. Others are Aragonese *arañón*, wild plum; *berro*, water cress; *brío*, vigor;
camino, road, way; *flecha*(?), arrow; *gato*, cat; *gavilla*,
sheaf; *grava*, gravel; *greña*, matted hair; *jamuga*, mule
chair; *lanza*, lance; *legua*, league; *losa*, flagstone; *ola*, wave;
pieza, piece; *roca*, rock; *taladro*, auger; *tamiz*, sieve; *tona*,
rind, cream on surface of milk (now used only in Galicia
and Portugal); *truhán*, scoundrel; *vasallo*, vassal; and the
verb *cambiar*, exchange. *Cabaña*, formerly held to be a
Celtic word, is now more often labeled as of unknown
origin. Most of these words have to do with material things,
few with hunting or war, though Livy mentions the Celts
as fine mercenaries (*History*, XXIV, 49). The Celts, then,
were a people who had lost their independence, both political and cultural, and who retained of their own language
only the names of objects which they felt to be theirs or
which they did not find in the Mediterranean area (e.g.,
abedul).

BIBLIOGRAPHY

Meyer-Lübke. *Introducción*, §§ 32–35.
Schulten, A. *Numantia*, I, 91 ff.

THE PHOENICIANS AND THE CARTHAGINIANS

The Phoenicians, carrying their trade around the Mediterranean coast line, arrived, by the eleventh century B.C. if we may believe the legend related by the historian Velleius Paterculus (*Compendium of Roman History*, I, 2, 6), and the corroborating statement (§ 134) of the *De mirabilibus auscultationibus* (formerly attributed to Aristotle), at southern Spain, where they set up "factories," or at least had ports of call, at Málaga (mentioned as a Phoenician settlement by Strabo), at Carteya (between Gibraltar and Algeciras; the site is now named El Rocadillo), at Adra (the ancient Abdera), at Almuñécar (anciently Sexi), and at Cádiz, which, as Gaddir, shortly became their richest and most prosperous city. If the Greek geographer tells the truth, it was second only to Rome in population. Then, too, there is the vague, indeterminate, and problematic Tartessos = Tarshish = Tharsis (near Huelva). Tartessos, possibly meaning "colonized regions," appears to have been the Phoenicians' name for southern Spain, or rather southwestern Spain. There was, it appears, probably at the mouth of the Guadalquivir, a settlement which bore the same name (cf. Strabo, *Geography,* III, 2, 11; Herodotus, *History,* I, 163). Some identify Tartessos with the Tarshish of the Bible (Ezekiel 27:12, "Tarshish was thy merchant by reason of the multitude of all kind of riches; with silver, iron, tin, and lead, they traded in thy fairs"; I Kings 10:22, "once in three years came the navy of Tarshish, bringing gold, and silver, ivory, and apes, and peacocks"; Jeremiah 10:9, "Silver spread into plates is brought from Tarshish"). On the other hand,

Pliny (*Natural History,* III, 3) says that the settlement of Carteya was called Tartessos by the Greeks. The Romans, also mistakenly, assumed that Gades was the same as Tartessos.

To Spain the Phoenicians brought the perfection of certain industries (mining, the salting of fish, the extraction of salt) and probably the art of writing, since most Iberian inscriptions use the Punic alphabet. From it they took the precious metals for which Spain has always been a storehouse (silver, gold, lead). These they traded for the tin of the Cassiterides (vaguely connected with both Cornwall and northwestern Spain, especially a group of small islands off the coast of Pontevedra)[6] and amber from the Baltic Sea.

About 500 B.C. Carthage, formerly a Phoenician colony, replaced Tyre and Sidon as the master of the Andalusian coast, incidentally destroying the city of Tartessos. The activities of the Carthaginians in Spain centered at the fine harbor of Cartagena or New Carthage (refounded *ca.* 243 B.C. by Hasdrubal, the son-in-law of Hamilcar Barca), although Hannibal penetrated at least as far to the west as Salamanca, which he captured in 217 B.C., and all the peninsula as far as the Duero and the Ebro was in their hands. Mahón in Minorca takes its name from Mago, the third son of Hamilcar, and youngest brother of Hannibal. The Romans, too, coveted the wealth and man power of Spain. The Second Punic War was provoked by an attack on the part of the Carthaginians on the city of Saguntum (Gk. Ζάκυνθος) near Valencia. Saguntum, originally an Iberian town but later settled by Greeks, the Romans claimed as

---

[6] Cf. Schulten, *Hispania,* pp. 42 and 74.

an ally. This war (218–201 B.C.) ended with the defeat of the Carthaginians, despite the victories of Hannibal in Italy after his conquest of Saguntum and subsequent march on Rome. The brilliant success of Publius Cornelius Scipio (afterward surnamed Africanus), who captured Cartagena in 210–209 B.C. (Polybius, *Histories,* I, 2–20; Livy, *History,* XXVI, 42), made an end of the Carthaginian domain in Spain.

The contributions of the Phoenicians or their successors the Carthaginians to the language of Spain are few. Some scholars believe that Hispania, the name favored by the Romans for Spain, has its root in a Semitic word meaning "hidden, concealed, remote," a not unsuitable designation for Spain from the point of view of the ancients. More poetic, and less probable, is the derivation suggested by St. Isidore, Hesperia, "the Western Land" (*Etymologiae,* XIV, 4, 28; cf. IX, 2, 126). Cádiz, the Roman Gades, was, to the traders from northern Africa, Gaddir, meaning "enclosure." Place names aside, there are only a very few Spanish words contributed by the Phoenicians and the Carthaginians, and they have passed through Latin: as *mapa, mata.*

BIBLIOGRAPHY

Bourciez. *Eléments,* § 65c.

Costa, Joaquín. *Estudios ibéricos,* Madrid, 1891–1895, Vol. I, *passim.*

Schulten, A. *Tartessos; contribución a la historia antigua de occidente,* Madrid, Revista de Occidente, 1924, *passim.*

THE GREEKS

Another seafaring people anxious for trade, the Greeks, probably came to the southern shores of Iberia in the seventh century B.C. Herodotus (*History,* IV, 152) relates that a Greek sailing ship from Samos which a storm had driven beyond the Pillars of Hercules "at last, by some special guiding providence, reached Tartessos. This trading town was in those days a virgin port unfrequented by merchants, and the Samians in consequence made by the return voyage a profit greater than any Greeks before their day" (Rawlinson's translation). Systematic search for the site of this city has been unsuccessful, though it was presumably near the mouth of the Guadalquivir, and the term Tartessos is more often applied to the whole of southwestern Spain, as has been said (p. 13). Another ancient point of contact was Mainake, at the mouth of the River Vélez near Málaga. Its ruins were still visible in the first century B.C. (Strabo, *Geography,* III, 4). However, the principal colonies of the Greeks, and they were the first actual colonizers of Spain, were settled from the base of Marseille along the northeastern coast, not far below the French frontier. The modern fishing village of Rosas occupies the site of Rhode; Ampurias (ruins) is Emporion, where Scipio landed during the Second Punic War. Of the defenses and plan of Emporion Livy gives a detailed account (*History,* XXXIV, 9). Farther south stands Denia (from the Roman name Dianium, for here stood a celebrated temple of Diana) to represent the Greek city of Artemisium or Hemeroskopeion. (Possibly its founding was contemporaneous with that of Mainake.)

Here Sertorius, the Roman general, later had his naval base. The Greek cities were in time Romanized, and it is unlikely that they made any specific additions to the Spanish vocabulary. In the advance of culture, however, their influence on the native races is plain in sculpture (the *dama de Elche*), pottery, vases, and architectural moldings. The earliest Iberian money coined is distinctly Greek in type. The introduction, or at least the cultivation, of the olive tree and the grapevine is usually credited to the Greeks.

Most of the Greek terms in Spanish found their way thence through Latin, and they adapted their vowel and consonant sounds to those of the latter speech. Among the vowels, υ and η became *u* and *e* in Latin: τύμβη > Latin (and Sp.) *tumba;* ἀποθήκη > Latin *apotheca* (Sp. *bodega*). φ,χ,θ,ζ were transcribed as *p, c, t, s:* φάλαγξ > Latin (and Sp.) *palanca;* χριστός > Latin *Cristus* (in inscriptions) > Sp. *Cristo;* κιθάρα > Latin *citera* (*Appendix Probi*) > Sp. *citara;* μᾶζα > Latin *massa* (Sp. *masa*). People of learning tried later to approximate more closely the real value of these Greek consonants by using *ph = f, ch, th, z* respectively: Φίλιππος > Latin *Philippus* (Sp. *Felipe*); χάρτης > Latin *charta* > Sp. *carta;* ῥυθμός > Latin *rhythmus* (Sp. *ritmo*); ζῳδιακός > Latin *zodiacus* (Sp. *zodiaco*); but the populace clung to *p, c, t:* κόλαφος > Latin *col(a)pus* (Sp. *golpe*); χάλιξ > Latin *calx* (Sp. *cal*). Similarly, by the learned, υ was rendered more exactly by *y = i; η* in time by *i:* ἀποθήκη > Sp. *botica;* κρύσταλλος > Latin *crystallum* (Sp. *cristal*).

To the Greek substantive ending *ία* corresponds the Latin *ĭa.* The former, doubtless thought more cultivated, has spread throughout Spanish, and is the only one used in modern formations (*demasía, habladuría, muchachería, nadería*). Thus μανία > Latin *mania* (cf. Eng. mania) > Spanish *manía*. *Maña* is probably derived from the Latin form with the short *i*. Yet most words of early introduction have retained the short *i*:ἐκκλησία > Latin *ecclesia* > Spanish *iglesia;* ἰστορία > Latin and Spanish *historia;* βυβλία > Latin and Spanish *biblia*. However, *Orgía* had a short *i* even in Greek, the correct Academy admits only *disentería* (though other authorities prefer the older form *disentería*), and the uninformed pronounce *lacería* with the stress on the *i*, all because *ía* seems more "proper." In some geographical names *ia* has given way to *ía*. Thus, though *Alejandria* and *Etiopia* were the usual pronunciation in the day of Lope de Vega, the current form is *Alejandría,* while there is still hesitation between *Etiopia* and *Etiopía.*

To list even a small part of the everyday words deriving ultimately from Greek (e.g., *barato, cada, cara, gobernar, madeja, máquina, playa, tío*) is obviously impractical in this book, but attention can be drawn to the great number of terms, employed in one or another branch of learning, which have come into the language at various times, especially during the sixteenth and early seventeenth centuries and again in the nineteenth and twentieth, when science made prodigious leaps, necessitating constantly a new terminology for every advance. Many of these words were adopted from a Latinized form, and many of them were made up for the occasion from Greek elements: *fonógrafo, pantógrafo, telegrafía; ángel, bautizar, diablo, obispo, paraíso, presbítero; astronomía, esfera, telescopio; botánica, física, química, filtro, rodio; antiséptico, cardíaco, artritis, neuritis; filosofía, gramática, frase, poema, drama; kilogramo, termómetro, decalitro,* and finally the neologisms of *hiperestesia, microparasitología, psicoterapia, psiquiatría.* Scientific terms like these last have often entered Spanish by way of translation of German treatises.

BIBLIOGRAPHY

CARPENTER, R. *The Greeks in Spain,* New York, Longmans, Green and Co., 1925 (Bryn Mawr Notes and Monographs, VI).

CUERVO, RUFINO J. *Apuntaciones críticas sobre el lenguaje bogotano,* séptima edición, Bogotá, Editorial "El gráfico," 1939, § 99.

MENÉNDEZ PIDAL. *Manual,* § 4, 2, and § 6, 4.

TORO Y GISBERT, M. *Ortología castellana de nombres propios,* Paris, Ollendorff, n.d.

♔ 3 ♔

Roman Spain

SPAIN IN THE ROMAN EMPIRE

AFTER the power of the Carthaginians was broken, there began the slow work of Romanizing the country. The task required nearly two centuries (201–19 B.C.), and in the same stretch of time the Empire had come to embrace all Italy, Greece, the area we now call France, the British Isles, a part of Germany, Rumania, and much of Asia Minor and North Africa. The resistance presented by the native Spaniards was less on the eastern coast and in the south, where foreign faces were no new thing, but increased rapidly as the legions pushed into the land of the Celtiberi and toward the mountainous home of the Cantabri and the Astures. The unwillingness of the native tribes to unite in a common cause (Strabo, *Geography,* III, 4, 5), though it perhaps made the outcome certain to be in the invader's favor, made the Romans' position the harder, for a guerrilla warfare was hazardous to an army which was accustomed to fighting in formation. In particular one Viriatus, a former shepherd, did manage to unite several tribes in the center and west, and for several years caused the enemy serious annoyance until his assassination, through treason, removed him (139 B.C.). The Romans founded Valencia for his soldiers.

Well known to historians is the siege of Numantia (Sp. Numancia), the capital of a federation of Celtiberian tribes, lying on the banks of the Duero above Soria in Old Castile. After 152 B.C. the Roman army was utterly defeated there on four separate occasions, but at last Scipio Aemilianus, after another year's maneuvering (134–133 B.C.), brought the Numantians to the extremity of firing their city and dying within its walls. On this subject Cervantes composed a patriotic tragedy *La Numancia* (not printed until 1784). Ascending the Ebro, we come to Calahorra in the province of Logroño, the scene of a siege by Afranius (71 B.C.) which was such that the famine there endured became a stock phrase, *hambre calagurritana*. In 19 B.C. Agrippa, the favorite of Augustus Caesar, led an army into the territory of the untamed Cantabri (*Cantabrum indoctum juga ferre nostra,* Horace, *Odes,* II, 6, 2), who, after heroic suffering, were shortly and finally subdued (cf. *Crónica general,* chaps. 136–137).

Civil discord in Rome had its repercussions in Spain, which was often the battleground for opposing factions from the homeland. Huesca, the ancient Osca, forty-odd miles north of Saragossa, was the military headquarters of Sertorius, who was arrayed against the party of Sulla (*ca.* 75 B.C.). Sertorius, who was of Spanish blood, even set up a government of his own, as generals will. At Lérida (Ilerda in those days; observe the element *ili*; p. 7), half way between Saragossa and Barcelona, but so remote that young Romans were threatened with rustication there (Horace, *Epistles,* I, 20, 13), Julius Caesar in 49 B.C. won a great victory over the adherents of Pompey. In Andalusia, Caesar again defeated the enemy at Munda (perhaps in the vicinity of Montilla, south of Córdoba) four years later.

The center of Roman life was the *municipium,* the city (the *colonia* or settlement is little different), and splendid must have been the examples in Spain of this phase of Roman organization. In the south the capital of Hispania Ulterior, and later of Baetica, was the thriving city of Corduba (Sp. Córdoba). Hispalis (Sp. Sevilla, Eng. Seville), too, was flourishing, as was nearby Itálica, of which only ruins remain. Other settlements in the rich agricultural area of Andalusia, which carried on a large export business with Rome, were Urso (Sp. Osuna), Ilipla (Sp. Niebla), Astigis (Sp. Ecija), Carmo (Sp. Carmona), Tukkis (Sp. Martos) (cf. Strabo, *Geography,* III, 2; Pliny, *Natural History,* III). Old coastal settlements (Ampurias; Sagunto; Cartagena; Málaga; Cádiz, rich and joyous, famous if not infamous throughout the Roman world) naturally retained their importance under the Romans. In the west of Andalusia were Emerita Augusta (Sp. Mérida) and Pax Augusta (Sp. Badajoz). In the northeast were Tarraco (Sp. Tarragona), the capital of Hispania Citerior (later Tarraconensis), where officials and soldiers from Italy usually landed, and Caesaraugusta (Sp. Zaragoza, Eng. Saragossa). In the northwest the principal cities were what is the present León, where Augustus quartered the Seventh Legion (*Legio Septima Gemina,* whence the name León), to keep the Astures "pacified"; Asturica Augusta (Sp. Astorga), which to Pliny the Elder, who may or may not have seen it, was a magnificent city (*Natural History,* III, 3); Lucus (Sp. Lugo), whose walls are said to be the most perfect of their kind, though they are not so familiar as those of Avila, which were constructed at the end of the eleventh century. At the northwest tip of the country Ardobicum Corunium or Ardobrica Caronium, captured by the Romans in 60 B.C., where the modern Torre de Hércules was originally a *pharos* (lighthouse) rebuilt in the reign of Tràjan, is Corunna (Sp. La Coruña), famed as the scene of more than one naval or military engagement in modern times.

In their customary thoroughgoing way the Romans connected their cities by a system of military highways which crisscrossed the country and which served also, be it observed, to spread the language of those who built them. Thirty-four are listed in the *Antonini itinerarium* of Antoninus Caracalla (?). The most ancient may be the so-called *Vía Hercúlea,* extending along the coast from the French border near Perpignan through Ampurias, Barcelona, Tarragona, Sagunto, and Valencia, thence to Cartagena. Another led from Tarragona through Lérida, Saragossa, Numancia, and Burgo de Osma to Astorga, thence to La Coruña. A secondary branch of this road led southward from Burgo de Osma (Lat. Uxama) toward Termes. It is this way that the exiled Cid passed in his journey toward Valencia (*la calçada de Quinea ívala traspassar, Poema de Mio Cid,* 400). From Mérida radiated causeways in all directions: the Via Lata (Sp. *Camino de la Plata*)—which so impressed Richard Ford—to Cáceres, Salamanca, an important junction point, Zamora, and Astorga; to Toledo, Alcalá de Henares, Sigüenza, and Saragossa, with a branch via Medellín to Córdoba, Antequera, and Málaga; to Seville and Cádiz. Thus Latin was carried to all parts of the country and the native languages were confined within increasingly narrow limits (cf. p. 7).

Politically Spain was at first divided into two provinces, Hispania Citerior, Nearer Spain, and Hispania Ulterior, Farther Spain. About 15 B.C. (or 27 B.C., according to other authorities) Augustus reorganized the grouping into the three provinces of Tarraconensis (the north, the center, the northwest), Baetica (the south), Lusitania (Portugal— approximately). By the time of Diocletian (245–313) the number had increased to five (Gallaecia and Cartaginense being the additional members). Citizenship, in varying degrees, was granted to native Spaniards first (*ca.* 73–74) by the emperor Vespasian (9–79), and then by Caracalla, whose decree (212) extended to all Roman subjects.

The effects of Roman conquest, with its unification of control under a central power as a consequence of the subjection of the disunited native tribes, were seen in the imposition of the Latin language, which was in time to evolve into Spanish, in the introduction of Roman law, and in all manifestations of the material civilization of the day (temples, baths, tombs, dwellings, circuses, amphitheaters, theaters, triumphal arches, roads, bridges, aqueducts), in agriculture and trade, as well as in Roman scientific, literary, and artistic culture. *Obra de romanos,* say the Spaniards of any undertaking which calls for time and work, and which is great of its sort. The enthusiasm with which Spaniards accepted Romanization appears in the number of men who removed to Rome, there to become celebrated. It is true that in the Roman epoch we cannot call by name any architect or sculptor who comes from Iberia, but for science and literature the case is different. Quintilian (35?–100?), whose treatise on rhetoric, the *Institutio oratoria* (in form, a textbook on public speaking; in content, the outline of a liberal education) was a prescribed dose for youth into the Middle Ages, was a native of Calahorra. The epigrammatist Martial (43–104) was born and died at Bilbilis (the site is on the hill now called Bambola), near Calatayud, in Aragon. After many years in Rome, a lady named Marcella having given him an estate at his native town (*Epigrams,* XII, 31, 8), he returned there, though from his description of the winter climate (I, 49) we may not be sure his gratitude was complete. The younger Pliny, be it said in passing, indelicately announces (*Epistles,* III, 21) that he provided the money for Martial's return to Spain. The elder Seneca (*ca.* 54 B.C.–A.D. 39), famous both for his rhetorical works and for his remarkable memory, was a native of Córdoba, where he lived most of his life, as was his better known son the Stoic philosopher and bloodthirsty dramatist (4 B.C.–A.D. 65). A nephew of the younger Seneca was Lucan (39–65), author of the long poem (the *Pharsalia*) dealing with the civil war between Caesar and Pompey. It is in the company of Horace and Ovid, though after them in order, that Dante places this Cordovan, who took his own life as a result of Nero's displeasure (*Inferno,* IV, 90). Columella, the chief writer on agriculture in the first century of the Christian era, was born in Cádiz. The earliest Roman geographer, Pomponius Mela, who flourished at the middle of the first century A.D., tells us himself (but the text of his *De situ orbis* is corrupt at this point, II, 6, 96) that he hailed from Tingentera or Cingentera, presumably on the bay of Algeciras. From Tarraco, or possibly from Calahorra, comes Prudentius (348–*ca.* 410), the greatest of the early Christian poets. In the Middle Ages great repute was accorded the *Historia evangelica,* a long poem in hexameters by the Spaniard Juvencus (fourth century).

Finally, it is fitting to record that Itálica, whose past is recalled by the early seventeenth-century poet Rodrigo Caro in his *Canción a las ruinas de Itálica,* is the place of origin of the emperor Trajan (52 or 53-117), who added Dacia (Rumania) to the Empire. The later emperors Marcus Aurelius (121-180) and Theodosius (346?-395) belonged to families whose blood was partly Spanish. No Roman province was so rich—Julius Caesar paid off all his debts and returned to Rome a rich man after one term there—and so cultivated as Spain, none so honored and privileged, none so important in Rome, where Lucius Cornelius Balbus Major of Cádiz was the first non-Roman to receive the rank of consul and where Caius Julius Hyginus, whom Suetonius reports as a native of Spain, was Augustus' chief librarian. In fact, the taste and style of the Cordovans came to be a vogue in Rome, though Cicero found their pronunciation not to his liking (*Cordubae natis poetis pingue quiddam sonantibus atque peregrinum,* poets born at Córdoba, whose speech had a somewhat thick and foreign accent, *Archias,* X, 26).

The Latin Spoken in Spain

The framework of Spanish, and a minimum of 60 per cent of its vocabulary, if the eighteenth-century estimate of the Benedictine Sarmiento be correct, derives from Latin, not from the pruned and cultivated language of literature, but from the everyday talk of legionaries, traders, *coloni,* and the like. This conversational Latin, that of the mass of the Roman folk, is not easy to know, since when setting down in writing any thought whatever we at once become grammar-conscious and try to write "correctly."

Customary sources of information for spoken Latin in all parts of Rome's empire are the slips of stone masons in cutting inscriptions, random observations of grammarians, who here and there frown upon innovations as is their wont, and comparison with the other languages which have their source in Latin. Colloquial forms occasionally appear in the comedies of Plautus. There are also a few late texts which reflect the popular speech, the *Satiricon* of Petronius Arbiter, of the time of Nero; the *Appendix Probi,* a list of correct and incorrect forms, of the third century A.D.; the *Silviae vel potius Aetheriae peregrinatio ad loca sancta,* the more interesting to us because the lady of the journey was likely a Spanish nun (fourth century A.D.). But in Spain, if one may judge by the *Corpus inscriptionum latinarum,* the cutters of inscriptions are exasperatingly grammatical, and such colloquial forms as they allow to escape them are common to the Romance languages rather than peculiar to Spanish. Grammarians or rhetoricians, and encyclopedists such as the elder Pliny (23–79) and especially St. Isidore of

Seville (560–636) contribute matter of interest. Thus the Roman naturalist says that in Spain earthen walls are called *formaceos* (Sp. *hormazos*) (*Natural History,* XXXV, 14, 48), that rabbits are called *cuniculi* (Sp. *conejos*) (VIII, 55, 81), and that there the bird we know as the bustard (Sp. *avetarda, avutarda*) was called *avis tarda* (X, 22, 29). St. Isidore, who for his devotion to learning is set down by Dante as an inhabitant of Paradise (*Paradiso,* X, 131: *Vedi oltre fiammeggiar l'ardente spiro d'Isidoro*), notes *antenatus > alnado,* stepson; *capanna > cabaña,* cabin; *catenatum > candado,* padlock; *mantum > manto,* cloak; *merendare > merendar,* lunch; *tabanus > tábano,* horsefly. Also mentioned in his *Etymologiae* are other words, Latinized in form, *burgus, camisia, saio,* etc., which are now known to have been carried south by Celts or Germanic invaders, or which are unknown in origin (as *cama*) and which do not concern us at this point (cf. pp. 8, 12). Quintilian speaks of *gurdus* (Sp. *gordo,* fat) in the sense of "obtuse" as originating in his native land: *gurdos, quos pro stolidis accipit vulgus, ex Hispania duxisse originem audivi* (*Institutes of Oratory,* I, 5, 57), but this word appears in other parts of Romance territory. *Canthus,* that is, Spanish *canto,* edge, corner, quarried stone, he considers of African or Spanish origin (I, 5, 88), but it is now thought to be of Greek ancestry. The "wooden bath-seat, which Augustus called by the Spanish name *dureta*" (Suetonius, *Octavius Augustus,* Holland's translation) appears to have left no descendants, nor is its antecedent history known. (Cf. E. Schwyzer, "*Hispanisch* dureta," in *Zeitschrift für vergleichende Sprachforschung,* Band 62 [1935], 199–203.)

In Spanish (and Portuguese), Latin words and meaning are found which do not appear in any number in French, Italian, or other Romance languages; if they do make an appearance, it is as mere Latinisms. Possibly, in accordance with the theory of Ascoli, this is because the Romans were present and settling in the Iberian peninsula approximately one hundred years earlier than in more northern countries (Gaul was not invaded until much later, southern Gaul in 123 B.C., northern Gaul in 58 B.C.),[1] possibly it is because the link between Spain and the Church has never been weakened, or possibly it is because it is the nature of the people to resist innovation—though these reasons can only be partial.

The Latin of Spain apparently favored the use of *amma* > *ama*, mistress; *caenum* > *cieno*, mire; *cereola* > *ciruela*, plum; *chordus + arius* > *cordero*, lamb; *columellus* > *colmillo*, eyetooth, fang; *collacteus* > *collazo*, foster brother, farm hand; *comedere* > *comer*, eat; a derivative of *cor*, *corazón*, heart; *cova* > *cueva*, cave, the post-Plautine form is more often *cavum*; *coxus* > *cojo*, lame; *cuius* > *cuyo*, whose; *dies* > *día*, day; *fabulare* > *hablar*, speak; *formosus* > *hermoso*, beautiful, the word survives in Rumanian also; *integrare* > *entregar*, deliver; *maturicare* > *madrugar*, rise early; *melimelum* > *membrillo*, quince; *metus* > *miedo*, fear; *metire* > *medir*, measure; the extension of the meaning of *mulier* to include wife; *mus caecus* > Old Spanish *murciégalo*, Modern Spanish *murciélago*, bat; *octuber* (the C.L. form is *october*) > *octubre*, October; *perfidia* > *porfía*, persistence; *pultarius* > *puchero*, stewpot;

---

[1] Cf. Meyer-Lübke, *Introducción*, § 19.

percontare > *preguntar,* question, a legal term like *integrare* above; *suffumare* > *sahumar,* smoke, perfume; *turpis* > *torpe,* slow, clumsy, shameful; *verrere* > *barrer,* sweep; except as learned terms, the loss of *canis,* dog, of *frater,* brother, and *soror,* sister; the shift in meaning of many words, such as *barba* (Lat. beard, Sp. beard, chin); *chalare,* to slacken, to lower, to let down > *callar,* silence or become silent; *laborare,* labor > *labrar,* restricted to meaning "till the soil," "work wood or stone or metal," "do women's handwork"; *magis* > *más,* meaning "more," as also in Rumanian; *passer* (Lat. sparrow, Sp. bird); *plicare,* fold > *llegar,* arrive, originally a nautical term meaning "furl the sails"; *quaerere,* seek > *querer,* meaning "wish, want, love"; *rostrum* > *rostro,* in the sense of "face" rather than beak or snout, mouth; *sensus* > *seso,* meaning "brain"; *sobrinus-a,* nephew–niece, rather than cousin; the passage of many verbs from the *ĕre* to the *ire* conjugation (*dicere* > *decir; petere* > *pedir;* etc.).

As knowledge of Spanish etymologies has become more exact, many words have lately been referred to a more satisfactory origin, but it must be said that there are only too many genuinely Spanish words whose provenance is still the object of discussion, in spite of intelligent guesses. In addition to those mentioned before there may be cited *anchoa, bahía, buscar* (of Germanic origin?), *chulo* (gypsy?), *escueto, galápago* (Arabic?), *garduña,*[2] *guapo, lindo, loco,*[3] *majo* (the social type), *muchacho, parra, perro, podenco, redoma, tirar, tomar, tuétano, vaho, zurdo.*

---

[2] Cf. L. Spitzer in *Neuphilologische Mitteilungen,* XXIV (1923), 150.
[3] Cf. C. C. Rice in *Hispanic Review,* III (1935), 162–163.

THE CHIEF CHARACTERISTICS OF SPOKEN LATIN

The languages spoken in Spain at and before the arrival of the Phoenicians, the Greeks, the Carthaginians, and the Romans, have influenced not at all the structure of Spanish, which is in this respect totally an importation. The idiom of the Augustan Age would have undergone in time the changes to which any living tongue is subject, but perhaps the tempo, if not the manner of modification, was increased, conservative as is Spanish,[4] by the difficulties the native peoples experienced with a delicately but systematically inflected speech unlike their own. It is evident in any case that Spanish is the product of the evolution of the Latin of daily intercourse. Vulgar Latin it is commonly called. I shall now essay to point out its chief features.

Accent.—It is fundamental that the stress has continued to the present day in Spanish upon the syllable which bore it during the period of the twelve Caesars and before (Lat. *spa'tula* > Sp. *espal'da;* Lat. *su'cidus* > Sp. *su'cio*). It is believed that preliterary Latin already had an accent which was primarily one of stress and that this was kept alive by the populace. The pitch accent of Greek may later, during classical times, have affected the language which drew from it so much of its intellectual inspiration, but by the fourth century A.D. grammarians point definitely to the triumph of accent of stress or intensity; for example: *Accentus in ea syllaba est quae plus sonat* (Servius).

Only occasionally does stress in Vulgar Latin differ sharply from that in Classic, or take a decided stand where

---

[4] " ... ninguno tiene autoridad para osar innovar alguna cosa con libertad," says Herrera, in his commentary to the edition of Garcilaso de la Vega.

the latter wavered. If in Classic Latin a vowel was followed
by one of the explosive consonants (*b, c, d, g, p, t*) + *l* or,
more often, *r*, its syllable could be either long or short, and
accordingly stressed or unstressed. Thus Classic Latin said
(if indeed the usage of poets be trustworthy evidence) either
in'tegrum or *inte'grum*. Vulgar Latin always stressed the
vowel in such a combination, probably as a consequence of
the tendency to insert a vocalic element between the explosive and the *l* or *r*: Spanish *ente'ro* (*íntegro* is plainly of
learned manufacture); compare **alecrem > alegre*. Spoken
Latin, too, tends to combine stressed *e* and *i* into a diphthong before another vowel, and the inclination to diphthongize successive vowels is still a pronounced trait in
Spanish. The Classic stress is on the *i* of *regina,* and there it
remained in early Spanish:

> *Non as miedo nin verguença de Rey nin Reyna,*
> *mudaste do te pagas cada dia ayna,*
> *huesped eres de muchos, non duras so cortina;*
> *como el fuego andas de vezina en vezina*
> > (*Libro de buen amor,* 391, fourteenth century);

Cógese la a *con la* i, *como en estas diciones:* gaita, baile; *y
puédese desatar, como en éstas:* vaina, caida (Nebrija, *Gramática,* I, 8); but the word today is of two syllables, with
the stress on the *e: reina.* The following pronunciations are
now accepted as correct: *perio'do* and *ocea'no* (three syllables in rapid pronunciation), though spelling lags behind;
período, océano. In accordance with this tendency the unlettered naturally pronounce *tiatro* (two syllables) instead of
teatro (three syllables), for them *trae* (two syllables) becomes *trai* (one syllable)—the form is already in Cervantes

(*El viejo celoso*)—*país* and *baúl* become *páis* and *bául,* and
ai (one syllable) replaces *ahí* (two syllables), at least in
Castile. Diphthongization in these and similar words has
been registered for New Mexico, Mexico, the Central American republics, and most of the South American republics.
Compare p. 236.

PHONOLOGY

Vowels.—The vowels of Classic Latin were characterized by
quantity, that is, the pronunciation of a long vowel simply
took longer than that of a short vowel. Sometime between
the second and fifth centuries of the Christian era, the difference of quantity was at last completely replaced by that
of quality: vowels were open or close according to the distance between the tongue and the hard palate. The long
vowels of Classic Latin became the close vowels of Vulgar
Latin, the short vowels of Classic Latin became the open
vowels of Vulgar Latin. Also, short *i* and long *e* came to
represent but one sound; similarly short *u* and long *o*. This
is shown by their confusion in inscriptions and late Latin
texts: *menus* for *minus, riges* for *reges, sob* for *sub, flus* for
flos,[5] and by subsequent developments in Spanish: Classic
Latin *pĭlum* > Vulgar Latin *pẹlo* > Spanish *pelo;* Classic
Latin *plēnum* > Vulgar Latin *plẹno* > Spanish *lleno;* Classic Latin *bŭllam* > Vulgar Latin *bọla* > Spanish *bola;*
Classic Latin *sōlem* > Vulgar Latin *sọle* > Spanish *sol.*
The confusion of *e* and *i, o* and *u,* is not limited to stressed
vowels (*anema, dibuisti, ridicola, Victurina*), and is still
frequent in Spanish (cf. p. 114).

---

[5] The fact is observed even by Lope de Vega, who certainly was not a student
of linguistics. See *El cuerdo loco,* publicada por José F. Montesinos, *Teatro antiguo
español,* Madrid, 1922, IV, 6–7.

The relation of quantity to quality may be summarized in the following table:

Classic Latin Vowels		Vulgar Latin Vowels
ă } ā }	. . . .	a
ĕ	. . . .	ę
ē } ĭ }	. . . .	ẹ
ī	. . . .	i
ŏ	. . . .	ǫ
ō } ŭ }	. . . .	ọ
ū	. . . .	u

Consonants.—The chief developments are the complete loss of *h*, an unstable sign of aspiration even in Classic Latin (it has, to be sure, been reintroduced into writing: Lat. *habere* > O.S. *aver* > M.S. *haber*); the loss of final *t* (*quievi = quievit,* on an inscription of the year 662); the loss of final *m* (it had been a weak sound at all times in Latin), except in words of one syllable where the nasal sound is represented by *n* (*cun, tan,* etc.); the tendency of intervocalic *b* to become fricative (especially from the second century A.D. on) rather than explosive, and consequently to be confused with *v* (*lebare* < *levare, iuvente* < *iubente*); the palatalization (that is, the raising of the front of the tongue so as to make the point of contact farther forward in the mouth) of *c, g* before *e, i: certum,* pronounced "kertum" in Classic Latin, but approximately "tserto" later in Vulgar Latin; *gentem,* the *g* occlusive in Classic Latin, but by the fourth century approximately like *y* in *yes;* the palatalization of *ci̯, ti̯, li̯, ni̯, di̯, gi̯* (though written evidence for Vulgar Latin is not abundantly available for this and the result appears only in Spanish), *radium* > *rayo, exagium* > *ensayo, humiliare* > *humillar* (the change of *li̯* ordinarily went farther: *mulierem* > *mujer;* cf. p. 97), *pineam* > *piña, minaciam* > Old Spanish *amenaça* > Modern Spanish *amenaza, tertiarium* > Old Spanish *terçero* > Modern Spanish *tercero;* the now general simplification of *ns, rs, ps, pt, monstrare* > *mostrar, aversum* > *avieso, ipse* > *ese, nepta* > *nieta.*

Syntactical phonetics.—Occasionally the form of a word depends upon its position within a breath group. This is hardly true of Classic Latin, but with the loss or decrease of inflected forms in Vulgar Latin words now tend to change with their syntactic environment. Thus if a word begins with *s* + consonant (usually *sc, sp, st*), and the preceding word ends in a consonant, there arises the habit of prefixing a front vowel (at first written *i*), probably because *s* had practically the value of a syllable: *cum scuto* > *cum iscuto* > *con escudo,* and analogically *ille scutum* > *el escudo.* Such a vowel, later written *e,* is first remarked by St. Isidore (according to Grandgent, *Vulgar Latin,* § 230), and the prefixed front vowel has become a characteristic of Spanish, to which "impure *s*" is an alien sound, demanding immediate modification: *Stephanum* > *Esteban, Squilacci* (the Neapolitan minister of Charles III) > *Esquilache, specimen* > *espécimen,* the English word *spleen* > *esplín, smoking* (= "tuxedo") > *esmoquin;* compare such innocuous pleasantries as: *Me he entregado por completo a este sport. ¿Es por ... higiene acaso? No; es por capricho* (Vital Aza, *La praviana,* X).

BIBLIOGRAPHY

Espinosa, Aurelio M. *Estudios sobre el español de Nuevo Méjico, traducción ...
de Amado Alonso y Angel Rosenblat,* Buenos Aires, 1930, *Biblioteca de dialectología hispanoamericana,* tomo I, §§ 8–12, Apéndice I: *Cambios acentuales,*
pp. 317–345.

Grandgent, C. H. *An Introduction to Vulgar Latin,* Boston, D. C. Heath and
Co., n.d. [1907], §§ 131–344. The paragraphing is the same in the Spanish
translation of Francisco de B. Moll, *Introducción al latín vulgar,* Madrid, 1928.

Kent, Roland G. *The Sounds of Latin,* second edition, revised, Baltimore, 1940
(Special Publications of the Linguistic Society of America), § 66.

Meyer-Lübke. *Introducción,* §§ 110–112.

Sturtevant, E. H. *The Pronunciation of Greek and Latin,* second edition, Phila-
delphia, 1940 (Special Publications of the Linguistic Society of America),
§§ 115 ff., 122 ff., and also chap. vii.

MORPHOLOGY

Nouns.—A trait of Vulgar Latin is the tendency toward
analytical expression of an idea. An indication of this tendency is the use of prepositions to define the relation of a
noun to other members of a sentence. Such precision was
perhaps most needful in the many and varied uses of the
dative and ablative. There is already in Classic Latin a
certain amount of competition between case endings and
prepositions, for example, *castris idoneum locum,* a place
suitable for a camp; *locus ad insidias aptior,* a place more
apt for lying in ambush; *tribus proxumis annis,* within the
last three years; *in diebus proximis decem,* within the last
ten days. The analytical construction prevailed in the
spoken idiom. The exactness of the function performed by
case endings was of course lessened by the disappearance
of final *m* and the confusion, in unstressed syllables, of *e*
and *i, o* and *u.* The result was that dative, accusative, ablative, and often the nominative (and vocative), too, sounded

alike (nom., acc., abl. *stella;* nom. *vinu,* dat. *vino,* acc. *vinu,* abl. *vino;* dat. *turri,* acc. *turre,* abl. *turre*). Here is another reason for rise of preposition and loss of declension.

Articles.—Noster sermo articulos non desiderat says Quintilian (I, 4, 19), and it is true that Classic Latin had no articles and did not feel the want of them. In the later years of the Empire the demonstratives *ille, ipse,* and even *hic,* lost their particular significance of nearness or remoteness, if it is permissible to judge by a context, and were reduced to indicating an individual among a class. This is to say, their function was that of the definite article: *illi seniores illas cappas quas reddere debent non commutent = no cambien los señores las capas que deben devolver* (St. Chrodegangus, in Muller and Taylor, *A Chrestomathy of Vulgar Latin,* p. 243); *descendit ipsa via et venit ad ipsam casam = bajó por el camino y vino a la casa* (cited by Bourciez, *op. cit.,* § 108a). Nouns indicative of abstract qualities or with a collective meaning, and consequently not designating an individual member of a group, were wont to do without the definite article even in early Spanish: *del rey non avie graçia (Poema de Mio Cid, 50), desondra de sus fijas no nos demanda oy (ibid., 3165), venido es a moros; exido es de cristianos (ibid., 566).* Spanish continues to avoid the definite article if individualization is not intended: *A menudo lógica y lengua coinciden* (Américo Castro), etc.

Even in Classic Latin *unus* was not infrequently used in the sense of "a certain," without particular numerical value, and thus approached an indefinite article: *cum uno gladiatore nequissimo,* with a [certain] very wretched gladiator (Cicero, *Philippicae,* II, 3, 7), *sicut unus paterfamilias his de rebus loquor,* just as a head of a family do I speak of these matters (Cicero, *De oratore,* I, 29, 132), and after the fourth century A.D. *unus* frankly assumes its present function. Spanish is still chary of *uno* when it might be considered a numeral (*cortar con cuchillo, leer gran parte de la noche, es cosa espantosa,* etc.); on the other hand, *con un entusiasmo sorprendente, de una bondad serena,* etc., are sometimes decried as gallicisms.

Comparison of adjectives.—There are in the Latin of literature two manners of comparison: by modification of the ending (*felix, felicior, felicissimus; miser, miserior, miserrimus; facilis, facilior, facillimus*), and by the use in certain classes of adjectives (e.g., those ending in *us* preceded by a vowel, and those ending in *alis, aris, icus, idus, ilis, inus, ivus, orus, timus, ulus, undus*) of *magis* and *maxime* (*idoneus, magis idoneus, maxime idoneus*). The analytical force of Vulgar Latin is here seen already at work, though its power did not extend to the strongly intrenched *melior, peior, maior, minor,* and the corresponding comparatives in early Spanish are *más feliz, más apto,* which shows the defeat in Vulgar Latin of the comparative ending. *Plus* (*plus formosus,* Nemesianus, *Eclogae,* third century) is only sporadic in early Spanish (*Non sovo plus vicioso nunqua, ni mas pagado,* Berceo, *Milagros de Nuestra Señora,* VI, 150d), and disappears thereafter.

The suffix *-issimus* has two meanings (e.g., as in *felicissimus,* very happy and happiest), but only the first survived. In Spanish it is rare at first, although it appears in inscriptions and sporadically as a pure Latinism in medieval writers like Berceo (*dulçissimo, Duelo de la Virgen,* 20d), but it was reintroduced, possibly from Italy, in the fifteenth century, and in the next it was abused by the fluent and flowery Luis de Granada (*¡oh altísima substancia, oh nobilísima esencia!*); the same author uses *inmensísimo* and *divinísimo,* which is not to say that *-ísimo* is not found in less learned styles at that time: *¡sabrosíssimo pan está!* says Lazarillo's hungry hidalgo (III); *¿Sois contento?—Contentíssimo,* in the *Diálogo de la lengua* (ed. cit., pp. 95–96).

Loss of tense forms.—The Classic Latin conjugation, complicated as it was, gave evidence of the process of simplification which has been the fate of the Indo-European languages. It lacked for example the dual number, the middle voice (but perhaps this is represented by the passive forms, or the deponent verbs) and the optative mood, all retained in Classic Greek. Time value predominated in its tense forms, but they still stood in some degree for verbal aspect (the attitude of the speaker toward the act).[6] This function of verb forms has not disappeared in Spanish: *hablaba* and *hablé* both refer to a past act, but the first views it as incomplete, the second as complete. Although all the Latin tense forms of both voices are preserved, in writing at least, to the end of the Empire, we can not escape the belief, since the Romance languages show no trace of some of them, that these were not in spoken use. Spanish, then, loses, in addition to the passive voice (*cantor, cantabar; moneor, monebar;* etc.), which may never have been colloquial, the future indicative (*cantabo, monebo,* etc.), and the imperfect subjunctive (*cantarem, monerem,* etc.); it combines the

---

[6] Cf. Otto Jespersen, *The Philosophy of Grammar,* New York, Henry Holt and Co., 1924, pp. 286 ff.; R. H. Keniston, "Verbal Aspect in Spanish," in *Hispania,* XIX (1936), 163 ff.

future perfect indicative (*cantavero, monuero,* etc.) and the perfect subjunctive (*cantaverim, monuerim,* etc.), which, differing only in the first person singular, were probably not very distinct to the Romans anyway. The substitution of the pluperfect subjunctive (*cantavissem, monuissem,* etc.) for the old imperfect generally throughout Romance territory, probably began in conditional sentences, the inherent unreality of which obscures actual time values.[7] Already in Classic Latin there was some hesitation between the *ēre* and the *ĕre* conjugations (*fulgēre, fulgĕre; scatēre, scatĕre*) and in Spain most of the *ĕre* verbs passed to the *ēre* (*cadere > caer, legere > leer, vertere > verter,* etc.); a good number, however, passed to the *-ire* (*dicere > decir, petere > pedir,* etc.). In some verbs both endings survive, with a difference in meaning (*competer,* be incumbent; *competir,* compete) or in social status (*hender,* split, is "correct," *hendir* is "vulgar").

A new future and a conditional.—The future indicative of Classic Latin was something of a compromise, inasmuch as the *-bo* of the first two conjugations (*cantabo, monebo*) is possibly derived from a verbal root meaning "be," while the forms of the third and fourth conjugations (*legam, audiam*) were originally borrowed from the optative mood. The future forms which were colloquial in Vulgar Latin have their basis in the idea of necessity. Passing from the *habeo etiam dicere,* "I have also to say, I can also say" (Sp. *tengo que decir, he de decir, puedo decir*) and the *de re publica nihil habeo ad te scribere,* "on public matters I can write you nothing," of Cicero (*Roscius Ame-*

---

[7] Cf. Bourciez, *Eléments,* § 136*b*; Grandgent, *Vulgar Latin,* § 118.

rinus, XXXV, 100; *Epistulae ad Atticum,* II, 22, 6), one reaches the *qui nasci habent,* who will be born (Sp. *los que han de nacer, los que nacerán*) of St. Jerome and similar forms of plain future value in other Church Fathers. By the seventh century the fusion of *habeo* and infinitive is documented: *daras* < *dare + habes* (*ille respondebat: non dabo. Iustinianus dicebat: daras;* Fredegarius).

To this new form for present time there arose a corresponding one for the past, as in the elder Seneca's *Venit ad me pater,* Father came to me; *Quid habui facere?,* What had I to do? or What could I do? (*Controversiae,* I, 1, 19). By gradual weakening, the infinitive + *habebam* comes to be the modern conditional: *Sanare te habebat Deus, si fatereris,* God would heal you, if you should confess (St. Augustine, *Serm. app.,* 253, 4; cited by Bourciez, *op. cit.,* § 257*b*).

A new passive voice.—According to one theory,[8] the disappearance of the Classic Latin passive forms began, at a relatively late date, with the confusion of the active and passive infinitive forms (*cantare, cantari, monere, moneri;* etc.; cf. p. 87). However this may be, it is no hard task to find in late Classic Latin writers the use of *esse* + the past participle in a way quite like that of the corresponding forms in Spanish. A distinction is at first observed between *interfectus est,* he was or has been killed, and *interfectus fuit,* he had been killed, but later they are used indiscriminately. The use of the past participle as a pure adjective, without verbal force, influenced the use of *sum* + the past participle as a present (cf. *Gallia est omnis divisa in partis tres*), *Candelae autem ecclesiasticae super ducentae paratae*

[8] H. Muller, "The Passive Voice in Vulgar Latin," in *Romanic Review,* XV (1924), 68–93.

sunt, Church candles, over two hundred, are provided (*Peregrinatio,* XXXVI, 2). If *sum* + the past participle is a present tense, then it is natural to build up a complete conjugation, using all tenses of *esse.* At the same time the need for the old passive forms is lessened by the employment of the reflexive form (*Myrina quae Sebastopolim se vocat;* Pliny, *Natural History,* V, 30). This use of the reflexive, later to become so general in Spanish, is already well established in the *Poema de Mio Cid* (*verán las moradas cómmo se fazen, afarto verán por los ojos cómmo se gana el pan,* 1643–1644; cf. 139, 1421, 1753, 1960, 3730).

A new perfect.—When the author of the *Bellum Civile* says (III, 89) *cohortes constitutas habebat,* the meaning is probably to be rendered in Spanish by *tenía colocadas las cohortes,* but when Cicero says *satis habeo deliberatum* the proper version is surely *bastante he deliberado.* This latter value supplanted the other in the course of time, but even in the *Poem of the Cid* it is not always easy to say whether *haber* is an auxiliary or an independent verb meaning "have or hold," the equivalent of *tener: Vedada lan conpra,* 62; *las armas avien presas,* 1001; *tierras de Borriana todas conquistas las ha,* 1093; *Nos puede repentir, que casadas·las ha amas,* 2617. The agreement of the past participle endured normally in Spanish into the fourteenth century; in certain phrases variability survives to the beginning of the sixteenth.

BIBLIOGRAPHY

BOURCIEZ. *Eléments,* §§ 108, 112; 81, 126, 245.

GRANDGENT. *Vulgar Latin,* §§ 56–57, 85–100, 101–130.

MULLER, H. F. and TAYLOR, PAULINE. *A Chrestomathy of Vulgar Latin,* New York, D. C. Heath and Co. [1932], pp. 29–69.

of the earlier Germanic invaders. Their coming *may* be commemorated in Catalonia (Sp. Cataluña), "the land of the Goths." The conquest of Spain was completed by Euric (Sp. Eurico), an able soldier and administrator, and not entirely uncivilized (died 486). To Euric is due a codification of Germanic law; the former subjects of Rome, however, were governed by their own laws, collected (506 A.D.) in the *Lex romana visigothorum,* the *Breviary* of Alaric II. During the first third of the sixth century the Visigoths were pressed from the north by the Franks who crossed over the Pyrenees, but the Franks were unable to maintain their foothold. Thus the Visigothic kingdom was concentrated in Spain. Toledo, since 192 B.C. in the hands of the Romans (whose historian Livy describes it as a "small city, but fortified by its location," *History,* XXV, 7), became its capital in the reign of Athanagild (Sp. Atanagildo, reigned 554–566) or in the reign of his son Leovigild (Sp. Leovigildo, died 586), who discontinued the fiction of allegiance to Rome. Aid was furnished to Athanagild by the Eastern Roman Empire of Justinian, and the Byzantines remained in southern and eastern Spain for nearly a century until Swintilla (Sp. Suintila) expelled them in 631.[1] The years following the rise of Athanagild and Leovigild were crowded with the subjection of the Swabians in Galicia (585), with contention between kings and nobles, and with religious difficulties. Reccared (Sp. Recáredo) accepted Roman Catholicism in 587, perhaps in the hope of aiding the political fusion of Goths and Hispano-Romans. Since the Visigoths tended to maintain themselves apart as a mili-

[1] See E. S. Bouchier, *Spain in the Roman Empire,* Oxford, B. H. Blackwell, 1914, chap. iv.

tary aristocracy, the question of amalgamation continued to be a problem in the last century of Visigothic domination, when both Chindaswinth (Sp. Chindasvinto, reigned 642–653) and Recceswinth (Sp. Recesvinto, reigned 653–672) took steps to combine the laws of the two peoples. The resulting work, when translated into Spanish in 1241, becomes the *Fuero Juzgo*. Wamba, the last great Visigothic sovereign (reigned 672–680), displayed splendid energy in his military victories, in the course of which he repelled an attack by the Moors. But by now decline was swift—the devil having dulled the wits of the wise, as the *Crónica general* has it (chap. 551). Witiza (died about 710) was succeeded after a struggle by Roderick, the last Goth, but this outcome was a hollow victory for Roderick, since his political adversaries brought from across the Strait help which was to remain for over 700 years.

The most brilliant period for the Visigoths was from 572–680, when their rulers were men of worth and force. What culture they had was almost entirely in the hands of the increasingly influential Catholic clergy, whose outstanding representatives are the encyclopedist St. Isidore of Seville, who has been mentioned (p. 28), and Orosius (born perhaps in Tarragona in the fifth century), whose *Universal History* (*Historiarum adversum paganos, libri VII*) was for centuries widely known throughout Europe.[2] The Visigothic churches of Asturias, let it be observed parenthetically, are of the greatest interest, architecturally.

The Visigoths, who preferred to reside in the country rather than in cities as was the Romans' taste, greatly en-

---

[2] Cf. Dante, *Paradiso*, X, 119–120.

larged the gulf between social classes, but in the matter of administration and in agricultural methods they did not profoundly modify the Roman system. Competent authorities find the social customs and the legal usages of the Visigoths prominent in the twelfth-century *Poema de Mio Cid.*[8] For Spaniards, however, to whom the very names of the Visigothic rulers, so un-Latin are they, are a source of jocularity, Visigothic has come to imply all that is reactionary, out of date, and behind the times, for example: *en tiempos del rey Wamba, godo,* and *ostrogodo* as applied by liberals to royalists during the wars of the early nineteenth century, and *niño gótico,* a modern slang phrase meaning a childish or puerile youth. A people whose main business was war, who were constantly quarreling among themselves, and whose chief accomplishment was to reduce Spain to the state of subdivision where it had been when the Romans found it, could hardly be expected to develop the inheritance of the Romans. In fact, the Roman language, always used by the Visigoths for official purposes, replaced their own speech, which, however, made many contributions to vocabulary, although not to syntax.

---

[8] Especially in the episode of the *Cortes de Toledo.* Cf. E. de Hinojosa, *Estudios sobre la historia del derecho español,* Madrid, 1903; *idem, El elemento germánico en el derecho español,* Madrid, 1915.

THE GERMANIC ELEMENT IN SPANISH

If a Germanic word found in Spain belongs originally to the Gothic dialect, it does not follow that the Visigoths introduced it there. The three hundred and more Germanic words in the Romance languages are a result of the intimate contact on several frontiers between German tribes and Roman soldiers and colonizers. Among the legionaries, too, were many Germani. These words were in use among the Romans long before the fall of the Empire in 476, and some of them (e.g., *burgus; cofea; harpa; sapo,* whence Spanish *jabón*) appear in late Latin writers. The form of the new words in Spanish does not indicate a dialectal provenance, rather it shows that they were absorbed in Latin early enough to undergo its evolution: Germ. *hosa* > *ǫsa* > Old Spanish *(h)uesa,* high boot. But if a term appears only in the Iberian peninsula, and not in France, Italy, or other Romance countries, there is some justification for saying that if the Visigoths did not carry it there, at least they kept it alive. Such words are *aleve,* treacherous; *aliso,* alder; *aya,* governess; *cundir,* spread; *escanciar,* pour wine; *eslabón,* link; *ganar,* gain, earn; *ganso,* goose; *lastar,* to pay or suffer for some one else; *sayón,* executioner; *tascar*(?), to champ; *toldo,* awning. Finally, it was through French that many Germanic terms of war and chivalry (O.S. *faraute,* messenger; O.S. *fonta,* shame; *orgullo,* pride) sifted down to Spain.

As "military" may be grouped *anca,* haunch; *bandera,* flag; *bandido,* bandit; *bando,* edict, faction; *blandir,* brandish; *blasón*(?), blazon; *botín,* booty; *brida,* bridle; *burgo* (mostly in proper nouns like *el Burgo de Osma, Burgos*), town; *cofia*, coif; *dardo*, dart; *esgrimir*, fence; *espiar*, spy; *espuela*, spur; *estribo*(?), stirrup; *guardar*, guard, keep; Old Spanish *guarir*, protect; Old Spanish *guarnir*, garrison, garnish (*guarecer* and *guarnecer* have a Latin inceptive ending); *guerra*, war; *guía*, guide; *hacha*, axe; *robar*, rob; *tregua*, truce; *yelmo*, helmet. Granting the term a certain elasticity, under "social" may be grouped *agasajar*, to treat with many attentions; *albergue*, shelter; *arpa*, harp; *banco*, bench; *barón*, baron and *varón*, male person (the older meaning); *blanco*, white (more directly from French?); *brasa*, live coal; *estaca*, stake; *estofa*, stuff; *falda*, skirt; *fieltro*, felt; *galardón*, guerdon, reward; *guadañar*, mow; *gris*, gray; *guante*, glove; *guiñar*, wink; Old Spanish *luva*, glove; *rico*, rich; *ropa*, clothing; *rueca*, distaff; *sopa*, soup; *tacaño*, stingy; *toalla*, towel. Not so readily classifiable are Old Spanish *ardido* or *fardido*, valiant; *arenga*, harangue; *arrancar*, tear away; *aspa*, cross; *bogar*, row; *bramar*, roar; *desmayar*, faint; *escarnio*, mockery; *esquivar*, avoid; *frambuesa* (later through French), raspberry; *fresco*, fresh, cool; *fruncir*, wrinkle; *gastar* (which is Lat. *vastare* contaminated with Ger. *wostjan*), waste; *grupo*, group; *guañir*(?), grunt; Old Spanish *guisa*, wise, manner; *marca*, mark; *lisonja* (by way of Provençal), flattery; *listo*, ready, quick; *lonja* (the building); *orgullo*, pride; the points of the compass: *norte*, *sur*, *este*, *oeste* (through French?); *trotar*, trot. Those names of men, and more infrequently of women, which do not come from the Church calendar are of this importation, *Alfonso, Bermudo, Elvira, Federico, Fernando, Francisco, Gonzalo, Matilde, Ramiro, Ricardo, Rodrigo*, as is also the termination *engo*, English *-ing* (*abolengo*). In closing the list, which is not intended to be complete, we note that words having to do with intellectual activities are not numerous here; those came from a warmer climate.

BIBLIOGRAPHY

GAMILLSCHEG, E. "Historia lingüística de los visigodos," in *Revista de filología española*, XIX (1932), 117–150, 229–260.

———. *Romania Germanica*, Band I, Berlin and Leipzig, 1934, 355–385.

MENÉNDEZ PIDAL. *Manual*, §§ 4, 3.

MEYER-LÜBKE. *Introducción*, §§ 36–46.

SACHS, G. *Die germanischen Ortsnamen in Spanien und Portugal*, Jena und Leipzig, W. Gronau, 1932.

(795) he and his son Louis successfully established the Spanish March as a part of the kingdom of the Franks. At last, by 732, the northward progress of the Arabs had been stayed at Poitiers, either by Charles Martel or by civil war behind in Spain. Spain then became an emirate, a province dependent on the Caliphate of Damascus. At the middle of the eighth century, having been dethroned by his rivals, and having fled to Spain, Abderrahman I (755–788), crossing from Africa, succeeded in setting up a government independent of Damascus, but the public peace continued to be disturbed by factional disputes. The transformation from subject emirate to caliphate was effected by the able Abderrahman III (reigned 912–961). Now, too, the seditious and the ambitious were quieted, and there began the century or more of splendor of the Caliphate of Córdoba, where, under Abderrahman and Hakam II (reigned 961–976), a degree of wealth and culture was attained which raised Spain to the height of the greatest European state. Brilliant, too, were the days of Hisham II (976–1008, 1009–1013), but power was in the hands of his mother's favorite, the general Almansur (Sp. Almanzor), who died at Medinaceli in 1002 (the battle of Calatañazor, celebrated in the ancient jingle *En Calatañazor perdió Almanzor el atamor,* appears to be a fiction). Shortly thereafter anarchy split the caliphate into a number of separate kingdoms known as Taifas (= factions). At the end of the eleventh century a religious sect from Africa, the Almoravides, "the devout ones,"(whose name appears in *maravedí* = belonging to the Almoravides) subjected the Taifas and took Valencia, which the relict of the Cid could no longer hold after 1102.

At the end of the first quarter of the twelfth century another tribe or sect, the Almohades, "the unitarians," had a more prolonged success and Spain became a part of the Empire of Morocco. In 1212 Alphonso VIII, miraculously guided over the Sierra Morena by St. Isidore dressed as a shepherd, won, with the assistance of French soldiery, a great victory at Las Navas de Tolosa, in the province of Jaén, putting the Christians in a position to undertake the domination of the plains of Andalusia. Córdoba fell to Ferdinand III, the Saint, in 1236, Seville in 1248. At the Salado (a rivulet which disembogues near Tarifa) Alphonso XI achieved a whopping victory in 1340. Moorish rule was rapidly being limited to the isolated kingdom and city of Granada; in properly modern style, Boabdil delivered up the keys of the city to Ferdinand on the second of January, 1492.

THE CULTURAL IMPULSE

The tolerance with which the newcomers normally treated the inhabitants of the invaded country was largely a matter of expediency. For them Spain was something of a financial speculation; they were not great in number; and the native landholding class, anxious to be undisturbed, soon came to terms. Mixed marriages were not unusual. Christians continued to live as such in Moorish territory. Arabic was the language of officialdom and of religion, but the language of the streets (and Arabs preferred the country) retained its identity. The Christians who lived among Moors (*mozárabes*) were the intermediaries between the two languages, and served to introduce Arabic words to Spanish. The same function was performed by Moors who knew Romance (*moros latinados, ladinos;* the latter word, < *latinum,* has come to mean sly, cunning, from the tendency of those knowing Spanish to use their knowledge to their own advantage), and by the *mudéjares,* that is, by Moors who lived under their own religion within Christian territory; this became more often permissible as the Reconquest advanced.[1]

It is said that during the years of Córdoba's magnificence the majority of Spaniards were literate. This may be an overstatement, but the cultivation of poetry, history, and philosophy, which last at times was frowned upon as under-

---

[1] Other social classes were the *renegados* or *muladíes,* Spanish Christians who embraced the faith of the Mohammedans. Since profession of this faith brought freedom to serfs, the Conquest was in this way facilitated. Moors upon whom conversion to Christianity was later forced were called *moriscos. Aljamía* is the term applied ordinarily to writings in the Spanish language with Arabic characters, but frequently it simply means Spanish as spoken by Moors.

mining religion, was intense. The greatest name among the philosophers is that of Averroës (1126–1198), who wrote a commentary upon Aristotle, and who is credited with re-introducing the Greek to western Europe.

Abderrahman III received as a gift from the Byzantine emperor a copy of the writings of Dioscorides, the Greek physician. A call for a translator brought the monk Nicholas in 951, and thereafter the translation of Greek works on medicine, astronomy, and mathematics went on apace. Not all works were translations by any means. A chapter on surgery in the medical encyclopedia of Abulcasis (936–1013) is considered to be among the most important contributions to the history of medicine. Trade, which was not with Europe, but with Egypt, Constantinople, and Asia Minor, is believed to have carried with it into Spain the idea of zero and its symbol, and the Arabic numerals, later conveyed into France together with the pendulum, by Gerbert, then a monk of Auvergne, later Pope Silvester II, who had studied in Córdoba. Rice, sugar cane, cotton, pomegranates, the silkworm, paper (instead of parchment)—first produced at Játiva, were introduced by the Arabs. It is not certain which of their innovations spread over Europe from Spain and which from their base in Sicily, where Frederick II (1194–1250), famed for his patronage of Arabic arts, learning, and science, lived at his court in Palermo rather as a Saracen than as a German. The medical school at Salerno, south of Naples, in particular, attracted students from many countries.

With prosperity and the consequent diffusion of culture came the establishment of schools, attended by students from the principal countries of Europe, and of libraries, especially in Córdoba, where that of Hakam II contained 400,000 volumes, as did another in Almería.

From Toledo, recaptured by Christian forces in 1085, and a center of communication between cultural Islam and the rest of Christian Spain, if not Europe, emanated the translations of Arabic scientific texts and of Greek authors (Aristotle, Euclid, Galen, Hippocrates, Ptolemy) which were the work of the translators of the Archbishop of Toledo, Raimundo (1126–1150). Here, too, were many Jewish scholars, who had been driven out of Andalusia. And so it is that the proudest boast of Arabic civilization is that it transmitted Greek learning to western Europe.

If Arabic has had no demonstrated impact upon the structure of what once was Latin, and very little upon word formation (final *i*, originally used as a suffix to form adjectives from proper nouns, is of Arabic origin: *zaquizamí*, garret; *zahorí*, soothsayer; *marroquí*, Moroccan; *maravedí*, the name of the money first manufactured in Toledo by Alphonso VII, in imitation of the coinage of the Almoravides), Arabic geographical names have replaced many Roman ones; in fact they dot the very map of Spain. Among such names are *Alcalá*, castle,[2] which settlement was called *Complutum* by the Romans; *Almadén*, mine; *Calatayud*, castle of Ayub, who founded it in the eighth century; *Gibraltar*, the hill (*gebel*) of Tarik; numerous names containing the

---

[2] As Don Quixote instructs Sancho (*Don Quixote*, II, 67), although a couple of his etymologies are at fault, initial *al* is a sign of probable Arabic origin, for *al* is the Arabic definite article, which has one form only for all genders and numbers. Before certain consonants the *l* is assimilated in Arabic, and the article thus is represented by *a* instead of *al*: *aceite, acémila, azúcar, adarme, azufre* (originally from Latin *sulfur*).

initial *Guad* < *wad*, river:[3] *Guadalajara*, river of stones; *Guadalquivir*, great river; *Guadarrama*, river of sand (the mountain range was anciently the *Montes Carpetani*); *Medinaceli*, possibly the "city (*Medina*) of Selim"; the river *Tajo* (since Arabic has no hard *g*, it replaced by an approximation the *g* of the Roman *Tagus*, just as *Galicia* became *Jalikiya*). *Zaragoza* is the product of Arabic corruption of *Caesaraugusta*, later *Cesaragosta*. The *Zocodover* of Toledo is the "village market" or the "market of the animals."

Among the terms of war of Saracen importation are *adalid*, chieftain; *adarga*, leather shield; *alarde*, military review, boasting; *albarda*, packsaddle; *alcaide*, governor of a castle; *alcázar* (but this is a corruption of the Latin word *castrum*), castle; *alférez*, ensign; *alforja*, saddlebag; *almena*, merlon; *atalaya*, watchtower; *atamor* (later to become *tambor*), drum; *lacayo*, lackey; *zaga*, rear. Having to do with civil government are *aduana*, customhouse; *albacea*, executor; *alcabala*, sales tax (which vexed Spaniards to the end of the eighteenth century); *alcalde*, mayor; *aldea*, village; *almacén*, storehouse; *almoneda*, auction; *arrabal*, suburb; *barrio*, district of city; terms of weight and measure: *adarme* (< Greek δραχμή), *azumbre, cahiz, fanega, quilate* (= carat), *quintal*. Building and housing are represented by *adobe*, sun-dried brick; *albañal*, sewer; *albañil*, mason; *alcantarilla*, sewer, drain; *alcoba*, bedroom; *alfarero*, potter; *alféizar*, sill; *andamio*, scaffolding; *azotea*, flat roof; *bazar* (a modern Gallicism?; strictly, it is of Persian origin), bazaar; *dársena*, wet dock; *mazmorra*, dungeon;

---

[3] For *Guadalupe*, Covarrubias says: *unos dizen que vale río de los Lobos a Lupo. Otros río de los Altramuzes que en Latín se llaman Lupinos.* This sounds too naïve to be true.

tahona, bakery; *zaguán*, vestibule. Related to furnishings are *alcuza*, container for olive oil; *alfiler*, pin; *alfombra*, carpet, rug; *almirez*, mortar; *almohada*, pillow; *azafate*, tray; *jofaina*, washbasin. For dress or adornment stand *alhaja*, jewel; *alpargata*, sandal; *ajorca*, bracelet; *arracada*, earring; *babucha*, slipper; *cenefa*, border; *gabán*, overcoat; and older terms like *ciclatón*, silk cloth, and *zaragüelles*, surviving as "sherryvallies" in our Southwest. *Ataúd*, coffin, is another Saracen importation.

The agriculture to which the Catholic and later sovereigns dealt such a farreaching blow by the expulsions appears in *aceite*, oil; *aceituna*, olive; *aceña*, flour mill run by water; *albaricoque* (but this contains *praecoquum*, which is Latin; Arabic, having no *p*, uses instead the related *b*), apricot; *alcachofa*, artichoke; *alfalfa*, alfalfa; *algodón*, cotton; *a(l)tramuz* (originally Greek), lupine; *arroz*, rice; *azafrán*, saffron; *azúcar*, sugar; *berenjena*, eggplant, of which Baltasar del Alcázar wittily sings; *chirivía* (originally Latin?), parsnip; *limón*, lemon; *naranja*, orange;[4] *sandía*, watermelon; *toronja*, grapefruit, early mentioned in the *Libro de buen amor*, 1443d (*Religiosa non casta es perdida toronja*), and the *Andanças e viajes* of Pero Tafur; *zanahoria*, carrot; and in flowers like *adelfa*, oleander; *albahaca*, sweet basil; *alhelí*, gillyflower; *azahar*, orangeflower; *azucena*, lily; and *jazmín*, jessamine. Extensive irrigation was necessary, and from this practice came the words *acequia*, irrigation ditch; *alberca*, reservoir; *aljibe*, cistern; and *noria*, chain pump. And in the fields an *alacrán*, scorpion, might be seen.

---

[4] Strictly, *limón* and *naranja* are Persian words.

In scientific progress, especially in medicine, which included botany and chemistry, and in mathematics, the Arabs showed the way to Europe: *albéitar*, veterinarian; *jaqueca*, headache; *jarope*, sirup; *momia* (through Latin?), mummy; *nuca*, nape of the neck; *alambique*, still; *alcanfor*, camphor; *alcohol*, alcohol; *alferecía*, epilepsy; *alfombrilla*, measles; *alquimia*, alchemy; *azogue*, quicksilver; *bórax*, borax; *cero*, zero; *cifra*, cipher, figure; *cenit*, zenith; *guarismo*, figure, digit; *nadir*, nadir.

Among the words of everyday use are *achaque*, complaint; *ahorrar* (*horro* = free), save; *albóndiga*, meat ball; *albricias*, reward for good news; *alfayate*, tailor; *alquiler*, rent, hire; *asesino* (probably through Italian), "one who has drunk of the hashish," a member of a murderous sect; *azul*, blue; *bellota*, acorn; *escarlata*, scarlet; *fulano* and *zutano*, so-and-so; *gandul*, given to loafing; *hasta*, until (influenced for its *s* perhaps by O.S. *faz* < *faciem* or by its correlative *desde*); *he*, behold (as in *he aquí*, etc.); *matar* (containing the root *mat*,[5] dead, which appears in "checkmate"), kill; *mezquino* (which may have come up from Sicily and through France), originally meaning "poor, miserable"; *mono*, monkey; *ojalá*, if Allah will; *res* (which has nothing to do with the Latin word of similar spelling), head of cattle; *zagal*, lad; *zalamero*, coaxing. To enlarge upon the above list is merely a matter of opening at the letters *j* or *z* a dictionary which provides etymologies, but among the Arabisms in Spanish will be found few verbs (*halagar, recamar, achacar?, escatimar?* See the *Hispanic Review*, VI [1938], 216–217; VII [1939], 337–344).

---

[5] Strictly, this is a Persian word.

BIBLIOGRAPHY

ALCALÁ, PEDRO DE. *El vocabulista de romance en arábigo,* Granada, 1505, or Petri Hispani, *De lingua arabica,* libri duo, Göttingen, 1883; there is also a reproduction, in microphotographic form, by the Hispanic Society of America, New York, 1928; this contains his *Arte para ligeramente saber la lengua arauiga, vocabulista y doctrina christiana,* Granada, 1504(?).

ASÍN PALACIOS, M. *Contribución a la toponimia árabe de España,* segunda edición, Madrid, 1944.

DOZY, R. and ENGELMANN, W. *Glossaire des mots espagnols et portugais dérivés de l'arabe,* deuxième édition, Leyden, Brill, 1869.

EGUÍLAZ Y YANGUAS, L. DE. *Glosario etimológico de las palabras españolas de origen oriental,* Granada, Imprenta de la Lealtad, 1886.

ENTWISTLE. *The Spanish Language,* pp. 125–134.

GONZÁLEZ PALENCIA, A. *Historia de la España musulmana,* segunda edición, Barcelona [1929], Colección Labor, no. 69, *passim.*

LOMBARD, A. "Die Bedeutungsentwicklung zweier ibero-romanischer Verba," in *Zeitschrift für Romanische Philologie,* LVI (1936), 637–643.

MENÉNDEZ PIDAL. *Manual,* §§ 4, 4.

MEYER-LÜBKE. *Introducción,* §§ 47–49.

SIMONET, F. J. *Glosario de voces ibéricas y latinas usadas entre los mozárabes,* Madrid, 1888.

STEIGER, A. *Contribución a la fonética del hispano-árabe y de los arabismos en el ibero-románico y el siciliano,* Madrid, 1932 (*Revista de filología española, Anejo XVII*).

TREND, J. B. "Arabic Words in Spanish and Portuguese," in *The Legacy of Islam,* edited by the late Sir Thomas Arnold, Oxford, Clarendon Press, 1931, pp. 19–27.

⚘ 6 ⚘

The Period of Old Spanish (To 1500)

Toward the Rise of Castile

By 718 the northward rush of the Arabs and Berbers, for the invaders were of both races, had swept them to the Biscayan coast at Gijón. The defeat inflicted at Covadonga in the same year, or between 721 and 725 according to a modern study, by Pelayo, aided by his band of refugees, and the activities of the Saracens in France, diverted the attention of the invaders from the northwest area, where a small Christian kingdom was established, with its capital first at Cangas de Onís, then at Oviedo, and finally at León.

Eventful was the miraculous discovery at Padrón of the body of St. James (see p. 7), whose bones the first archbishop, Diego Gelmírez, is reported to have incorporated into the foundations of the cathedral, perhaps, as some one has said, to confound the researches of the skeptical. Among the numerous devout legends which shortly sprang up is that of the appearance of the saint, mounted on a white horse, before Ramiro I of Asturias and León at the supposed battle of Clavijo (near Calahorra in the province of Logroño) in 844. From then on Santiago was accepted as the patron saint of Spain, and of cavalrymen in particular, whose war cry became *¡Santiago y cierra, España!*, Saint James and attack, Spain! The pilgrimages that were soon established, which were at their height in the twelfth and thirteenth centuries and were mentioned by Chaucer (*Canterbury Tales,* "Prologue") and by Dante (*Paradiso,* XXV, 18), led to a great strengthening and consolidation of the Christian spirit. It is apropos to recall that the prose *Historia Karoli Magni et Rotholandi* or *Pseudo-Turpin* was written in the early twelfth century as part of a longer work advertising Compostela to prospective visitors. The route followed by the majority of the pilgrims, the *camino francés,* led from Roncevaux and Pamplona, or from Somport and Jaca, to Estella, Logroño, Burgos, Sahagún, Astorga, Ponferrada, and thence to Santiago.

Castile was at first a dependency of the kings of León; its "capital" was Amaya, on the upper Pisuerga, and Count Fernán González was one of its early Christian governors. León was at its height under Ramiro II (930–950), but the devastating raids of Almanzor, who, after a campaign in which Zamora fell, assumed his title (*Al mansur = defendedor, defendimiento, Crónica general,* chaps. 734, 747), reduced it to a waste. The feeling for Castilian independence is represented by Count Fernán González (died 970), in whose time the land of castles became practically free from its western master. The two crowns became one, for the moment, when Ferdinand I (1037–1065), who was of Navarrese origin, defeated his Leonese brother-in-law, but the political union did not become permanent until 1217. A growing feeling of regionalism, a difference in spirit, is considered to have been accentuated by the fact that León was repopulated by mozárabes, Castile by settlers from Cantabria. Ferdinand's son Alphonso VI (1072–1109) restored Toledo to Christian hands, and further progress toward the Reconquest was made by Alphonso VIII, Ferdinand III, and Alphonso XI (cf. p. 55). In the meantime, Alphonso X, the Learned (1252–1284), pursued literature rather than the infidel. As the founder of Castilian prose, he had scholars compile and translate into Spanish the historical (*Grande et general estoria; Primera crónica general,* continued, after chap. 627, by Alphonso's son, Sancho IV), legal (*Las siete partidas*), and scientific (*Libros del saber de astronomía, Tablas alfonsíes, El lapidario,* etc.) works which contained the totality of the knowledge of the period. At Alphonso's literary court were troubadours from France, and Alphonso himself composed religious poetry (*Las cantigas de Santa María*) in the Galician dialect, the medium of lyric poetry at that time, which had been carried to Galicia from southern France along the *camino francés,* the French Road or Way of Saint James. In towns on this route entire districts were populated by French emigrants. Already in the reign of his father, Fernando III el Santo (1217–1252), Spanish had been recognized as official for notarial documents and royal diplomas.

Civil war was continued by Peter el Cruel (1350–1369) and his half-brother Henry of Trastamara (1369–1379), who took his name from an ancient castle in Galicia. The weakness of the monarchy and the consequent prevalence of anarchy are but too evident throughout this period. In turning from this subject it is interesting to note that in 1388 at Briviesca (northeast of Burgos), King John I conferred the title of *Príncipe de Asturias,* Prince of the Asturias (since borne by the heir to the Spanish throne), on his eldest son, at the request of John of Gaunt, Duke of Lancaster, before the prince's marriage to the Englishman's daughter. In the early fifteenth century the government was controlled by a minister, Alvaro de Luna, the nobles being, as always, troublesome. Isabel, the sister of Enrique IV, was placed upon the throne of Castile in 1474 by the nobles on the ground that Enrique's heir Juana was the daughter of the queen by the royal favorite Beltrán de la Cueva (hence Juana was dubbed *la Beltraneja*).

Of the history of Aragon only a few points concern us here. At the end of the thirteenth century, having reached out first for Majorca, Aragon had extended its sway to Sicily, thanks to the great Catalan mercenary Roger de Flor (died 1306), who later aided the Roman emperor of Constantinople against the Turks. The jealousy of the Byzantine natives led to treachery and to retribution by the Catalan adventurers which has become a stereotyped phrase (*venganza catalana*). Over a century later the queen of Naples invited Alphonso V (1416–1458) to aid her against the French house of Anjou. Shortly thereafter, the Italian kingdom became an Aragonese possession, and Alphonso remained permanently in Naples, where his reputation depends on his patronage of literature and the arts. Ferdinand V, having married Isabel of Castile in 1469, became king of Aragon ten years later. The joint rule (*tanto monta, monta tanto, Isabel como Fernando*) of the Catholic Kings marks the beginning of the history of Spain as a great nation in modern times. The nobles were crushed, the crown assuming the rank of grand master of the ancient military orders (Calatrava, 1487; Santiago, 1493; Alcántara, 1494; Montesa,

1587). The Santa Hermandad was revived and reorganized by Isabel in 1476 to form in the end the nucleus of a country-wide police force. Countless administrative reforms were introduced. In 1478 the Inquisition was established. The remaining possessions of the Moors were taken, after a war of ten years. Naples was more firmly attached to the crown through the successes of Gonzalo de Córdoba, "the Great Captain"; and, in 1512, that portion of Navarre which lay south of the Pyrenees was added by Ferdinand to Spanish holdings.

The Spread of Castilian

The use of the vernacular, and it is now time to call it Spanish, continued throughout the Moorish domination. Latin may be said to have become Spanish when the authority of Rome weakened to such a degree that local tendencies of speech went unchecked among the ruling classes. The date may be set at the fifth or sixth century A.D. (cf. Bourciez, *Eléments,* § 137; Grandgent, *Vulgar Latin,* § 3).

The Arabs who came early to Spain married Spanish women, and women cherish their native language within their homes. The upper classes of both races were bilingual, and even in the law court the proceedings might be conducted in Romance. Knowledge of this everyday language (Mozarabic) is scanty, since it must be collected piecemeal from the chance remarks of Arabic historians, from their transcription of place names, from its occasional insertion, for the exigencies of meter or for purposes of jocularity, into poetry, and from rare glossaries. It remained in the south, except when Mozarabs trekked northward pressed by the fanatical Almoravides and Almohades, and, as its development was arrested, it shows archaic features: it retains the diphthongs *ai, au, ei* (cf. *yenáir* instead of *enero, lauxa* instead of *losa, Junqueira* instead of *Junquera*); initial *ge, gi,* and *j* before an unstressed vowel (*januarium* > *yenáir*); initial *pl* (*plantagine* > *plantáin*); the unvoiced intervocalic consonants (*totum* > *toto*); the *t* < *ct* (*lactem* > *leite*); the stage of *ll* < *c'l* (*cuniculum* > *conello*); and it preserves *mb* (*Columbaria* > *Colombaira*). The Mozarabic dialect appears to have survived in Toledo into the thirteenth century, although the date and manner of its disappearance are not yet clear.

The Castilian dialect was extended through the founding of Burgos, the "head of Castile," about 884, in a strategic position with its back to the mountains, and through the eminence of its citizens. Alphonso VI annexed La Rioja in 1076; Segovia and Avila were repossessed at about the same time as Toledo (1085), to which the court was removed in 1087. That the central part of the country was largely repopulated by immigrants from the north is shown by the names of many villages in the area surrounding Burgos and Osma: Bascones, Basconcillos, Bascunaña, Villabascones; and, in Avila and Segovia, Gallegos, Castellanos, Castellanillos, Aragoneses.

It was through a king of Navarre (Sancho the Great, 1027–1035) that the Benedictine monks of Cluny, soon to be so favored by Alphonso VI, came into Spain. It was in Navarre that the Visigothic ritual was first replaced by the Roman; it was there that the Carolingian or French style of handwriting, the *letra francesa,* was substituted for the Visigothic. The monks of the great Benedictine houses of San Pedro de Cardeña, San Pedro de Arlanza, Oña, Sahagún, Santo Domingo de Silos, and San Millán de la Cogolla (a favorite pilgrimage place for Castilians), even through their preference for Latin over the vernacular diminished the prestige of León and Leonese, which dialect was the real heir of the language of the Visigothic epoch. The probably abundant development of epic poetry in the eleventh and twelfth centuries served also to confirm the position of Castilian. The intensity of the feeling of nationality which animated the counts of the plains of Burgos and their followers[1] led them to reject the written law of the *Fuero Juzgo,* which held in León, Toledo, and among the Mozarabs generally. Settlers from Roman Cantabria, which comprised northern Old Castile and the province of Santander (La Montaña and Campóo), and settlers from La Rioja, a region of Castilian influence, pushing south and southwestward to Toledo, had, with the help of a flourishing literature, brought Castilian to the commanding position.

It was not until 1925 that the conservative Royal Spanish Academy, whole role is to "purify, fix, and lend splendor" (*limpia, fija, y da esplendor*) to the chief language of Spain, saw fit to designate its grammar and dictionary as of the Spanish rather than of the Castilian language. This is not to say that the terms necessarily are synonymous; Castilian may be the speech of the lower ranks of society in Old and New Castile. Spanish, in the words of Menéndez Pidal, is "the product of many-centuried collaboration of cultivated men from all Hispanic regions." In the technical discussion of the growth of Spanish it is the dialect of Castile which will be the main topic, at the expense of the other principal subdivisions of the language, Leonese and Navarro-Aragonese.

[1] See ... *de toda Spanna Castylla es mejor ... Aun Castylla Vieja ... mejor es que lo al* (*Poema de Fernán González,* 156a, 157ab).

BIBLIOGRAPHY

ALONSO, A. *Castellano, Español, Idioma Nacional,* Buenos Aires, 1938 (Instituto de Filología ... de la Universidad de Buenos Aires).

MENÉNDEZ PIDAL. *Orígenes, passim.* (The same author's *El idioma español en sus primeros tiempos,* Madrid, Editorial Voluntad, 1927, or Buenos Aires, *Colección austral* [no. 250], 1942, reprints without notes, pp. 434 ff. of the *Orígenes.*)

The Earliest Texts and Early Literary Texts

A manuscript of the late ninth or tenth century from the monastery of San Millán de la Cogolla (in the western part of the province of Logroño) contains, between the lines and on the margin of the Latin text, equivalents in Romance, though with somewhat Latinized spelling. There are two comments in Basque; these (nos. 31 and 42) may be independent of the text. These running commentaries or glosses, the *Glosas Emilianenses,* are the first Spanish text. From them it appears that by that date the existence and the special function of the colloquial speech could no longer be ignored.

In the British Museum there is another manuscript, of the second half of the tenth century, from the monastery of Santo Domingo de Silos, southeast of Burgos, which likewise contains explanations of the Latin text in the vulgar speech; these are the *Glosas Silenses.* Representative glosses from the *Glosas Silenses* and from the *Glosas Emilianenses* are given in the following table; the *glosa* is in the right-hand column.

Number of Glosa	Glosas Emilianenses	Glosa
3	suscitabi	lebantai
29	inueniebit	aflarat [hallará]
30	incolomes	sanos et salbos
65	adtendat	katet
103	et tu ibis	etuiras [y tu irás]
107	terribilem	paboroso uel temeroso
110	donec	ata quando
140	quid agas	ke faras [qué harás]

Number of Glosa	Glosas Silenses	Glosa
24	abluit	labat
57	interitu	muerte
72	esse	sedere [ser]
86	quod	por ke
93	interficiat	matare
218	habeat	ajat [haya]
223	abunculi	tio
248	ad nubtias	a las uotas
304	igitur	de inde
351	ferre	leuare

Such texts as are found in Spanish in the tenth, eleventh, and twelfth centuries are usually legal documents (church registers, deeds, laws, *fueros*); literature before 1200, mostly arid *cronicones*, continued to be in Latin. The major exponents of this historical writing are, in later generations, Lucas, bishop of Túy (on the Portuguese border, south of Vigo), whose *Cronicon mundi* was finished in 1236; and Rodrigo Jiménez de Rada, archbishop of Toledo, whose *Historia gothica* was completed in 1243.

The highly developed state of the language, already shaped, not very dissimilar to that of the present, as seen in the first monuments of literature, is in striking contrast to the notarial documents of the tenth to twelfth centuries. Monumental indeed in its granitic solidity is the oldest work of Spanish literature extant, the epic *Poema de Mio Cid* of 3735 verses. The composition of this work is assigned authoritatively but somewhat arbitrarily to the year 1140, principally on the basis of historical reference. Dealing also with a national hero, but cast in a less popular form, is the *Poema de Fernán González*, written supposedly at the monastery of San Pedro de Arlanza about 1236. The existence of several other poems on epic subjects is evidenced in various indirect ways, as, for example, by their incorporation in prose chronicles, but we have not their original text.

Compared—if inconclusively—to Gallic church dramas both in French and Latin, and probably another product of the influence of the Cluniac clergy in Spain, is the most ancient specimen of the drama, the incomplete *Auto* or *Misterio de los reyes magos* (146–147 verses), of the thirteenth or perhaps even the twelfth century, which is extant, like the poems of the Cid and of Count Fernán González, in but one manuscript.

In 1251, by order of the then prince Alphonso the Learned, whose position in the establishment of Spanish prose has been previously referred to (p. 65), there was translated the *Calila y Dimna,* a collection of moral tales of Indian origin, whose chief actors are the two *lobos cervales* or lynxes who give the work its name. A transitional work from the saintly legend to the romance of chivalry is the long prose *Libro del Caballero Cifar* (or *Zifar*), of the earliest part of the fourteenth century. A long step forward in content and language are the fifty or fifty-one tales, still owing much to Arabic storytellers, of the *Conde Lucanor,* or *Libro de los enxiemplos del Conde Lucanor et de Patronio* (1328–1335), by the nephew of Alphonso X, Juan Manuel, who is the first to show a definitely personal, if an unemotional, style. The *Conde Lucanor* was printed first in 1575 by Argote de Molina.

With San Millán de la Cogolla in La Rioja is associated the unoriginal, occasionally naïve, occasionally inspired, occasionally humorous monk Gonzalo de Berceo (active

1220–1242), the first Spanish poet known by name. In the metrical form in which his religious poems are written, in the counted syllables of monorhymed quatrains which men of learning used, are two other poems of the thirteenth century, by unknown authors, the lengthy *Libro de Alixandre* of over 10,000 verses, dealing with Alexander the Great, and the *Libro de Apolonio* of 2624 verses, which has to do with the hero of a late Greek romance, Appolonius, Prince of Tyre. In Berceo's monkish work occur passages truly lyrical, but the first lyric in Castilian is a poem of 162 verses which is obviously southern French in inspiration. I mean the *Razón de amor,* of the thirteenth century, slight and tasteful.

Belonging to the first half of the fourteenth century is one of the three most important books in Spanish literature (in the opinion of its greatest critic), the long miscellany in varied verse, the *Libro de buen amor* of Juan Ruiz, the archpriest of Hita, a village near Guadalajara, whose personality leaps out from almost every page. The long, moralizing *Rimado de palacio* (probably meaning "Rhymed Account of Life at Court") by Pedro López de Ayala (1332–1407), the great political figure, is a more sober work, showing a more critical spirit. This grand chancellor of Castile, like Alphonso X, or, rather, like the latter's ghost writers, composed important historical works, and translated some classical authors (Livy, Boethius), but, leaving for later pages the discussion of the revival of Antiquity in the fifteenth century, I hurry on to remark that another jovial archpriest, Martínez de Toledo, from Talavera, is the first to find the language of conversation worthy of reproduction in literature, in the *Corbacho* (a title borrowed from Boccaccio) or *Reprobación del amor mundano,* completed in 1438.

BIBLIOGRAPHY

FORD, J. D. M. *Old Spanish Readings,* Boston, Ginn and Company [1906, 1911].

MÉRIMÉE, E., and MORLEY, S. GRISWOLD. *A History of Spanish Literature,* New York, Henry Holt and Company [1930], pp. 8–89.

MENÉNDEZ PIDAL. *Orígenes,* pp. 1 ff.

ZAUNER, A. *Altspanisches Elementarbuch,* zweite umgearbeitete Auflage, Heidelberg, C. Winter, 1921.

THE MATTER OF ORTHOGRAPHY

Such new sounds as evolved out of Vulgar Latin presented problems of spelling, especially in non-Latin names of people and of places, which scribes of the tenth to twelfth and even thirteenth centuries solved in a variety of ways. Their system of spelling survived until the period of activity of the scholars of Alphonso the Learned, whose orthography continues, essentially, to the present day, in spite of attempted reforms by Nebrija and later grammarians of the sixteenth and the seventeenth centuries.

Vowels.—The new Romance diphthongs *ie* < *ę* and *ue* (and earlier *uo*) < *ǫ* left copyists in some perplexity. Now one vowel is reproduced, now the other. Even as late as the *Auto de los reyes magos, morto* (< *mortum*) and *pusto* (< *positum*) are in rhyme (vv. 109–110). Similarly for *ie*, there are both *e* and *i: celo* and *cilo* = *cielo, tirra* (rhyming with *guer[r]a*) = *tierra, seglo* = Old Spanish *sieglo* > Modern Spanish *siglo, marauila* = Old Spanish *marabiella* and *strela* = *estrella, strelero* and *quiro* (= *quiero*) in rhyme (vv. 36, 41, 23–24, 43, 1–2, 52–53). But this hesitation has practically vanished by the beginning of the thirteenth century.

I and J, U and V.—To stand for *y* = consonant, as in *iam*, the Romans of the Empire often used a long form of *i*. From this long *i* has arisen the letter *j*; the definitive differentiation took place after the invention of printing, as did the distinction between *u* and *v,* which were originally, in Roman times, two forms of writing the vowel *u.* The early grammarian, Nebrija (p. 137) is the first to make the distinction and printers in the Low Countries were the earliest to adopt the idea generally. (See L. Kukenheim, *Contributions à l'histoire de la grammaire italienne, espagnole et française à l'époque de la renaissance*, Amsterdam, 1932, pp. 32 and 36.)

Y (originally the capital form of *upsilon*) was borrowed by Latin from the Greek alphabet to reproduce the sound of that Greek letter. With the passing of time *y* came to be interchangeable with *i*: *yr, yfante, ynfiernos*, etc. In the initial position Lope de Vega, for example, prefers *y*, but elsewhere he writes either *i* or *y* (*soi, soy, quereis, beys*). The modern spheres of *i* and *y* were defined by the Royal Spanish Academy as late as 1815, since which date *y* appears (except occasionally on the Pacific coast of South America) as a vowel only in the conjunction *y* and, with semivocalic value, as the second element of a final diphthong (*hay, soy, ley*, etc.). Spellings like *Ynés, Ysabel, Ygnacio*, and the like are therefore obsolete. Compare p. 189.

Consonants.—The new consonantal sounds were (as is usual in the Romance languages) mostly palatal.

In Castile, for the sound of *ñ* the competition was between *ni* and *nn*: *sennor = señor, connomento < cognomentum, vinias = viñas;* compare *adelinnando < linea* (*Poema de Mio Cid*, 2237). *Nn*, which was abbreviated as *n̄*, hence our *ñ*, prevailed to the extent that *España, extraña*, and *Alemaña = Alemania* rhyme in Castillejo's *Contra los que dejan los metros castellanos* (before 1550). Phonetic spellings like *ñeto = nieto* and *ñeso = ni eso* are found among the untutored today. In documents from Navarre, Aragon, and eastern Spain generally the symbol was at first *ng* or *gn*: *uingas = viñas, Castagne = Castaña*.

For palatalized *l,* Castilian, when it did not use the etymological *li* (*filio, mulier*), regularly chose *ll* (*muller*), but often used a single *l* (*kabalo*). Per Abbat, the copyist of the sole manuscript of the *Poema de Mio Cid,* vacillates disconcertingly between *l* and *ll,* and in the late fifteenth century Nebrija is aware of variation when he says (*Orthographía,* VII): Escreuimos esso mesmo en algunos lugares l senzilla, ꝛ pronunciamos la doblada, como quando alos nombres femininos que comiençan en a, ... *dezimos* con doblada l: ellalma, ellaguja, ellaçada, pero *escreuimos* el alma, el aguja, el açada; con las otras vocales lo uno ꝛ lo otro escriuimos ꝛ pronunciamos, como diziendo: la espada, el espada, ell espada (the italics are not in the original). In eastern Spain the symbol for palatal *l* in the oldest manuscripts was *lg: valge = valle* (La Rioja), *Gilgelmus = Guillermo.*

For the Old Spanish sound of [ž] (as in azure) or [ŷ] (as in Jones) notarial documents used *li: relias = rejas;* often *g: concego = concejo, Uallego = Vallejo;* and *gg: figgos = fijos, bieggo = viejo, ualleggo = vallejo.* G was used also for the sound of *y* = consonant (as in *iam*): *magore = maiore;* since Classic Latin *ge, gi* > Vulgar Latin *y.* (Cf. p. 91.) Further illustrations of the confusion of orthographical *i, g,* and *y* from the *Poema de Mio Cid* are *aiude* (221) vs. *ajuda* (2103); *corneia* (11); *consego* (85), *consegar* (1256), in which both *i* and *g* < *li;* and *mensage* (1278) vs. *mensaie* (627, 975, 1188, 1834, 2600). The use of *g* for either [ž], [ŷ], or [y] had become less frequent by the middle of the thirteenth century.

For the sound of *ch* [č] (as in church), which the Latinist Nebrija thought required a new symbol, the oldest symbols were *g*: *Sangiz* = *Sánchez* or *Sánchiz,* or, rarely, *gg*: *Didac Sanggeç* = *Diego Sánchez,* but *ch,* perhaps borrowed from France, where it had long been in use, appears in Spain at the end of the eleventh century, and rapidly becomes the accepted symbol for this sound.

The sound of [š] (as in shoot) is written over all the country as *x,* or not infrequently at first, as *sc*: *Xemeniz* = *Ximénez, Scavierri* = *Xavier,* or, sporadically, as *ss*: *issie* = *exía* (Berceo).

The tendency at the beginning is to use *z* to describe the phoneme yielded by *ce, ci,* and *ti* + vowel: *conzedo* = *concedo, razionem* = *rationem.* In the Visigothic style of handwriting (*letra visigoda*) *z* often had at the top a large hook in the form of *c,* which was likely to occupy the space of the entire line, causing the body of the letter to descend to the line below. This use of two forms of one and the same letter, for one sound, continued with the introduction of the French style (*letra francesa*), but in time the *z* came to be a mere flourish, that is, a *cedilla,* or "little *z,*" at the bottom of the *c.* From the early years of the thirteenth century it became customary to use *ç* for the unvoiced sound of *ts* [ŝ] (as in boots): Old Spanish *çinco, z* for the corresponding voiced equivalent, *dz* [ẑ] (as in adze): Old Spanish *fazer,* but in the manuscript of the *Poema de Mio Cid* this distinction is not yet clearly observed.

The confusion of *b* and *v* (*u*) is increasingly frequent: *salbos* = *salvos, suscitabi* glossed as *lebantai, hauet* = *habet, uona* = *bono, viba* (*Poema de Mio Cid,* 1754) and *biva* (*ibid.,* 1038) = *viva.* Old Spanish later tended to use *b* for the occlusive sound in absolute initial position: *vota* > *boda, u* for the fricative sound in the intervocalic position: *beued* = *bebed* (*Poema de Mio Cid,* 1025), but regularity of observance has been interfered with by the claims of tradition, which has clung to the Latin spelling. Thus Old Spanish *beuer* (< *bibere*) and *biuir* (< *vivere*) have restored the original consonants, and we now write *beber* and *vivir.* Into the seventeenth century, however, *-aba* of the imperfect indicative was still normally written *-aua.*

A special and striking use of *b* with the value of consonantal *u* = *v* is shown by the standard Old Spanish forms *debda* = *deuda, cibdad* = *ciudad, cabteloso* = *cauteloso,* and so forth. The consonant had not yet become vocalized in the first half of the sixteenth century, at least not after the back vowels *o* and *u,* into which it was in time absorbed, for of such forms as *dubda* (< *dubitam,* M. S. *duda*), Valdés says in his *Diálogo de la lengua* (ed cit., p. 109): *toda mi vida los he scrito y pronunciado con b* (cf. p. 238).

There are a few consistent minor differences between the orthography of Old Spanish and that of the Golden Age and later times. Old Spanish is more accurate phonetically in the spelling of the sound of *erre,* which is written as *rr* or *R* (*buena rrazon, muebles e Rayzes, sonrrisos mio Cid*), though the rights of etymology are not entirely ignored. The precise nasal sound pronounced before a *b* or *p* depends nowadays largely upon the rate of articulation, and either an *m* or an *n* will result, according as there is or is not assimilation to the labial.[2] From the medieval period into the seventeenth century, with decreasing frequency, this phoneme, whatever its actual value, is written *n* + *b, p: canpo, el burga-*

---

[2] Cf. Navarro Tomás, *Manual,* § 87.

lés conplido, Ponpeyo, canbiar, anbos, etc. In the older texts words which had an initial *h* in Latin are written without this soundless symbol: *auer* < *habere, onrra* = *honra,* and it is often improperly added: *Hyremos* = *Iremos* (*Poema de Mio Cid,* 1224). The influence of learning restored the original spelling: *haber, honra,* and probably no mistake is more widespread now than the prefixing of a superfluous *hache: hechar* = *echar.* "Let's see if you write *amor* with an *h*" (*A ver si pones amor con hache*), says a teasing sister to her brother in a contemporary comedy (Martínez Sierra, *Sueño de una noche de agosto,* I). The use of *h* in *hueso* < *ossum, huevo* < *ovum,* and most other words beginning with *hue,* is due to the fact that the symbols *u* and *v* were used for both vowel *u* and consonant *v.* The *h* therefore was a device to indicate that the vocalic value was intended (Nebrija, *Orthographía,* IV), as it may have been also in *hielo* < *gelum, hiedra* < *ederam,* and *hierba* < *herbam.* In the two last, however, the variant spellings *yedra* and *yerba* have gained the upper hand, but *yelo* is obsolete.

BIBLIOGRAPHY

Cuervo. "Disquisiciones sobre antigua ortografía y pronunciación castellanas, II," in *Revue Hispanique,* V (1898), 273–313, or in *Disquisiciones filológicas,* tomo I, Bogotá, Editorial Centro, 1939, pp. 131–206.
Menéndez Pidal. *Orígenes,* §§ 1 ff.

EVOLUTION OF SOUNDS

It is a basic principle for the historical study of speech sounds that *under the same conditions any one sound* of the parent language will yield one and only one sound at any given time in the derived language.

VOWELS

Stressed.—Characteristic of Castile are: the early establishment (by the tenth century) of the diphthongs *ie* < ę and *ue* < ǫ while the remainder of Spain wavered between several variant forms, at least for ǫ; the prompt disappearance of the step *ei* in the evolution of *a + i*; the prevalence there of *illo-a* < *iello-a* < *ęllum-am*. Some of these and other traits call for discussion.

The diphthongization of ǫ progresses everywhere in Romance territory, but the rapidity with which this occurs and the conditions of the change differ among and within the several languages which continue Vulgar Latin. In the western parts of the area belonging to the Leonese dialect the step *uo* (e.g., *puode, luogo*), which precedes *ue* (though not directly) is still in use. The primitive stages of the language of Spain show *uo* in León and Aragon, where it is usual, and in Castile, where it is not the rule. Here *ue* is already established by the tenth century. The original form of the *Poema de Mio Cid*, if we accept its probable composition in the province of Soria near Aragonese influence and if we assume that its assonances were meant to be perfect, would seem to call for *uo*, which the copyist may have modernized or Castilianized into *ue*, since *fuert* (1330, 2696,

2843), *puede*(*n*) (2009, 2920, 3468), *muert* (2676, 2774, 3641, 3688), *aluen* (2696), *fuent* (2700), *despues* (3706), all occur in passages assonating in *ó*. There is reason[3] for believing in the existence of *uo* at the time of composition also of the *Auto de los reyes magos* and of the brief *Disputa del alma y el cuerpo*.[4]

Ue is reduced to *e*, provided the nature of the consonants preceding be such as to provoke the elimination of the labial *u*. Thus *fruente* (< *frontem*), *flueco* (< *floccum*), *pruebo* (< *probo*), which contain two labial sounds (*f* or *p, u*) of which the second (*u*) is both preceded and followed by articulations which are made in the front of the mouth (*r* or *l, e*), simplify their form to *frente* (*fruente* still appears in the *Corbacho*, III, 6, composed before 1438), *fleco* (*flueco* still in the 1619 edition of *Guzmán de Alfarache*, also in the 1758 edition of Isla's *Fray Gerundio*, I, 3; IV, 3, twice), and *prebo* (which nowadays is dialectal).

For a somewhat similar reason the termination *iello-a* < *ęllum-am* has been reduced to *illo-a*: Castilla < Castiella < *Castella*. The reduction does not become frequent in writing until the fourteenth century; there are sporadic examples long before. We may deduce that the palatalization

---

[3] Cf. R. Menéndez Pidal, *Cantar de Mio Cid*, Madrid, 1908, I, 144-145.

[4] The belief that the stress was originally on the first vowel of the diphthong (*íe, úo*) is discussed by R. Menéndez Pidal, *Orígenes*, § 22. Cf. also E. Staaff, "Réflexions sur la diphthongaison en espagnol," in *Studier i modern Sprakvetenskap*, X (1928), Upsala, 115–130. For the opposite opinion cf. several papers by J. D. M. Ford, "Some considerations on diphthongs and triphthongs," in *Homenaje ofrecido a Menéndez Pidal*, Madrid, 1924, II, 29–33; "The Passage of Vulgar Latin Close *u* to French Rounded *i* (*ü, y*) Is Purely a Romance Phenomenon," in *Mélanges Antoine Thomas*, Paris, 1927, 157–163; "The accent in diphthongs created by the 'breaking' of a simple stressed vowel," in *Mélanges de philologie offerts a Jean-Jacques Salverda de Grave*, Groningen, 1933, pp. 104–105.

of intervocalic *ll,* assuming it became general during the thirteenth century, since the written language requires a fairly long period to catch up with the innovations of the spoken, carried with it the lifting and absorption of *e,* a disturbing element between two sounds of the same relative point of articulation, the palatals *í* and *ll.* Given the nature of Castilian *s* (p. 161), the simplification of *vesperam* > Old Spanish *viéspera* > *víspera* and of *pressam* > Old Spanish *priesa* > *prisa* may arise out of the same phonetic situation.

Already evident in the Augustan Age, when it is the subject of jokes and puns, is the substitution of *o* as the halfway point between the extremes of openness and closeness of *au: aut* > *o, paucum* > *poco; faucem* > *hoz,* narrows. This change is later than the voicing of the intervocalic consonants and had become general in Castile by the beginning of the eleventh century. Just as the *r* of *parte* prevents the change of *t* to *d,* so the *u* of *pauco* hinders the passage of *c* to *g* (as in *pacare* > *pagar*). In other words, *au* remained as a diphthong until after the period of evolution of the intervocalic consonants. Yet in *causam* > *cosa* the change must have taken place early, for *cosa* rhymes in Old Spanish with the ending *-osa* (cf. p. 158). By failing to raise the tip of the tongue, *u* was pronounced instead of *l,* and the *au* which thus arose in Vulgar Latin also > *o: falcem* > *hoz,* sickle; *balbum* > *bobo;* compare *dulcem* > Old Spanish *duz* or *duçe.*

Another of the characteristics of Castilian in contrast to Aragonese and Leonese is the disturbing influence upon both stressed and initial vowels of the sound of *i̯* as either the first or second element of a diphthong. This sound, tech-

nically named *yod* (which is the name for the letter *y* in
the Hebrew alphabet) and written either *i* or *e,* may be as
old as the colloquial pronunciation of the Classic Latin form
of a word; it may arise in Vulgar Latin or Spanish, as in the
evolution of certain consonant sounds (*ct, c'l, x*). That final
i (as in *feci*) has a like effect, or that *u* in a diphthong (as in
lingua) has this effect is questionable or exceptional. With
respect to the stressed vowels, ordinarily *yod* checks the
diphthongization of *ę* and *ǫ: pectum > pecho; Valeria >
Valera; noctem > noche; oculum > ojo;* it draws the openness of *a* and the closeness of *i* together into the intermediate
sound of *e: caseum > caiso > queiso > queso; sapiat >
saipa > seipa > sepa; primarium > primairo > primeiro >
primero; laxu + s > laixos > leixos > lejos.* But a *yod*
which early palatalized the preceding consonant usually
does not affect the vowel: *scǫrteum > escuerzo,* and *lęn-
teum > lienzo. Yod* makes the unstressed vowel of a preceding syllable closer by one degree (*a > e; e > i; o > u*):
*lactucam > lechuga; mentieron > mintieron; morió >
murió.* This rule has an important application in the preterite, imperfect subjunctive, future subjunctive, and gerund
of radical-changing verbs of the second and third classes, of
which the modern forms are already well entrenched in the
Poema de Mio Cid: adurmio (405), *firio* (963), *espidio*
(1067), *murieremos* (687), *sirviessen* (3155), etc. The steps
between the Classic Latin or Vulgar Latin form and the
modern Castilian are represented in the primitive dialects;
they survive in northwestern Spain (*freisno, queiso*) and
in Portuguese (*saiba, primeiro*), the speech of the center of
the country standing independently apart, as is its wont.

Intertonic.—Those vowels have disappeared which, being neither in the first nor the last syllable of a word, precede the principal stress, as in *capitalem,* or succeed it, as in *solidum,* except for *a,* which is ordinarily resistant enough to remain, though it is not infrequently weakened to *e:* Vulgar Latin *comperare < comparare, citera < cithara;* and dialectal Spanish *almenaque, bracelete, testerudo,* etc. The disappearance of the posttonic vowel (*solidum*) had become general by the tenth century. The emperor Augustus held *calidus* to be affected, as against *caldus,* and forms like *postus < positus, balneum < balineum* are already in Classic Latin. The process was intensified in Spanish: *delicatum > delgado; litteram > letra; columellum > colmillo; rapidum >* Old Spanish *raudo,* which has now been replaced, except in the language of poetry, by the Latinism *rápido.* But *a* survives: *mirabilia > maravilla; sabanum > sábana.*

Now, if the syntactic relation between the words of a phrase is close enough for them to be felt as a unit, the vowels which precede or follow the chief stress will be slurred over until they are lost. In this way *bon*um *diem > buen día; un*um *de illos > un dellos,* regular in Old Spanish, while we now say *uno de ellos; Dom(i)n*um *Carolus > Don Carlos; Sanct*um *Paulum > San(t) Pablo; mult*um *male > muy mal; me*um *librum > mi libro; primari*um *librum > primer libro; a man*o *salva > a mansalva; a fuer*o *de > a fuer de;* etc. In the earlier usage names like *Fernando* drop their final vowel (and then the preceding consonant, for a different reason) only when used in immediate conjunction with the family name: *Fernán González* but *Ovo* *nonbre Fernando, el conde don Fernando.* Compare *Hernán Cortés* and *Hernando del Pulgar.* Compare *don Pero* but *Per Bermúdez* in the *Poema de Mio Cid.* Thus are born the apocopated forms of the present day; the modern plurals of the adjectives in question probably owe their form to the fact that pluralization destroys the unity necessary for the excision of the intertonic vowel. There is also the problem of frequency of use. But *a* normally remains without change: *bonam noctem > buena noche,* unless the wear and tear of daily use be excessive: in popular usage *en casa de > en ca(s) de; compare María Gutiérrez > Mari Gutiérrez,* Old Spanish *García Pérez > Garci Pérez.* The occasional apocopation of *primera, tercera, postrera* (e.g., *tercer noche*) may, however, be analogical.

Final.—A, e, and *o* are the only final vowels native to Spanish: *animam > alma; scribit > escribe; manum > mano. Tribu, análisis,* etc., have not gone through the changes of sound requisite to a genuinely popular word. Necessarily after the simple consonants, and optionally after many grouped consonants, final *e* sloughed off in early Spanish: *panem > pan; cantare > cantar; salem > sal; piscem > pez; dicit > diz; sitim > sed; vicem > vez; habui > obe > of(f)* (*Poema de Mio Cid,* 3320–3321); *noctem > noch; gentem > yent; salvasti > salvest.* The apocopated and the modern forms are both in use in the *Poema de Mio Cid* (*noch* vs. *noche; nuef* vs. *nueve; part* vs. *parte;* etc.), but in the fourteenth century the tendency to retain *e,* except after *d, l, n, r, s,* and *z,* became dominant in the standard speech, and the other form is now to be observed only in a few instances: *val = valle,* in proper names like *Valverde,*

Valdemoro, Valdepeñas; cal = calle in *Caldebayona, Cal de Abades* (Vélez de Guevara, *El diablo cojuelo,* X and VII); *mont(t) = monte,* in *Monforte, Moncayo; duz = dulce* in *palo duz,* licorice; etc. However, that there is still uncertainty about retaining or dropping the final *e* appears in dialectal forms like *clas, huéspede, rede, tien, trébole,* which are widely used in Spain and in Spanish America.

BIBLIOGRAPHY

BOURCIEZ. *Eléments,* §§ 331–334.

ESPINOSA, AURELIO M. *Estudios sobre el español de Nuevo Méjico,* § 199, note.

FORD, J. D. M. *Old Spanish Readings,* pp. ix–xxiv.

HANSSEN. *Gramática histórica,* §§ 47–102.

MENÉNDEZ PIDAL. *Orígenes,* §§ 12 ff.

———. *Manual,* §§ 5–31.

ZEITLIN, M. A. "La apócope de la -a final átona en español," in *Hispanic Review,* VII (1939), 242–246.

CONSONANTS

Initial.—In works of literature of the fifteenth century initial *f* of Latin gives way before *h: facere >* Old Spanish *fazer > hacer; farinam > harina; fidem > fe > he* (in the O. S. phrase *a la he*). There are, to be sure, signs of the transformation in the *Libro de buen amor,* the manuscripts of which are believed to be of the fourteenth century: *Henares* (170*b,* 1107*c*), *herrén* (1092*b*), *hosco* (1215*c*), *heuilla* (1004*a*), *Hita* (575*a*), etc. Possibly it is because the labial quality of *u* reinforced *f,* whether labiodental or bilabial, that *f* has been preserved, at least in literary language, before *ue: fuego, fuella, fuente, fuera, fuero, fuerte, fuerza.* But forms with *hue* (*huego, huera,* etc.) have been frequent in the speech of the unlettered from the period of Juan del

Encina (1468?–1529?) and Lucas Fernández (1474?–1542) to the present Spanish of Spain, Mexico, New Mexico, Colombia, and elsewhere. Such an *h* was aspirated, that is, pronounced: *la pronunciamos hiriendo en la garganta,* says Nebrija in the *Gramática* (I, 5). It prevents synalepha in the poetry of Garcilaso de la Vega, Luis de León, and the Sevillan Herrera, which means either that it still had sound, or at least that the tradition of its sound was still alive: *mas ¿qué / haré que el alma ya barrunta* (11 syl.; *2a Egloga*), *las horas del vivir le va / hurtando* (11 syl.; *Noche serena*), *los que en él se / hallaron* (7 syl.; *Canción por la victoria de Lepanto*). But a change was in process. In a poem laudatory of the Catholic Kings (*ca.* 1492), the political (but not the linguistic) union of Castile and Aragon is symbolized in the *hinojo* = fern: *Llámala Castilla ynojo / qu'es su letra de Ysabel ... llámala Aragón fenojo / qu'es su letra de Fernando*. That the speech of Castilla la Vieja differed in this respect from the speech of the rest of Spain is further confirmed by the remark of a grammarian who says (1578) that in Old Castile people say *alagar*, in Toledo *halagar*.[5] In 1611 a lexicographer (Covarrubias, in the *Tesoro*, sub *h*) declares that those who do not pronounce the initial consonant of *heno* and *humo* are "pusillanimous, negligent, and weak-chested," *pusilánimes, descuidados y de pecho flaco*. The aspiration of *h* < *f* is still to be heard in this twentieth century in many parts of Spain (notably the South, the provinces of Santander, southern Salamanca, western Toledo, Extremadura) and in Spanish America. Now and then both forms, with *f* and *h,* have remained in the lan-

[5] Cf. Menéndez Pidal, *Orígenes*, pp. 238–239.

guage, with differing meaning: *filum* > *filo* = cutting edge, *hilo* = thread; *formam* > *forma* = form, *horma* = mould, last, as in the adage *hallar la horma de su zapato,* to meet one's match. ¿Quién es *Morros d'aca*? [= *haca*] ... ¡Si al menos hubiera usted dicho *Morros de jaca!* says the old schoolmaster to one of his discouraging pupils in *La barraca,* VI. In a few words this archaic pronunciation, now represented by *j,* has been accepted as correct Castilian: Andalusian *juerga* is the same word, historically, as Castilian *huelga;* similar are *jamelgo* and *jolgorio* (also written *holgorio*). *Las Hurdes* (that most primitive region of Spain) is preferably written *Las Jurdes.*

The reason for the passage of *f* to *h,* which is not universal in Spain, since it is lacking in the western part of Asturias, the western part of León, and in Upper Aragon, has been the subject of controversy. It *may* stand for the evolution of a bilabial *f,* which without difficulty becomes aspirate *h* by opening the lips, and which *may* have existed among the Romans, since such a sound is found in some Italian dialects and is not unknown to Spanish. It probably has no connection with Germanic *h,* which was too weak to maintain itself; words from this source (*hacha,* O. S. *faraute* or *haraute,* O. S. *fardido,* O. S. *fonta*), which were most often written with *f* in Old Spanish texts, are likely to be later borrowings from French. Starting from the basis that Basque, which formerly had an aspirate *h,* has no *f* (or *v*), for which it now substitutes *p,* or, having acquired *f,* misuses it (*¿Qué te farece a ti el médico nuevo?—La frática es lo que palta.—Pues es hombre listo, hombre de alguna portuna; tiene su fiano en casa,* Baroja, *Zalacaín el aventurero,* III), and recognizing the early use of *h* for *f* in notarial texts of the eleventh to thirteenth centuries (the *h* gradually spreading south from Cantabria, near the Basque country, late in its Romanization), many scholars hold that the spread of aspirate *h*, deriving from the pre-Roman speech of north-central Spain, accompanied the Reconquest, and the recovery of the center of Spain by Castilian, fanning out from a point north of Burgos.[6]

The history of initial *j*, and also of *g* + *e, i*, which already in Vulgar Latin had become *y* (p. 36), varies with the following vowel, and according as the latter is stressed or not.

Before stressed *a, e, i, j, ge, gi* > *y*: *jacet* > *yace; gentem* > Old Spanish *yent(e)*, which has been replaced by *gente*, wherein *g* may be a Latinism or a symbol of an alternate development [ŷ]. Before stressed *o, u, j* > *j* orthographically, [ŷ] phonetically; the pronunciation later passed through a series of changes which will be detailed elsewhere (p. 160): *jovis* > *jueves; junium* > *junio*.

Before unstressed *a, e, i, j* disappears, as does also *g* before *e, i*: *januarium* > *jenuarium* > *enero; geniculum* > *genuculum* > *(h)inojo; genista* > *(h)iniesta; germanum* > *(h)ermano*. The *y* which is expected, and which is abundantly documented in the tenth to twelfth centuries (*iermano, yermano*), has been absorbed into the front vowel *e* (both being palatal sounds). The *h* of *hermano, hiniesta*, and *hinojo* would appear to be a mere scribal device. Before unstressed back vowels, *j* > [ŷ]: *judaeum* > *judío*.

The divergence of result (*yace, yent[e]* vs. *jueves, junio*)

[6] Confusion of *f* and aspirate *h* is a living phenomenon; cf. Espinosa, *Estudios sobre el español de Nuevo Méjico*, §§ 121 and 129. For the presence of bilabial *f* in both Spain and Spanish America, see *ibid*. pp. 137–138, note.

calls for comment. The presence of *j* in place names over all Spain (*Junco, Junquera*), the restriction to the south and center of forms in *y* (*Yunco, Yuncos, Yunquera*), and the existence sometimes of two forms (O.S. *yurar* and *jurar,* O.S. *yamás* and *jamás, yunta* and *junta*), leads to the suspicion that *y* is an early step in the evolution of the sound, and that Castile has passed beyond it.

The study of *j* and *g + e, i* is rendered difficult by the interchangeable use in medieval manuscripts of *i, j,* and *y*. It is not always possible to be sure that one has correctly evaluated the symbol. Even nowadays words like *jónico,* Ionic and *jota,* iota, for example, may simply represent the imperial Latin spellings *jonicus* and *jota*. The *j* of *majestad* certainly is that of *majestas-tatis;* the less learned *mayor < majorem* represents the normal evolution of intervocalic *j*.

Only partial, in view of the number of words unchanged (*placer, planta, plata, plato, plaza, plomo, pluma; claro, clase, clavo,* etc., etc.)· has been the success of the passage of *pl* and *cl* to *ll; planum > llano; clavem > llave; clamare > llamar*. *Fl* either remains unchanged: *flaccum > flaco;* reduces to *l: flaccidum > lacio;* or, in a very few words, palatalizes as do *pl* and *cl: flammam > llama*. The process would have begun with the intensification of the palatal nature of the *l* (forms like *ķllave = ķlyave* and *plleno = plyeno* occur in Upper Aragon), with the later effacement of the preceding occlusive consonant. In the evolution of *pl, cl, fl,* Castilian has, exceptionally, been more conservative than its western neighbor, for in Portuguese, Galician, and western Leonese *planum > chão, chanu,* "shãu," "tchau," or "tsanu," etc.

Intervocalic.—In the business of phonetic innovation Castile is usually enterprising, but she is backward in the voicing of intervocalic consonants, to judge from the evidence of the retention of Latin spellings before the Cid and Alphonso the Learned (when the process is complete). Relatively, the change usually takes place before the loss of the intertonic vowels: *comitem* > *conde;* compare *pontem* > *puente.*[7] Absolutely, most of the earliest instances are from Andalusian inscriptions of the second half of the seventh century: *pontivicatus* (665). Yet there are rare illustrations from the second century A.D. Illustrative of the change are *minutum* > *menudo* ($t > d$); *saponem* > *jabón* ($p > b$); *ficum* > *higo* ($c + a, o, u > g$); *facere* > Old Spanish *fazer* ($c + e, i$ > O.S. z [$\hat{z}$]); compare (*filius*) *Didaci* > **Dida-z(e)* > *Díaz* (the genitive ending, vowel + *ci*, was extended to proper names which did not have it originally, and in this way arose family names like *Álvarez, Núñez, Pérez, Ruiz, Sánchez, Velázquez,* etc.); *profectum* > *provecho* ($f > v$). In some words the consonant evolved normally (*praedicare* > *predigar*) (in the *Crónica general*), but the Latin form has prevailed (*predicar*).

Of the voiced consonants of Latin only four demand attention.

D usually vanishes: *pedonem* (originally, "one who has flat feet") > *peón; fiduciam* > Old Spanish *fiuza; ad + i(n)sulare* > *aislar; crudum* > *cruo* (in the *Caballero Cifar*); *desnudum* > *desnuyo* (in the *Conde Lucanor* and in the *Crónica general*). In the two last the *d* of good Latin

---

[7] Since the unvoiced double consonants of Classic Latin merely reduce to the corresponding simple consonant in Spanish, we may also deduce that the simplification did not take place until after the period of voicing of the single consonants: *flaccum* > *flaco*, whereas *lacum* > *lago*.

orthography is now written: *crudo, desnudo* (the *y* of *des-nuyo* merely indicates hiatus between the vowels, though *v* would be expected).

Continuing a process already begun in Classic Latin (*parvum* > *parum; si vis* > *sis*), and continued in Vulgar Latin (*avus non aus,* demands the *Appendiz Probi;* cf. nos. 62, 73, 174, 176), the fricative sound of *b* or *v*, usually written *u* in Old Spanish, tended to be passed over in contact with the sounds, also labial, of *i* and *u: rivum* > *río; sibi* > *sí; privado* > Old Spanish *priado; -ibam* > *-ía* (e.g., *audibam* > *oía*); *gingivam* > *encía;* Old Spanish *Gonçaluo* > *Gonzalo;* Arabic *atabut* > *ataúd.* Conversely, this sound may be wrongly introduced as a glide: *judicium* > *juuizio* (*Poema de Mio Cid,* 3226, 3239, 3259) for Old Spanish *juizio* > *juicio;* compare *anchova* vs. *anchoa.*

Not native to the Romans but to the Sabines and the Greeks respectively are *asinus* and *caseus, rosa. Casa,* originally a hut, cabin, or cottage, was borrowed from the dialects of southern Italy. In general, words containing *s* between vowels were not usual in Latin, for the sound (which was originally like English *z*) early passed to *r* by the process of rhotacism. Such *s*'s as remained in Latin, through simplification of *s*'s of various origins, were in all probability pronounced like *s* in loose (authorities differ!), but in Old Spanish they were pronounced like *s* in lose, as is shown, for example, by the fact that the Spanish Jews represent *s* by symbols of their alphabet which approximate the sound of the English *z,* and by the later statements of grammarians (cf. p. 158). In early Spanish poetry *s* and *ss* do not rhyme, nor does either one rhyme with *ç* or *z.*

The unvoiced variety (*s* in loose) was carefully written *ss: fablasse, tolliesse; que ssea* < *que sea, fuesse* < *fue* + *se* (for initial *s* was always unvoiced); compare *falsso, pienssan,* where *ss* makes clear that the sound was not *ç*.

G often remains unchanged before *a, o, u: rugam* > *arruga; augustum* > *agosto.* At times, however, relaxation of its articulation is carried as far as the *y*-stage: *sagum* > *sayo;* at other times relaxation continues to the point of disappearance, especially before a back vowel: *Calagurrem* > *Calahorra; Magonem* > *Mahón; cucumerem* > *cogombro* > *cohombro;* possibly *hac hora* > Old Spanish *agora* > *ahora. G* + *e, i* > *y,* which is combined with the vowel, especially if the latter follows and is stressed: *magistrum* > **ma(y)estro* > *maestro; rugitum* > **ru(y)ido* > *ruido; vigilare* > **ve(y)elare* > *velar; magis* > Old Spanish *mayes, mais* or *maes* > *mas,* only the stressed vowel surviving in this word so frequently used in unstressed position. Intervocalic *g* disappears sporadically in rapid speech, whatever the nature of the adjacent vowels; compare the popular forms *jugar* > *juar; juguete* > *juete; luego* > *lueo; migaja* > *meaja, miaja.*

Substitution of related sounds.—The majority of sound changes are gradual, and appear in "ear words," passed down by word of mouth from generation to generation, from century to century. Equally old may be changes resulting from the sudden substitution of a sound by one that is related to it in point or manner of articulation. The resulting forms are frequent in popular Spanish. For the most part, such substitutions are sporadic and short-lived in the standard language (*dictado has de decir, que no litado;*

Don Quixote, I, 21; cf. *ibid.,* II, 7), but some of them have become permanent.

Confusion of occlusives occurs in the ancient *cattum* > *gato; vulpeja* > *gulpeja* (*Libro de buen amor,* 87a, 329b, etc.); *buhardilla* > *guardilla; buñuelo* > *muñuelo;* confusion of fricatives in *aguja* > *abuja; Felipe* > *Celipe;* confusion of dentals in *lintel* > *dintel; ninguno* > *denguno* (popular only); compare Classic Latin *olere* (verb), but *odor* (noun); *dacruma* preceded *lacrima,* as *dingua* did *lingua.*

Similar in their point of articulation (the sockets of the upper teeth) are *n, l,* and *r,* and consequently they are liable to confusion.

L > *r; r* > *l; pallidum* > *pardo; rarum* > *ralo; practicam* > *plática; Bernardo* > *Bernal* (cf. p. 86).

N > *l; l* > *n: Barcinonem* > *Barcelona; communicare* > *comulgar; mille grana* > *milgrana* > *mingrana* > *minglana,* which Valdés dismisses as no longer in use (*op. cit.,* p. 170); *Nebrija* > *Lebrija* (a town overlooking the marshlands south of Seville, the birthplace of the grammarian Nebrija); Arabic *laʿib* > *naipe.*

N > *r: sanguinem* > *sangne* (frequent in Berceo) > *sangre.*

Grouped.—Among the consonant sounds unknown to Classic Latin is that of Spanish *ch* [*ĉ*]. The passage of *ct* to *ch* is essentially a mutual approximation of the points of articulation of *c* and *t. C,* having become fricative rather than occlusive, passes from the velar to the postpalatal to the prepalatal position. The resulting *i̦* effects the change of *a* to *e.* At this stage two Spanish dialects stop (Aragonese and

Western Leonese *feito* < *factum*), as do French and Portuguese. *T*, under the force of the prepalatal *c*, palatalizes into the affricate [ĉ]: *feycho* (*Orígenes*, § 15, 6). Lastly, the two palatals combine: *fecho*. The process often is only partial: *pectine* > *peine; delectare* > *deleitar;* *affactare > *afeitar;* or the difficulty of the oppositely placed sounds overcome in another manner: *pacta* > *pauta; actu* > *auto; efectu* > *efeto, efeito, efeuto, efezto* in popular style; *carácter* > *caráter, caráiter, caráuter, carázter* among the illiterate; *tractare* > *tratar; respectum* > *respeto*. Words of late introduction or in learned use showed a semilearned stage in the seventeenth century, when *efeto, perfeto,* or other solutions like *lición* < *lectionem; afición* < *affectionem,* etc., were the usual forms. Latinizing influences here have restored the *c* (*efecto, perfecto*) except in a few words like *obiectum* > *objeto; luctum* > *luto*. By comparable processes of approximation of points of articulation *gn* > *ñ: lignum* > *leño,* and, after the palatalization of *l* (> *i*), *-ult* > *-uch: multum* > *mucho; a(u)scultat* > *escucha*.

Widespread in the Romance languages is the evolution of *li̯*. The first step was the palatalization, resulting from the pronunciation of *i* as a semivowel, of *li̯* to palatal *l: lieva* > *lleva; humiliare* > *humillar; Eulaliam* > *Ulalia* > *Olalla*. Aragonese retains the *ll*-form (*folia* > *fuella*). But *ll* is unstable. Intensification of the articulation narrows the passage of the breath through the mouth to produce [ŷ]: *folia* > *folla* > Old Spanish *foja; similiare* > *semellar* > *semejar; molliare* > *mollar* > *mojar;* compare *collecta* > Old Spanish *cogecha*. On the other hand, negligence in lifting the tonguetip to the sockets of the upper teeth yields the passage of *ll* to *y* (*yeísmo*). Modern Leonese shows the *y*-form (*folia* > *fueya*). Intervocalic (and initial) *y*, whatever its origin, is nowadays frequently pronounced as [ŷ], or more often as [ž], in New Castile, Andalusia, in parts of Mexico (especially the region of Puebla), in Argentina generally, and indeed in most parts of Spanish America. (Cf. p. 160.)

By enunciating the *c* or *g* farther forward in the mouth, whereby the ensuing *i̯* affects the *l*, the same effect of palatalization results from *c'l*, *g'l* and also from *t'l*, *d'l* (which to the ear is almost the same sound): *auriculam* > *oreja; cuniculum* > *conejo; regulam* > *reja*, plowshare; *rotulare* > *arrojar; radulam* > *raja*, splinter, slice, crack.

With the disappearance of the intertonic vowels, there resulted combinations of consonants not native to the Latin language. A readjustment was necessary when a nasal sound was followed by *l, r*. Just as in English chimney > chimley > chimbley, so *m'l* > *mbl: tremulare* > *temblar; ni + me + la* > *nimbla* (*Poema de Mio Cid*, 3286); *m'r* > *mbr: memorare* > Old Spanish *membrar; n'r* > *ndr: ven(i)ré* > *vendré* (this difficult consonant combination was simplified also by the exchange of position of *n* and *r*: O.S. *verné*, or by strongly trilling the *r*: O.S. *venrré*); *m'n, m'r* > *mbr:* *faminem* (the C.L. form is *famen*) > *famne* (as everywhere in Berceo) > *famre* > *fambre* > *hambre*. The *b* and the *d* "make themselves" in the course of transition from nasal to alveolar. This is true even in Arabic words: *al + hamra* > *Alhambra*, the reddish; *ramla* > *rambla*, sandy spot, the name of the boulevards in Barcelona.

As illustrations of Castilian phonetic independence and preëminence, the evolution of *mb* > *m* (also found in

Aragonese) and *sc, st + e, i* > Old Spanish *ç + e, i* will serve to close this discussion.

Ordinarily, position at the beginning of a syllable is more likely to survive than position at the end of a syllable, but perhaps, having articulated a bilabial sound (*m*), it is an "economy of effort" merely to prolong it, rather than to raise the soft palate and to open and close the lips for the *b,* also bilabial: *lambere > lamer; plumbum > plomo; ambos >* Old Spanish *amos.* Here, as so often, the revival of classical learning and the spread of printing caused the rejection of normal phonetic evolution, and *ambos* has been restored. But the general rule is valid, for the unschooled say *tamién,* instead of *también < tam + bene.*

Nescium > Old Spanish *ne(s)çio > necio; parescere >* Old Spanish *pare(s)çer > parecer; piscem > peçe > pez* and *peje; ustium >* Old Spanish *uço; cum angustia >* Old Spanish *congoxa > congoja.* Forms in Old Spanish *(s)ç* are good Castilian, those in *j* are proper to its rivals on either side, León and Aragon, though originally many examples of both forms probably existed in one and the same area.

BIBLIOGRAPHY

BOURCIEZ. *Eléments,* §§ 335–341.

ESPINOSA, AURELIO M. *Estudios sobre el español de Nuevo Méjico,* § 159, and notes, pp. 440–469.

ESPINOSA, AURELIO M., hijo, and Rodríguez Castellano, L. "La aspiración de 'h' en el sur y oeste de España," in *Revista de filología española,* XXIII (1936), 225–254, 337–378.

FORD, J. D. M. *Old Spanish Readings,* pp. xxv–xliii, and "The Old Spanish Sibilants," *Harvard Studies and Notes in Philology and Literature,* VII (Boston, 1900), 107 ff.

HANSSEN. *Gramática histórica,* §§ 103–160.

MENÉNDEZ PIDAL. *Orígenes,* §§ 41 ff.; *Manual,* §§ 32–72.

EVOLUTION OF FORMS

DEFINITE ARTICLE

By the dropping of the final *e,* and the resultant lack of proper position (p. 83) for the evolution of the sound of palatalized *l, ille > el. Illo(s), illa(s) > lo(s), la(s).* The initial vowel of *illo(s), illa(s)* suffered the fate of an intertonic vowel (cf. p. 86). Secondary reasons for the obliteration of the first syllable were the tendency of *l* to absorb an adjacent vowel (cf. such pronunciations as *'l campo*),[8] and the fact that it was the second syllable which distinguished the gender, and hence the use, of the word.

The object pronouns arise from practically the same Vulgar Latin forms as the definite articles, with the addition of *illī(s) > le(s).* The dialectal (Aragonese) indirect object forms *li* and *lis* may represent the archaic period in which *ī* had not become *e.* In the early stages of the language, object pronouns ordinarily did not begin a breath group: *Video illum > Véolo; fablarunt illis > habláronles;* compare *Válgame Dios* or *Dios me valga* as present-day alternatives, and early phrases such as *venido les* (= *le + es*) *mensaje* of the *Poema de Mio Cid* (975, 1419, etc.). The initial vowel therefore was here, too, treated as intertonic.

The conjunction of two *a*'s, or, at first, of *a* and *e,* and rarely *a* and *o,* effected their fusion: *illam aquam > ela-agua > el agua,* and by the same process were produced *el hermana, del otra parte (Conde Lucanor,* XXVII). This natural phonetic evolution was remarked by Valdés, who says that *el arca, el ama, el ala* were *por evitar el mal sonido*

---

[8] Espinosa, *Estudios sobre el español de Nuevo Méjico,* pp. 431 ff.

que hazen dos aes juntas (*Diálogo de la lengua*, p. 77). To
the end of the fifteenth century there were three acceptable
forms of the feminine singular definite article: *el, ell, la
espada* (p. 78). Before *a,* stressed or unstressed, *el* continued
to be used in the seventeenth century (*el artillería, el alforza,
el aguja, el ayuda,* etc.), but nowadays convention has further restricted *el* to use before stressed *a* of nouns only:
el agua, but *la arena* and *la alta casa.* By the 1600's *ell* was
relegated to popular usage: *ell agua* (Vélez de Guevara, *La
serrana de la vera,* 752).

<h3 style="text-align:center">NOUNS</h3>

The three groups of Classic Latin nouns (for the third and
fifth declensions are but varieties of the second and fourth
respectively) continue through Vulgar Latin into Spanish as
the *a*-group (*agua*), the *o*-group (*vino*), and the group ending in *e* (*carne*) or in a consonant (*pan*). There are a few,
relatively very few, shifts such as *passerem > pájaro; cu-
prum > cobre; diem > día,*[9] the final *a* of which may result
from the tendency to confuse *a* and *e* in unstressed syllables
(cf. *mía > mie* and the verbal ending *ia > ie,* p. 113), or
from the fact that *diem* was of both masculine and feminine
gender, at least in the singular, and assumed the corresponding feminine ending, -*a.* There were occasional difficulties
of gender, such as *el, la calor, color*—the feminine, which
was usual in Old Spanish in abstract nouns ending in -*or,*
rarely shows itself now in the dignified pages of "correct"
Spanish, except to be sure in *la labor,* but observe *la calor
es mucha* (Benavente, *Alfilerazos,* I, 1)—*el, la azúcar;* with

---

[9] Cf. K. Pietsch, *Two Old Spanish Versions of the Disticha Catonis,* p. 38.

or without a change of meaning: *el* or *la puente*, the bridge (*el* is the rule nowadays); *el orden*, the arrangement, *la orden*, the command or religious or military order. Other words of variable gender without change of meaning are *fin, linde, mar, margen, mimbre, tilde, tizne*. Illustrations of variable gender with change of meaning are too numerous to list. Neuter plurals in *-a* are treated like any *a*-declension nouns: *festa > fiesta; vota > boda*, but the plural notion is occasionally felt in the Spanish word: *ligna > leña*, firewood, kindling; *lignum > leño*, stick of wood. Collectively, fruit is *fruta*, but the product of any fruit-bearing tree or plant is known as its *fruto: la manzana es el fruto del manzano*. Numerous doublets in *-o* and *-a* have been created within Spanish and then their distinction is the product of convention. Thus *huerto* (smaller than a *huerta*), orchard; *huerta*, vegetable garden, fruit- and vegetable-growing district; *lomo*, loin, back of animals; *loma*, broad-topped hill; *río*, river; *ría*, estuary; etc., etc.

The form of most substantives harks back most directly to the accusative of the Classic Latin noun. Through clerical influence the nominative appears in *Dios, Carlos,* and Old Spanish *Pablos*. The singular forms of the definite article (p. 100) and of the demonstratives *ese < ipse* and *este < iste* also go back to the subject case of Classic Latin. The genitive is seen in the names of week days: *martis (diem) > martes; jovis (diem) >jueves; veneris (diem) > viernes*. By association with these, *lunae (diem)* has taken on an *s* to become *lunes*, and *mercuri (diem)* with shift of stress *> miércoles*. The genitive appears also in *Fuero Juzgo < Forum Judicum*, Forum of the Judges, and in a few place names: *Santander*

< *Sancti Hemeteri* (the accusative form would yield **San-tander[i]o*). In the invocation of *Santi Yagüe* (< *Sancte Jacobe*) may be traced a vocative, whereas *Santiago* shows the normal accusative provenance.

PERSONAL PRONOUNS

As typical of the Old Spanish period there is first *ge*, which is equivalent to Modern Spanish *se* (when not reflexive): *aquel que ge la diesse* (*Poema de Mio Cid*, 26) = *aquel que se la diese, era mucho mejor que quitargelo* (Fernando del Pulgar, *Claros varones de Castilla*, 1486) = *era mucho mejor que quitárselo*. By much the same stages as those which effected the evolution of *mulierem* > Old Spanish *mug(i)er* (p. 97), *Petrum (il)lī illum* (or *illam, illos, illas*) *dat* > *Pedro gelo* (or *gela, gelos, gelas*) *da*. The *ll* of *illum* did not palatalize (p. 83) or remain palatized, if it did so, because, the object pronoun forms *lo* < *illum, la* < *illam*, etc., having in most cases lost their initial vowel (which becomes intertonic in a breath group) before the period of palatalization (p. 84), their *l* had assumed its permanent form. For the plural, the same form (*ge*) was used, perhaps in part through the influence of reflexive phrases like *lavósela a sí mismo* and *laváronsela a sí mismos,* perhaps because of the association with the more common singular which brings about the ancient and still frequent use of *le* for *les: Le tengo miedo a las mujeres* (Ricardo León, *Casta de hidalgos,* VIII); *la misma risa que le producen a los chicos* (Julio Camba, *El descubrimiento de la sonrisa*).[10] *Ge* continued in general use to the end of the fifteenth century, at

---

[10] Cf. R. J. Cuervo, *Apuntaciones críticas sobre el lenguaje bogotano*, § 335; J. Casares, *Crítica efímera*, I, 107 ff.

which time it is frequent in the *Cárcel de amor* (1492) and the *Celestina* (1499), but it dies out in Spain in the first third of the following century. By this time its pronunciation was presumably quite like that of the reflexive *se* (cf. p. 162), it was therefore similarly spelled, and its identity was thus lost. In rural Santo Domingo, however, it is still in use (P. Henríquez Ureña, *El español en Santo Domingo,* Buenos Aires, 1940, pp. 41 and 173).

Pronoun object forms ending in *e* (*me, le, se, te*), lacking stress of their own, attached themselves, as did all pronoun object forms, to a following word beginning with a vowel, or more often to a preceding word ending in one, and modified their form in consequence. Only in the earliest literary texts may we read forms like *Vedada lan conpra* (*Poema de Mio Cid,* 62) = *Vedada le han conpra; bien landa el cauallo* (*ibid.,* 778) = *bien le anda el caballo.* The stubborn retention of the vowel in writing has in all likelihood acted to preserve it in speaking, but the uneducated elide the *e* even now: *m'alegro = me alegro; l'habrá dicho = le habrá dicho; sa reío = se ha reído* (Arniches). Entirely absent today is the attachment of the pronoun to a preceding vowel, especially with *que* and *no: Quandol vieron de pie* (*Poema de Mio Cid,* 1757) = *Cuando le vieron de pie; Diot con la lança* (*ibid.,* 353) = *Dióte con la lanza; Muchol tengo por torpe qui non conosçe la verdad* (*ibid.,* 1526) = *Mucho le tengo por torpe quien no conoce la verdad; nol cunplia lo quel prometiera* (*Conde Lucanor,* XI) = *No le cumplía lo que le prometiera.* These forms do not represent a kind of shorthand but the actual pronunciation, since a consonant thus left in the final position evolves as does any other final consonant: *sin salue el Criador* (*Poema de Mio Cid,* 2960) = *así me salue el Criador* (cf. p. 36); *nimbla messo* (*ibid.,* 3286) = *ni me la messó* (cf. p. 98); *toveldo* (*ibid.,* 3322) = *túvetelo* (cf. p. 111). In writing, the enclitic form of *le* survived into the fourteenth century, that of *me, se, te* is found almost solely in the *Poema de Mio Cid.*

INDEFINITES

In indefinite adjectives and pronouns there was a great inclination toward new uses or new formations. Only illustrative cases will be considered here.

Instead of *aliud* a more colloquial form was *alid* > Old Spanish *al: Achesto es i non es al* (*Auto de los reyes magos,* 14), *Non han de fazer al* (*Crónica general,* chap. 737). Often combined with *lo* (*lo al = lo otro*), *al* becomes obsolete in the sixteenth century, at which time Valdés says he prefers *otra cosa.*

The original prepositional use of *cada* < κατά with distributive force ("in the proportion of") appears as late as the seventeenth century, but it may, in the previous century, represent the revival of interest in the classical languages: *Dejando en los fuertes cada dos compañías* (Hurtado de Mendoza), that is, two companies for each fort; *dando a cada uno su parte, que ... fueron cada tres mil ducados en dinero* (*Don Quixote,* I, 39), that is, 3000 ducats to each one; compare *cada dos días,* once every two days.

Unable perhaps to survive the competition of (*de*) + *allí, dende,* and of *de* + *el* (*le*), *ella, ello, i* (*y*) < *hic* or *ibi* and *ende* < *inde* did not outlive the fifteenth century: *y estaba doña Ximena* (*Poema de Mio Cid,* 239) = *allí estaba doña*

Jimena; fallose ende bien (*Conde Lucanor,* end of each *enxiemplo*) = *se halló bien en ello* or *de ello.*

The affirmative meaning of (*rem*) *natam,* anything existing > *nada* today is observable in the use of *nada* in rhetorical questions or exclamations: *¿Hay nada más hermoso?*, but even in the *Poema de Mio Cid* its sentence always contains a *non: ca non me priso a ella fijo de mugier nada* (3285); *mugier nada* is equivalent to *ninguna mujer nacida.* A bit closer to the original significance is *Ueer lo e otra vegada, si es uertad o si es nada* (*Auto de los reyes magos,* 46–47), I shall see it again, [see] whether it is real or [whether it is] anything.

The similarity of form of *quien* < *quem* and *alguien* < *aliquem,* which latter (*alguien*) bore the stress on its last syllable in Old Spanish and even in the Golden Age (Correas, *Arte grande de la lengua castellana,* edition of Viñaza, p. 89); the influence of *qui* in shaping the Old Spanish pronouns *nadi, otri,* and the archaic *elli* (frequent in Berceo) = *él,* led to a veritable medley of forms, *nadi, nadie, nadien, naidie, naidien, naide; otro, otri, otrien, otrie,* of which only two, *nadie* and *otro,* are (and have been since the early sixteenth century) part of standard Castilian, though *naide* is current and many of the others are in use by the populace.

The regular equivalent in Old Spanish for *hominem* is *omne.* The use of *omne* = *hombre* as an indefinite subject (*omne non puede escusar la muerte* says Count Fernán González, in the *Crónica general,* chap. 689) without stress of its own (hence the lack of diphthongization) collapses in the sixteenth century before the extension of the impersonal reflexive construction.

CONJUNCTIONS

Investigation of the history of *y* (*i*) < *et* is rendered difficult by the use in the medieval period of a sign *τ* , whose actual sound value is not always certain, although it may sometimes be surprised by a copyist's slip, *Esto τ yo en debdo* (*Poema de Mio Cid*, 225) = *Esto he yo en deudo,* and therefore *τ = e. Et* was ordinarily without stress and did not diphthongize in Castilian as a general rule. Irrespective of the possibility of formation of *ie* < *et,* the modern *y* (*i*) seems to have arisen in association with a vowel sound, hiatus being abhorrent to Spanish, which tries to unite two successive vowels into one syllable (p. 34), *vino e*(*t*) *agua* > *vino i* (*y*) *agua; oro e*(*t*) *plata* > *oro i* (*y*) *plata. Y,* then, appeared first only when adjacent to a vowel (only before *e* originally), and up to 1500 it is not usual elsewhere. Since then it has spread to all positions, except that convention requires the original *e* (to avoid hiatus!) before the sound of vocalic *i: padre e hijo,* but *madera y hierro.*

Aut > *o,* which when adjacent to a vowel developed into *u,* for the same reason and in the same way as *e* > *i* (*y*): *uno o otro* > *uno u otro; fablan o escuchan* > *fablan u escuchan.* Here, however, the form for a special circumstance has not been extended, in correct Castilian at least, to general use. On the other hand, those writers who are not grammar conscious, from Santa Teresa (who never uses *o*), Quevedo, Lope de Vega, Rojas Zorrilla (*que en dos años u dos siglos; Cada qual lo que le toca,* 328), Vélez de Guevara (*diez u doce, El diablo cojuelo,* II), and Calderón (... *viento / u del centro en lo profundo, El mágico prodigioso,* III, 14), on, have known no limitation of its employment, but use it in all positions: *U, conjunción, se usa mucho en el hablar, yo la escribo como se habla, aunque otros escriben siempre O,* says Correas (*Vocabulario de refranes,* sub *u*). From modern "popular" style come *es caridad u es envidia, si hago bien u hago mal, entra usté u cierro.*

The modern usage for both *i* and *u* is already recommended by Valdés (*Diálogo,* pp. 104 and 107), because only before *e* and *o* respectively do *i* and *u* "sound well" to him, although Castilians, he admits, sin by the general use of *u.*

VERBS

Endings.—The phonetic law by which a final *e* disappeared (p. 87) was as valid for verb forms as for any other part of speech, hence *viene > vien; tiene > tien;* Old Spanish *dize > diz;* Old Spanish *plaze > plaz;* etc. But the tendency toward leveling, which is most pronounced in the morphology of verbs, soon demanded the return of the vowel, the only correct forms now being *viene, tiene, dice, place,* etc., whereas no such necessity is felt for substantives: *panem > pan; pacem > paz.*

The second personal plural termination *tis > des* wherever it occurred (present indicative and subjunctive, imperfect indicative and subjunctive, future indicative and subjunctive, conditional): *fabulatis > fablades; fabulabatis > fablauades; fablar + (hab)etis > fablaredes; fabularitis > fablár(e)des;* etc. For *-er* and *-ir* verbs the forms are entirely parallel. In the course of the fifteenth century, the *d* vanished in the present tenses and in the future indicative, and *i* replaced *e* through imitation of the corresponding Latin form or, in the present tenses, because it avoided the hiatus distasteful to Spanish (and the first step is for *e* and *o* in this position to become *i* and *u* respectively): *fablades > fablaes > fabláis; fablaredes > fablarés; comedes > comés; comeredes > comerés; vivides > vivís; viviredes > vivirés.* The forms in *é* (*fablarés, comés, vivirés,* etc.) are characteristic of the fifteenth century and represent the tendency of adjacent *e*'s to coalesce; the forms in *éis* (*fablaréis, coméis, viviréis,* etc.) probably represent the alternate change of *ées* to *éis*. Forms like *estades, érades, iredes* are still used in certain areas where the Leonese dialect is spoken.

In the preterite indicative the second person singular form often added an *s*, which in most tense forms belongs by right of etymology to this person and number: *¿Qué as* [= *has*]? *¿Sentistes algo?* (*Calila y Dimna,* p. 46, l. 4 of Allen's edition). In their partiality to medieval "color" Romantic dramatists found this form in *s* particularly desirable, presumably because it often added a syllable necessary to a verse: *tender osastes el vuelo* (Zorrilla, *Don Juan Tenorio,* la parte, III, 3); *y tú feliz que hallastes en la muerte* (Espronceda, *A Teresa*), but its use is frequent today, for even such a literary light as José Echegaray says *tú aceptastes* (*O locura o santidad,* end), *perdistes,* and *te pusistes* (*Un crítico incipiente,* I, 2 and II, 5), perhaps inadvertently publishing an admission that his earlier career was not in the field of letters. The second person singular of *-ar* verbs frequently showed *e: fablest(e),* which form lingers on the north coast of Spain, as does likewise the termination *-emos* for the first person plural: *¡Qué papel firmemos nunca ni tú*

ni yo! (Pereda, *De tal palo, tal astilla,* X); *Lleguemos, Sa-
quemos* (Pereda, *Don Gonzalo,* XXVI). The plural number in the second person invariably ended in *tes,* as it should
have as heir to *-tis: fablastes, comistes, vivistes.* Of *-er* and
-ir verbs, the first two persons plural developed perhaps
through the continuance into Vulgar Latin of *ĭ(v)ĭmus,
ĭ(v)ĭstis,* perhaps by formal association with the third person in *-ieron,* an *ie: comiemos, viviemos,* etc.; these forms
are not yet obsolete in Asturias.

The imperfect and future subjunctive forms of the first
and third person often appear shorn of their final *e: fablasse
> fablás; comiesse > comiés; fablare > fablar* (not to be
confused with the infinitive); *comiere > comier;* etc. In
the future subjunctive of these two tenses the first person
singular occasionally (but not in the *Poema de Mio Cid*)
terminated in *o: Si vna uez salliero* (Berceo, *Vida de Santa
Oria,* 103*c*), recalling that this Spanish tense form represents two tenses of Classic Latin, the future perfect indicative and the perfect subjunctive (p. 42).

By the principle of syncopation in the matter of intertonic vowels, *fabláredes, comiéredes,* etc. *> fablardes, comierdes,* etc. These contractions were acceptable to Nebrija
(*Gramática,* V, 9) and endured to the seventeenth century
(1619 edition of *Guzmán de Alfarache, passim*). But so
little known were they to Romantics like Villalta and
Espronceda that they took them for singulars: *Y si, lector,
dijerdes ser comento, Como me lo contaron, te lo cuento*
(*Estudiante de Salamanca,* end).

The omission, through the complete relaxation of its
articulation, of final *d,* and the inconsistent, when not non-

existent, use of accent marks in older Spanish yields as imperative forms *fablá, comé, viví* (still correctly used in the seventeenth century), often written *fabla, come, vivi*. At other times negligence in bringing the tip of the tongue near the edge of the upper teeth yielded forms like *quedai* < *quedad; miraime* < *miradme;* etc., these being in use by the uneducated at the present time. (For the vocalization of *d*, compare *paire* < *padre; Peiro* < *Pedro; pieira* < *piedra;* and the opposite change in *odredes* < *oiredes, Poema de Mio Cid*, 70, etc.) The metathesis of *d* and *n* (*fablandos* < *fabladnos*), is no longer usual even in the fourteenth century, but that of *d* and *l* (*fablaldes* < *fabladles; comeldo* < *comedlo; escribilde* < *escribidle*) was still current in the *Siglo de oro* (*persuadilda, hacelde*, Alarcón, *La verdad sospechosa*, III, 6).

Present tense.—Of *ser, dar, estar, ir,* the present indicative form of the first person singular was regularly, up to the sixteenth century, *so* < *sum; do* < *do; estó* < *sto; vo* < *vado* (?), respectively. At this time the forms with *y* came into general use, although they appear already in the *Libro de buen amor* (76a, 307b, 1028b), the *Corbacho,* and in the poetry of the Marquis of Santillana. Nebrija is aware of this appended letter, and he considers it a mere adornment: *algunas veces por hermosura añadimos i sobre la o, como diziendo do doi*, etc. (*Gramática*, V, 6). Possibly he means that *y* serves to avoid hiatus. Several explanations have been advanced to account for the *y;* perhaps the most conventional is that *so, do, estó,* and *vo* merely follow the example of Old Spanish *hei* (*hey*). From Classic Latin *habeo,* Vulgar Latin *haio,* through loss of its *o* when used in close syntactical relation to following words, came Old Spanish *hei* (*hey*) > *he* (pp. 85 and 86). Another explanation, that of Professor Ford, is that the *y* represents a glide sound resulting when *yo* was appended to the verb form: *so* + *yo* > *soi̯* + *yo*. *Soy* was then extended to general use. Perhaps the *y* appeared first as a glide sound before a vowel: *so español* > *soy español*, then became general. The dropping of the *o* of *sapio* > *saipo* > *sei* > *sé* is comparable to that of *haio*.

The *g* of *tengo* < *teneo*; *pongo* < *pono*; *salgo* < *salio*; *vengo* < *venio* probably represents the imitation by these verbs of such Latin forms as *cingo, fingo, frango, jungo, pango, pingo, plango, tango,* and Old Spanish *digo* and *fago*. Possibly, too, there was an unconscious desire to keep the verb stem intact without palatalizing its *n* or *l*. In the course of the 1500's *cayo* (< *cadeo*), *oyo* (< *audio*), *trayo* (< *traho*), *valo* (< **valo*), *aso* (from the Germanic verb *sazian* > *asir*) were driven out by *caigo, oigo, traigo, valgo,* and *asgo*. The tendency to insert *g* into forms of the present tense is illustrated by modern ungrammatical forms *creiga* < *crea*; *haiga* (very common!) < *haya*; *leiga* < *lea*; *vaiga* < *vaya*; *veiga* < *vea*, etc. The replacement of *y* by *g* may have been hastened by the occasional complete relaxation in Spanish of *g* to *y* (p. 95) and the subsequent notion that *g* was more correct than *y*.

For the verbs discussed in the preceding paragraph, the present subjunctive forms in Old Spanish were *caya, oya, traya, vala, asa*.

Imperfect indicative.—Whether because -*ebam* and -*ibam* were confused in speech in late Vulgar Latin, or because of the influence of *habebam* > **abea* > *abia*, both in Spanish yielded -*ia*.[11] The latter normally in Old Spanish became *ie* by the approximation of *a* to *i* (p. 85), so that, for an -*er* or *ir* verb (e.g., *escriuir*), the imperfect indicative forms were *escriuia, escriuies, escriuie, escriuiemos, escriuiedes, escriuien* (the retention of the *a* in the first person singular may be apparent only and may result from the relative scarcity of this person and number in estimating statistically the most frequent forms). There existed concurrently a complete set of forms in -*ia,* the modern ones, which by the fifteenth century, being the choice of grammarians in their closer similarity to Latin, displaced those in -*ie* in the standard language, the latter being relegated to dialects (Asturias, Zamora), where they are still in use.

In the -*ie* forms the stress was, at least at first, on the *i*, as shown by the dropping of the *e* (p. 108): *sey < seie < seia* (*Poema de Mio Cid,* 1840, 2278). But the avoidance of hiatus once again transferred the stress to the more open vowel. The pronunciation *ié* is deduced from rhymes like *fasien* [= *hacían*], *desien* [= *decían*], *detyen* [= *detiene*], *bien* (*Libro de buen amor,* 1309) or *sabiemos* [= *sabíamos*], *viniemos* [= *vinimos*], *auemos* [= *habemos*], *fisiemos* [= *hicimos*] (*Libro de Alixandre,* 2268) and by its presence today in the linguistically archaic region of Astorga.

Preterit.—Forms of this tense, regular or irregular, continue with a good degree of fidelity those of Latin. An important group which has, within the life of Spanish, undergone modification is that of the forms derived from *a . . . ui* (C.L. *habui, placui, sapui,* etc.). The preliterary

---

[11] In the opinion of many scholars, *ẹa > ia:* Classic Latin *viam >* Vulgar Latin **vẹa >* Spanish *vía.*

aubi spread in Spanish to a lengthy list: *andove* < *andar;* *cope* < *caber;* Old Spanish *crove* < *creer; estove* < *estar;* Old Spanish *sove* < *ser; tove* < *tener;* in addition to *hove* < *habui; plogue* < *placui; sope* < *sapui.* The use of *u* (*anduve, cupe, estuve, plugue, supe, tuve*) had become regular by 1500. *Nebrija* (*Gramática*, V, 4 and 6) mentions the older forms in *o* almost solely for *haber* in combination with a past participle (*ove amado*), though he hesitates when the vowel is not stressed (*uviesse, oviera*). The use of *u* has been variously explained as due to association with the *u* of *-ude* (*pude,* O.S. *estude,* O.S. *andude*) and *puse;* as beginning in the third person plural, where the presence of a *yod* (e.g., *sopieron*) acted to make closer the vowel of the syllable preceding, from the third person the *u* spread to the remaining persons and numbers; as resulting from the confusion in unstressed syllables (e.g., *sopiste, sopimos, sopistes, sopieron*) of *u* and *o* (p. 236), then it spread to those forms in which the stem vowel is stressed (e.g., *sope, sopo*).

Future indicative and conditional.—From the *Poema de Mio Cid* to the seventeenth century both the synthetic form in which fusion of infinitive and the present indicative of *haver* is complete (e.g., *me dirá*), and the older and analytic "split" form (e.g., *decir me ha*) were in use, occurring even in one and the same sentence: *el obispo do Jerome soltura nos dará / dezir nos ha la missa ... (Poema de Mio Cid,* 1688–1689); *yo me untaré con él, e quando viniere, fallarme ha sana (Conde Lucanor,* XXVII). It is of course possible that the meaning is not entirely the same, the "split" form corresponding to the inevitability expressed now by *haber de* + infinitive (*ha de decirnos la misa, ha de hallarme*). The older form is still frequent in Cervantes: *casarme he con ella* (*El celoso extremeño*); *vernos hemos* (*Rinconete y Cortadillo*); *comeros heis* (*Don Quixote*, II, 42); but its use later in the century (*echarle ha el tiempo, hallarla heis, haceros heis* in *El criticón*, I, 10, III, 9, and III, 11, respectively) was doubtless consciously archaic, inasmuch as it is often introduced into the speech of rustics.

Future indicative forms of -*er* and -*ir* verbs, if the latter were not book words, usually dropped their intertonic *e* or *i* (p. 86): *com(e)r + he > combré* (*Poema de Mio Cid*, 1021); *deb(e)r + he > debré* (*debré* is colloquial today, but formerly it was an acceptable form); *entender + edes > entendredes* (*Conde Lucanor*, XXV); *mor(i)r + hemos > morremos* (*Poema de Mio Cid*, 2795); *pod(e)r + he > podré*; *repent(i)r + ha > repintrá* (*Poema de Mio Cid*, 1079); *sab(e)r + he > sabré*; *sal(i)r + ha > saldrá* (which, if we may believe Valdés, *op. cit.*, p. 176, was not yet generally used in his day); *ten(e)r + he > tendré* (also in use in O.S. were *terné* and *tenrré*); *viv(i)r + hedes > vivredes* (*Conde Lucanor*, III); etc. The influence of standardization has, for the most part, restored the *e* or *i*, the dropping of which was phonetically normal. Of the dozen modern future indicative forms which are irregular (they are not at all so, historically), ten are verbs in such frequent use as to have resisted any effort toward standardization. *Haré* is formed on the Vulgar Latin infinitive **fare*; *diré* is probably built on a Vulgar Latin infinitive **dire*.

The formation of the conditional or "past future" parallels that of the future in every respect. Moreover, the *a* of the ending (that is, the remnant of the imperfect indicative of *haber*) usually weakens to *e*, yielding *me fablarie, fablar me ie* (*ye*), etc.; compare *veriedes* = *veríais* (*Poema de Mio Cid*, 170); *fer lo ien* = *lo harían* (*ibid.*, 1250). Further, the *e* may be dropped in the second personal plural: *fablarides, comerides*, etc., according to Nebrija (*Gramática*, V, 9), but these forms are not common in texts. Both the analytic and the synthetic forms occur in the earliest literary texts: *quanta riquiza tiene aver la yemos nos* [= *nosotros la habríamos*] ... *nunqua avrie derecho de nos* (*Poema de Mio Cid*, 2663 and 2665). The intertonic *e* or *i* of the infinitive is dropped: *començó a cuydar que vendría* [= *vendería*] *aquella olla de miel* (*Conde Lucanor*, VII). The analytic form is no rarity in Cervantes: *llevarme hían* (*La gitanilla*); *espantarse hía* (*El viejo celoso*); *responderles hía yo* (*Don Quixote*, I, 47, end), but was probably old-fashioned even then.

Infinitive.—The assimilation of *rl* to *ll* (e.g., *hablarle* > *hablalle*) is already practiced, at least orthographically, in the *Poema de Mio Cid* (833, 1070, 1778, 2967; cf. 579, 1284). Early evidence on the actual pronunciation is furnished by Nebrija (*Orthographía*, VII) who says that *ll* in such forms has *aquel son que diximos ser proprio de nuestra lengua*—palatalized *l*, that is. Possibly as a fashion, *hablalle*, etc., became popular in the first half of the sixteenth century, Garcilaso de la Vega being addicted to it, while Valdés preferred to keep the *r* (*Diálogo*, p. 126) and it continued into the next century (e.g., *qué de cosas tengo que contalle*, Quevedo, *El buscón*, XV; *si no es para servillas*, Vélez de Guevara, *El diablo cojuelo*, II). At the present time it is used in poetry and occurs in speech in southern Spain.

Past participle.—The form of past participles looks directly to that of the Latin etyma: *auditum > oído; apertum > abierto; factum > fecho; prehensum > preso; scriptum > escrito.* A few Latin past participles survive only as adjectives: *bibitum > beodo; strictum > estrecho; tensum > tieso.* The suffix *udo < utum* was often employed, before the fifteenth century, in verbs which had not *-utum* in the parent language: *metudo (Poema de Mio Cid,* 844, 914), *vençudo (ibid.,* 3644, 3691) for *metido* and *vençido* respectively; the latter forms also occur in the same text (74, 784, etc.). Nowadays it is restricted to adjectives like *agudo, forzudo, huesudo,* etc.

BIBLIOGRAPHY

Bourciez. *Eléments,* §§ 353–376.
Ford, J. D. M. *Old Spanish Readings,* pp. 119 ff.
Hanssen. *Gramática histórica,* §§ 161–452.
Menéndez Pidal. *Manual,* §§ 73–130.

Evolution of Constructions

WORD ORDER

One of the striking features of the Spanish language in its written form is the extreme flexibility of its word order. No small part in this freedom of arrangement is played by the development of the use of *a* before certain types of direct objects. This characteristic of Spanish syntax probably does not owe its origin to the necessity (given the loss of case endings and the liberty of word order) of distinguishing object from subject; it may be due to association with the *a* of indirect objects, beginning possibly with personal pronouns: *A mí han hablado > (Me) han hablado a mí,* whence *Me ven > Me ven a mí.* In time the use of *a* spread to nouns, *(Le) ven a Juan.* In this respect Spanish may be the heir of Latin, which tended to construe some of its verbs with the dative case, preferring to consider the object as consciously sharing in the act rather than caused or objectively affected by it. There seems to be no criterion for judging whether, in *Juan sirve a su amo, servir* means "serve" (transitive) or "be of service" (intransitive). Confusion with *a* of indirect object seems the most likely explanation for the Spanish accusative *a.* Although in Old Spanish the niceties of its employment are of course not yet observed to the point where successive generations of grammarians have brought it today, the employment of *a* in the earliest texts is already established: *Tú que a todos guías, Reçiben al que en buen ora nasco, Salvest a Daniel, Hy gañó a Colada, Más quiero a Valençia que tierras de Carrión* (*Poema de Mio Cid*, 241, 245, 340, 1010, 3474). But usage is by no means rigidly fixed: *Veremos vuestra mugier (ibid.,* 210); *Veré a la mugier (ibid.,* 228); *quería provar a tres sus fijos, ovo provado así todos sus amigos, levó a su muger a su casa, levaron la novia a casa de su marido* (*Conde Lucanor,* XXIV, XLVIII, XXVII, XXXV, respectively).

Being weak of stress, needing some word to support themselves upon, object pronouns of Old Spanish ordinarily did not stand at the beginning of their sense group: *Partiós de la puerta, Acogénsele omnes* (*Poema de Mio Cid,* 51, 134); *Vuestra vertud me vala; Ya lo vedes; que nadi nol diessen posada (ibid.,* 221, 114, 25); *era su voluntad de se partir desta tierra* (*Conde Lucanor,* I). This rule was regularly observed up to the sixteenth century, at which time a sense group like *Le veo* is practically nonexistent, but now, except for affirmative wishes or commands (*Válgame Dios, Tráigame pan*), it is limited to dialect or literary style at the beginning of a sentence or clause: e.g., *Quedóse un rato meditabundo* (Bello, *Gramática,* §§ 906–908). Yet there are signs of its survival generally: *Cerca de las mesas veíanse las perchas* (Pérez Galdós, *Miau,* XXI). The close relation between the auxiliaries *deber, ir, poder, querer,* and their dependent infinitive, constituting as they do a series of periphrastic conjugations, results in the logical anteposition of object pronouns (*que lo debía dejar, quisol besar las manos*). Preposition to the main verb (e.g., *lo puedo hacer*) continued to be the use prevailing up to the nineteenth century, but it is now perhaps more frequent in speaking than in writing.[12] The weakness of stress of object pronouns was such that their exact position was not rigidly set, and other

---

[12] Cf. Rodolfo Lenz, *op. cit.,* §§ 247, 255.

words might be interposed between them and the verb: *Nunqua vos yo merescí* (*Crónica general,* chap. 736) = *Nunca yo os merecí, unos omes que me non aman mucho* (*Conde Lucanor,* XXVI) = *unos hombres que no me aman mucho, que ge lo non ventassen* (*Poema de Mio Cid,* 151) = *que non se lo descubriesen.* This phenomenon dies out rapidly after the fourteenth century, but there are sporadic occurrences in the sixteenth.

Another prominent characteristic of word order in Spanish is the postponement of subject to verb or of the verb to final position in its sense group: *Sospiró myo Cid* (*Poema de Mio Cid,* 6); *Un`dia se apartó el Conde Lucanor con Patronio* (*Conde Lucanor,* III); *quando por todo esto non lo dexase, contól la razón porque allí viniera, quando el mercadero aquello oyó* (*ibid.,* I, XI, XXXVI). Relegation of the verb to the end of the clause became a fetish upon revival of interest in Classic authors during the fifteenth and sixteenth centuries: *por esta razon de avariçia muchas de las tales infinitos e diversos males cometen: que si dineros, joyas preçiosas e otros arreos intervengan o dados les sean, es dubda que a la mas fuerte non derruequen* (*El corbacho,* II, 1); *En dar poder a natura que de tan perfecta hermosura te dotase, y hacer a mi inmérito tanta merced que verte alcanzase, y en tan conveniente lugar, que mi secreto dolor manifestarte pudiese* (*La Celestina,* beginning). Preference for the end position continues to the present.

NEGATION

By modern usage only one negative may stand before the verb: *No veo nada* or *Nada veo,* but until the end of the fifteenth century the customary construction knew no such restriction: *Ninguno non responde* (*Poema de Mio Cid,* 2305), *Nadie no me quiere* (*La Celestina,* IX of the 1501 edition). A survival of the ancient practice appears in *Don Quixote,* where the redundant *no,* however, does not immediately follow the other negative: *como ninguno de nosotros no entendía el arábigo* (I, 40); *que nunca otra tal no habían visto ni oído decir* (II, 56).

In all languages there seems to be recourse to objects of small value for the purpose of making negation more emphatic, and Spanish is no exception. Old Spanish texts do not make extensive use of the three terms familiar to every one today, *ardite,* a coin; *bledo,* wild amaranth; and *comino,* cummin seed, but the list includes coins, fruits, vegetables, nuts, living creatures: *A todos los debaxo no tenia en una blanca* [a coin] (*La Celestina,* VII of the 1501 edition); *Quanto dexo no lo preçio un figo* [fig] (*Poema de Mio Cid,* 77); *agora non vale una faua* [bean] (*Libro de buen amor,* 897d); *por papas e por Reyes non das un vil nuez* (*ibid.,* 1521d); *Non li creçio un punto* (Berceo, *Milagros de Nuestra Señora,* 212d); *Non daria un baso* [i.e., *vaso*] *de agua del rio* (*Libro de Alixandre,* 2591c of Paris MS).

MOODS AND TENSES

A trick of popular poetry is the inexact use of tenses, the requirements of rhythm and versification being more important than temporal precision. In ballads, above all, the flavor imparted by the substitution of imperfect for present may be caught: *Cada vez que el moro pierde, bien perdía una ciudad* (*Romance de Moriana,* beginning *Moriana en un castillo*), and this substitution can usually be laid to metrical exigencies: *A cazar va el caballero / A cazar como solía* (*Romance de la infantina*). Another common substitution is that of conditional for future: *Buen Conde, si allá non ides / Daros hían por traidor (ibid.*). To the present day, Spanish has used the imperfect, when speaking of present time, in order to moderate the force of a statement, and the *Este niño es un imbécil. Merecía que le diesen un puntapié* of Palacio Valdés (*La hija de Natalia*, II, 7) is paralleled by *Yo, que esto vos gané, bien mereçía calças* in the *Poema de Mio Cid*, 190.

Not surviving (except for *vamos*) into the modern period is the use of the present subjunctive (without introductory *que*) with the effect of the imperative: *Por Raquel e Vidas vayadesme* [= *idme*] *privado* (*Poema de Mio Cid*, 89); *Non vos tardedes, mandedes* [= *mandad*] *ensillar* (*ibid.*, 317; cf. 254, 257, 307, 977, 991, etc., etc.); *Digas* [= *Di*] *tú, el marinero* (Gil Vicente, *Canción*). The line of demarcation between wish and command is not always easy to draw, as appears in the last illustration especially, but Old Spanish gave preference to the former concept.

In *si* clauses which involve no uncertainty, and in temporal clauses of future reference, the use of the future subjunctive is the rule: *si nos muriéremos en campo, en castiello nos entrarán; / si venciéremos la batalla, creçremos en rictad* (*Poema de Mio Cid*, 687–688); *mientra que visquiéredes, bien se fará lo to* (*ibid.*, 409), but it is, already in this early text, subject to the competition of the present indicative or subjunctive, which was later to drive it into obsolescence: *ca si non comedes, non veredes cristianos* (*ibid.*, 1033b);

mientra que vivades, non seredes menguados (*ibid.*, 158).
The future subjunctive is also used in Old Spanish in adjective clauses of hypothetical antecedent or of future reference: *de lo que ovieren huebos, sírvalas a so sabor* (*Poema de
Mio Cid*, 2639). Unlike their sister languages, French and
Italian, Spanish and Portuguese have not continued the
employment of the future indicative in adverbial clauses of
time, and the *quando los gallos cantarán* (v. 316), of Mio
Cid's instructions to his men hardly knows descendants.

   In Spanish syntax the infinitive takes a subject and this
phenomenon has no lack of heirs nor of early ancestry: *para
las estorias se fazer bien e derechamente son neçesarias tres
cosas* (Pérez de Guzmán, *Generaciones y semblanzas,* prologue) ; *sin lo tu merescer* (Martínez de Toledo,*El corbacho,*
I, 1) ; *es causa del marido separarse de la muger* (*ibid.*, I,
15). This extremely concise construction (cf. *antes de mar-
charme yo* vs. *antes que yo me marchara*), filling somewhat
the same need as the personal infinitive of Portuguese, is
used now by literate and illiterate alike: *Se fué p'allá sin yo
saberlo* (Benavente, *Señora ama,* II, 1, end) ; *se maravillaba
de Su Merced quererle deshonrar así* (Menéndez Pidal, *La
España del Cid,* IV, 3, 3).

   Deriving from a pluperfect indicative of Classic Latin,
the verb form in *-ra* was in its proper precinct in Old Spanish in *fizo enbiar por la tienda que dexara* [= *había dejado*]
allá (*Poema de Mio Cid,* 624), in *ca assil dieran* [= *habían
dado*] *la fe e gelo auien jurado* (*ibid.*, 163, also 2011), and
in *la pregunta quel fiziera e que la avía fallado* (*Conde
Lucanor,* L). In the *romances* the use of the *-ra* form in
principal clauses, with the time value of either pluperfect

or preterit, is a characteristic trait: *Dellos* [= Some of them] *me dejó mi padre, Dellos me ganara yo* (*Romance del conde Fernán González,* beginning *Buen conde Fernán González*); ... *Diérale calzas de grana* (*Romance del Conde Claros,* beginning *Media noche era por filo*). Once again Valdés frowns, condemning this indicative use as antiquated (*Diálogo,* pp. 245–246), and indeed it is rare in the sixteenth century, and in the seventeenth practically disappeared from existence (if we discount its presence in the historical writings of Mariana, as one of the archaic turns which he introduced from his reading of the chronicles to give his work a touch of venerability). Sporadic occurrences there are: *del mismo modo que saliera ... le metió allá* (*El criticón,* III, 5). It reappears in Jovellanos and Meléndez Valdés at the end of the eighteenth century. Later it was to be favored (in relative clauses) by the Romantics (p. 203), but to use it in principal clauses is now the mark of dialect (Galician, Asturian), though it was not always so: *Et el escudero casara poco tiempo avía* (*Conde Lucanor,* L), *ca él visquiera* [= *había vivido*] *muy grand tiempo con él* (*ibid.*).

The history of the *-ra* form in conditional sentences is a separate problem. The Classic Latin writers, seemingly with the object of gaining increased vividness by saying "had" rather than "would have," use, though not frequently, the *-ra* form in the result clause of conditional sentences, retaining its past perfect meaning: *si modum orationi posuisset ... animos audientium impleverat* (Tacitus, *Annals,* IV, 9, 1), that is, "would have filled"; *Praeclare viceramus, nisi ... Lepidus recepisset Antonium* (Cicero, *Epistulae ad familiares,* XII, 10, 3), that is, "would have won." Such usage, still with past meaning, is continued in the early Spanish texts: *si ellos le viessen, non escapara de muert* (*Poema de Mio Cid*, 2774), if they had seen him, he would not have escaped death; *si yo non uviás, el moro te jugara mal* (*ibid.*, 3319), if I had not arrived, the Moor would have left you badly off. The *-ra* form is not long in appearing in the *si* clause: *Sy essora se tornaran, fueran byen aventurados* (*Poema de Fernán González*, 136d; cf. 138c, 531d, 536c, 678d, etc.), but only in the fourteenth century does its use as a simple tense form become at all common: *pues él por omne lo escogiera* [= *había escogido*] *que bien entendía que non fuera* [= *sería*] *él omne si esto non fiziera* [= *hiciera*] (*Conde Lucanor*, XXV). The compound form is at least as old as Berceo: *Si ante lo sopiessen, / No li ovieran fecho* [= *hubieran hecho*] *esso* ... (*Milagros de Nuestra Señora*, 148d), but even in Cervantes and Mateo Alemán both the *-ra* form, and more rarely the *-se*, which also was originally pluperfect in time (p. 42), continue to function as perfect tenses (though not exclusively): *Si Cardenio no se le quitaran, él acabara la guerra del gigante* (*Don Quixote*, I, 35), where *quitara* = *hubiera quitado; acabara* = *hubiera* or *habría acabado; Si no fuera por el huésped, allí fuera la de Mazagatos* (*La ilustre fregona*), where *fuera* = *hubiera sido; No sé si despertara tan presto, si los panderos y bayles no me recordaran* (*Guzmán de Alfarache*, I, 3), where *despertara* = *hubiera* or *habría despertado; recordaran* = *hubieran* or *habrían recordado*. Since the context is the sole criterion for determining whether the form is to be judged pluperfect or imperfect, decision is often difficult, but the original time value of the *-ra* or *-se* form may occasionally be observed in modern Spanish: *La cosa hubiera sido inter-minable, si la corregidora ... no dijese* [= *hubiese dicho*] (Alarcón, *El sombrero de tres picos*, XXXIII).

PASSIVE, REFLEXIVE, ETC.

Combinations like *es muerto, es venido, es hecho,* and others are now in the minority; indeed a certain comic touch is sometimes lent by the use of *Somos muertos* (Arniches, *El terrible Pérez,* I, 9), *Esto es hecho,* etc., because they recall the rhetoric of the older stage. But the rule, and not the exception, for Old Spanish, is the use of *ser* with the past participle of neuter verbs: *en buen ora fuestes* [= *fuisteis*] *naçido, por las parias fué entrado, Exido es de Burgos* (*Poema de Mio Cid,* 71, 109, 201; but cf. *a Valençia an entrado,* 2247). The agent of a passive verb is regularly introduced by *de* at this time (*mis dueñas de quien so yo servida, Poema de Mio Cid,* 270; *dexadas seredes de nos, ibid.,* 2716), whether the act be explicit or implicit. Latterly *por* tends to occupy this role of *de* in most cases. As a variant for the passive voice, the reflexive form, which after 1500 outstrips the "true" passive, is already in evidence in the earliest monuments; *non se faze assí el mercado* (*Poema de Mio Cid,* 139), *verán las moradas cómmo se fazen, afarto verán por los ojos cómmo se gana el pan* (*ibid.,* 1642–1643), *en este logar se acaba esta razón* (*ibid.,* 3730, cf. 409); the very Spanish prominence of the emotional "dative of interest" is also illustrated here: *non saben qué se an* [= *se tienen*], *Rogad al Criador que vos biva algunt año* (*ibid.,* 1086, 1754). But the so-called "impersonal" reflexive, used when treating of persons, not things (*se le ve, se les humilla a los podero-*

sos, etc.), scarcely appears before 1500. Persistently, however, Spanish has preserved the use of the third personal plural form to indicate an indefinite subject: *O [= Donde] dizen Castejon ... , a uno que dizien mio Cid Ruy Diaz de Bivar (Poema de Mio Cid,* 435, 628).

Granting that before 1500 *haber* regularly had the independent meanings which are now the property of *tener,* it is not an easy matter to determine whether *vedada lan conpra (Poema de Mio Cid,* 62) corresponds to *le tienen vedada compra* or *le han vedado compra.* However, agreement of the past participle with *haber* is obligatory in the *Auto de los reyes magos* (3, 100, 146); it is optional in the *Poema de Mio Cid* (e.g., *Arribado han las naves,* 1629; *cogida han la tienda,* 2706), compare *el conde Ferrant Gonsales avía passados muchos trabajos (Conde Lucanor,* XVI), *habiendo leídas e oídas muchas grandes cosas (El victorial,* p. 28 of the edition of R. Iglesia), and traces of it survive until shortly after 1500.

Minor phenomena.—There are problems of the evolution of Spanish syntax which this is not the place to discuss. It may be mentioned that the characteristically Spanish turn of phrase, *lo* + adjective or adverb, is as old as the oldest literary texts (*lo to [= tuyo], lo nuestro, lo so* in the *Poema de Mio Cid,* 409, 1118, 1557); not *hacer* but *haber* is the usual word in expressions of time even in the sixteenth century: *pocos días ha, oy ha siete semanas,* etc., and therefore the *poco tiempo hacía* of E. Juliá's edition of the *Conde Lucanor* (Madrid, 1933, p. 297), is at once suspect, and the more so since Knust–Birch-Hirschfeld reads *avía* (p. 233); *estar* + adjective is used only twice in the *Cid,* and the second time the meaning is plainly the basic "stood" (*bien puede estar rico*, 1304; *Firme estido* [= *estuvo*] *Per Bermudoz*, 3629); in the *Conde Lucanor*, *ser* alternates with *estar* in the expression of condition (*ser triste*, XLIV; *estar triste*, XLII, XLV) and of location (*era en muy grant peligro*, I; *aquel peligro en que estava*, I), but by 1500 the modern limits of these two verbs are definitely marked out; agreement with the sense rather than the form has always been prominent: *que nadi nol diessen posada* (*Poema de Mio Cid*, 25; cf. 34, 59, 151), "that they shouldn't give him lodging, any one of them"; *cada uno por si sos dones avien dados* (*ibid.*, 2259), "they had given their presents, each one separately." This lack of agreement is more apparent than real, however, for, as the translation into English attempts to show, *nadi* and *cada uno* are appositives of a really plural subject. This quite explainable trick of expression is still a feature of the language: *La gente del pueblo valemos más que todos esos duques y marqueses* (Baroja, *La feria de los discretos*, XXVI), *que nadie nos demos por entendidos* (Benavente, *La escuela de las princesas*, I, 10). It is sometimes carried to unexpected lengths: *¡Quién no hubiéramos hecho otro tanto!* (Benavente, *Señora ama*, II, 3), "Who of us wouldn't have done likewise!"

Vocabulary

In the manufacture of his chronicles and scientific treatises the great stabilizer of the early Spanish language, Alphonso X, the Learned, perforce introduced or at least popularized a quantity of Latin and Arabic words as his compilers translated Classic and Mohammedan texts. Often definitions' of these terms are included with their introduction: *rector* (*que quier tanto decir como regidor del estudio,* that is, of the community of teachers and students), *bedel* (*la universidat de los escolares debe haber un mensagero que llaman en latín bidellus*), *teatro* (*un grand corral redondo que llamauan en latín teatro*), *descripción* (*est escreuir de las yentes es llamado en latín descriptio*), *monarquía* (*que quiere tanto dezir cuemo un omne seer sennor de tod el mundo*); *almohades en el castellano tanto quiere dezir como ayuntados, fizo ell un grand libro ... al que ellos llaman alcorán.*

It is, however, from France, the only country whose soil touches that of the Iberian peninsula, that most of the early importations came. Invited, it appears, by the early kings of Navarre, the monks of Cluny (their abbey was founded at Cluny in Burgundy in 910), established their first convent in 1022 at Leyre, southeast of Pamplona, the burial place of early Navarrese rulers. Their center was Sahagún or San Facundo, between Palencia and León. The influence of the French monks soon made itself felt in the substitution of the Roman ritual for the Mozarabic, the introduction of the Carolingian style of handwriting, the restoration of Latin to its high place—with the presumable checking of the prestige of the vernacular—the translation and imitation of French literary works (*Auto de los reyes magos, Disputa del alma y el cuerpo, Libro de los tres reyes de oriente, Vida de Santa María Egipciaqua, Razón de amor con los denuestos del agua y el vino, Elena y María, Danza de la muerte;* the shadow cast by France on the origin of the major epics is not for discussion here), the continuance of the wars against the Moors, especially in the reign of Alphonso I of Aragon, the Battler. In the Toledo of Alphonso VI many of the court and the church officials were French. Indeed, three of Alphonso's wives (he had five) were French princesses, the zealous Constance, daughter of Robert of Burgundy, being the best known, and Alphonso married two of his daughters to counts of Burgundy (*Crónica general,* chaps. 847 and 871). The strings of pilgrims, and the purveyors to them, traveling over the *camino francés* leading to Santiago, brought in still more of France's men, goods, ways, and language.

Some of the Gallicisms (their origin is shown by their form) which thus early were adopted by Spanish are *ardiment = ánimo,* valor (it does not concern us here that the word is basically Germanic with the addition of a Latin substantive termination); *bajel; barnax* (*Poema de Mio Cid*), that is, Old French *barnage; coraje* (*Libro de buen amor, 278b*); *cosiment=merced,* favor; *derranchar=*French *déranger; doncel; fol, follía* (Berceo) < French *folie; fraile* (Berceo, *Conde Lucanor*); *jamón* (*Libro de Alixandre,* 2.050c of the Paris MS), *jardín* (included in Nebrija's early Spanish dictionary, 1495); *jaula* (*Crónica general*); *jayán; hereje* (in the *Conde Lucanor*); *lesonja* or *lisonja; lenguaje;*

linaje (the last three words also are in the *Conde Lucanor*);
maison (Berceo); *manjar* (in the Mozarabic poet Abencuzmán); *mensaje* (*Poema de Mio Cid*); *monje; omenaje* (*Poema de Mio Cid*); *palafré* (*Poema de Mio Cid*); *paje* (listed by Nebrija); *sergente = sargento; usaje* (*Poema de Mio Cid*); *vergel* (*Poema de Mio Cid*); *vianda* (*Poema de Mio Cid*). The Spanish forms *Enrico* and *Filipo* were early displaced by the Gallicized *Enrique* and *Felipe*. The frequency of the French ending *aje* < *aticum* did not, however, drive out the native Old Spanish *adgo* > *azgo* (e.g., *maioraticum* > O.S. *mayoradgo* > M.S. *mayorazgo*), yet *adgo* at no time appears in the *Poema de Mio Cid*. French, also, is the suffix *ete, ote,* so frequent in Juan Ruiz (*librete,* French *livret;* also in the *Conde Lucanor,* XLVI).

The following list comprises words which nowadays are exiled to the linguistic suburbs of works of literature, where their quaintness gives them entrée, or to the linguistic slums, the speech of the *pueblo.* This is a list, capable of ready expansion and not including terms whose history has been specifically treated heretofore, of words or meanings which were a normal part of the Old Spanish vocabulary: *aguardar* in the meaning of "accompany"; *acuçia = diligencia; agora = ahora; aína = pronto; ansí = así; aquese = ese; aqueste = este; asaz = bastante; asconder = esconder; asmar = estimar, pensar; asperar = esperar; ayuso = abajo; ca = porque; castigar* with the sense of "warn" or "advise"; *catar; cobijar; cras = mañana; cuidar* meaning "believe" or "think"; *cuita, dellos ... dellos,* some ... others; *de que, desque = después que; exir = salir; fiuza = confianza; guisa,* formerly much used in adverbial phrases: *fiera guisa = fiera-*

mente, a fea guisa = feamente; haber with the value of *tener; finiestra = ventana; lazrar = sufrir; luengo* (preserved in the saying *de luengas vías, luengas mentiras*); *levar = levantar; lisiar = herir, lastimar; maguer = aunque; o* (and *do*), *onde = donde; otrosí = además; pensar de* + infinitive *= disponerse a, empezar a; rahez = vil; recordar = despertar; suso = arriba; toller = quitar; tornar; vegada = vez; ya* (< Arabic?) as an exclamation; *yantar = comer al mediodía;* etc., etc. Some of these (*asconder, asperar*) and other ancient words or phrases still flourish unchecked in the speech of the people, and there words and meanings held to be long dead may arise to confound the rash: *¡De que* [*= Después que*] *ellos lleguen, veréis cómo se alegra esto!* (Arniches, *El amigo Melquiades*, I, 1); compare *Y de que he despachado las viandas, pienso que es necesario* (Azorín, *Los pueblos, La Andalucía trágica*, II).

BIBLIOGRAPHY

Castro, Américo. *Lengua, enseñanza y literatura*, pp. 102 ff.

Menéndez Pidal. *Manual*, §§ 4, 5.

Oelschläger, V. R. B. *A Medieval Spanish Word-List (A Preliminary Dated Vocabulary of First Appearances up to Berceo)*, The University of Wisconsin Press, Madison [1940].

Procter, E. S. "The Scientific Works of the Court of Alfonso X of Castile: The King and His Collaborators," in *Modern Language Review*, XL (1945), 12–29.

Valdés. *Diálogo de la lengua*, pp. 158 ff.

Van Scoy, H. A. "Alfonso X as a Lexicographer," in *Hispanic Review*, VIII (1940), 277–284.

☞ 7 ☜

The Period of Spanish Ascendancy (1500–1700)

THE GROWING INTEREST IN SPANISH, THE NATIONAL LANGUAGE

TYPICAL of the Renaissance in the concentration of a restless curiosity upon the individual, both the individual man and the individual nation, is the attention devoted to the modern languages, which until then had not been deemed deserving of notice. The new dignity of the vernaculars owed something to the political development of the modern nations; the separate speeches of these nations displaced Latin, the international language, as their governments did the authority of Rome, and became instruments of their sovereign status. Yet more essentially characteristic of the Renaissance and its interest in the discovery of man's reality is the attraction held by all that was popular and spontaneous. Hence the study and the defense of the living languages, expressed in grammars and dictionaries, collections of proverbs, of ballads, of anecdotes (Luis Zapata, *Miscelánea,* between 1592 and 1595; Melchor de Santa Cruz, *Floresta española,* 1574; Juan Rufo, *Los seiscientos apotegmas,* 1596, etc.), and treatises on metrics (Rengifo, *Arte poética española,* 1592).

Castiglione's *Cortegiano,* 1528, which was translated into Spanish in 1534 by Boscán at the suggestion of Garcilaso de la Vega, had an enormous influence upon manners. Three chapters (6, 7, and 8 of Book I) of this treatise are devoted to adequacy and propriety of speech. Propriety of speech, it is affirmed, needs to be cultivated, and one's thoughts, spoken or written, should be expressed in terms proper and select, not empty but harmonious, and—above all—in use, even by the populace. Ancient words must be rejected, because it would be an error to continue to eat acorns, like the ancients, now that there is an abundance of wheat (chap. 7 of Boscán's translation; the reference to acorns and wheat is a commonplace of the time). Previously, Nebrija himself had spent seven years (1463–1470) in Italy, mostly at Bologna, where he absorbed the humanistic ideas prevailing there. Italian students of the classics and of grammar carried the new ideas to Spain even before 1484, when Marineo Sículo left Italy to teach for twelve years at the University of Salamanca, then to become a member of the Court of Ferdinand and Isabel. At court, too, was Pietro Martire d'Anghiera (whom the Spaniards called Pedro Mártir), the chronicler who introduced classical studies to the nobles (cf. p. 183). Then, too, there is the pupil of Politian, the Portuguese Arias Barbosa, professor of Greek at Salamanca. By whatever means the philological theories and practices of the Italian humanists were conveyed to Spain (p. 183), it is true that in the first thirty years of the sixteenth century, under the influence of these new modes, Spanish was stripped of much of its ancient costume and began to emerge as the language of the present day.[1]

---

[1] It is not without profit to reread chapter iii of Part V, "Language as the Basis of Social Intercourse," in Jacob Burckhardt's *The Civilization of the Renaissance in Italy.*

The first grammar in any modern language was the Spanish grammar (*Gramática de la lengua castellana*, Salamanca, 1492) of Antonio de Nebrija, who printed also a separate work on spelling (*Reglas de orthographía*) in 1517. Nebrija's grammar was followed by many other grammatical treatises in the sixteenth and seventeenth centuries, such as the *Util y breve institution para aprender ... la lengua Hespañola,* Louvain, 1555; the *Arte breve y compendiosa* of a certain Cristóbal de Villalón, printed in Antwerp, 1558; the anonymous *Gramática de la lengua vulgar española,* Louvain, 1559; Juan de la Cuesta's *Libro y tratado para enseñar ... todo romance castellano ... Alcalá,* 1589; the *Ortografía castellana* of Mateo Alemán, published in Mexico (1609); the comparative grammar of Latin, Greek, and Castilian, *Trilingüe de tres artes de las tres lenguas castellana, latina i griega,* Salamanca, 1627, of Gonzalo Correas; etc., etc.[2]

The first Latin-Spanish dictionary, the *Universal vocabulario en latín y en romance* (Seville, 1490) of Alfonso Fernández de Palencia was put in the shade by Nebrija's Latin-Spanish and Spanish-Latin vocabularies (*Dictionarium latino-hispanicum,* 1492, and *Interpretación de las palabras castellanas en latín, ca.* 1495, respectively). His larger (?) dictionary, however, was never put into print. The erasmista Juan Lorenzo Palmireno, who also collected proverbs (*El estudioso cortesano,* 1573), printed a *Vocabulario del humanista,* in Valencia, 1569. Alonso Sánchez de la Ballesta contributed a *Dictionario de vocablos castellanos* (Salamanca, 1587). Useful as a guide to the language of its day,

---

[2] I defer for later discussion the Spanish grammars, dictionaries, etc., printed outside Spanish territory.

in spite of its awkward arrangement, is the *Tesoro de la lengua castellana o española* (Madrid, 1611)[3] of Sebastián de Covarrubias, which in its second edition (Madrid, 1673–1674) is preceded by an essay entitled *Del origen y principio de la lengua castellana* (1606) of Bernardo de Ald(e)rete. The latter shows some signs of a historical approach and might even be called the founder of historical grammar in Spain.

In the course of his pursuit of knowledge, the *estudio de la ciencia* of which Fernando del Pulgar speaks (p. 141 below), the Marquis of Santillana collected (though its authorship is questioned) the *Refranes que dizen las viejas tras el huego ordenados por la orden del A B C*. The *Diálogo de la lengua* of Valdés, probably the most valuable of all contemporary treatments of questions of language, quotes numerous adages and holds them up as the standard, because, Valdés says (*Diálogo,* p. 44) in them *se vee mucho bien la puridad de la lengua castellana*. The unusually long list of *refraneros* includes the *Refranes o proverbios en romance* (1555) of Hernán Núñez, called the *Comendador griego* because of his prowess as a Greek scholar and his office in the Order of Santiago, the *Philosophía vulgar* (1568) of Juan de Mal Lara, the humanist of Seville, and the *Vocabulario de refranes* of Master Gonzalo Correas (died 1631), which was not printed until 1906 (second edition, 1924). In their enthusiasm (or craze) for proverbs these and other compilers may have had the example of Erasmus, whose *Adagia* had increased from eight hundred in the edition

---

[3] A microphotographic reproduction has been made of this work by the Hispanic Society of America, New York, 1927.

of 1500, when their author did not know Greek, to three thousand eight hundred in the Venice print of 1508.[4]

Even slang, the language of low life, of thieves, beggars, gangsters, and gypsies, was dignified by the appearance in 1609 of Juan Hidalgo's *Vocabulario de germanía,* reprinted in 1737 by Mayáns y Siscar. To Juan Hidalgo also is due a collection of ballads in the *germanía* or thieves' jargon: *Romances de germanía de varios autores,* in the same volume as the *Vocabulario.* The argot of this underworld appears occasionally in the *jácaras,* rogue ballads, of Quevedo, who had a weakness for low characters.

Early in the course of his literary labors and the civil disturbances in which he was involved, Alphonso the Learned is supposed, without good reason, to have decreed, at the Cortes of 1253, that the usage of Toledo should set the standard for the meaning of a Spanish word. Juan de Valdés prides himself on being *criado en el reino de Toledo* (*Diálogo,* p. 65); poor Sancho Panza, on being rebuked by Don Quixote for another slip, objects that a poor rustic can not fairly be forced to talk like a Toledan (*Don Quixote,* II, 19); and Gracián in his allegorical novel *El criticón* (I, 10), calls Toledo the *escuela del bien hablar.* Although Burgos had just claims and some defenders, Toledo was (need it be said?) often the seat of the Spanish court from the date of the capture of Toledo by Alphonso VI (1085) to the establishment of the capital at Madrid by Philip II in 1561. It is still the seat of the Spanish Church. The fact that it was

[4] For bibliography of the *refraneros* see J. Hurtado y A. González Palencia, *Historia de la literatura española,* tercera edición, Madrid, 1932, § 415; E. Mérimée-S. Griswold Morley, *A History of Spanish Literature,* New York [1930], pp. 191–192, 287.

the residence of the king, which would seem to account sufficiently for its importance, is listed last by Melchor de Santa Cruz (in the *Floresta*), who presumably lays greater stress on its location in the center of the country, its remoteness from the sea, the absence of foreigners, the very cleverness (*habilidad y buen ingenio*) of its residents, either because of the thinness of its air or the climate (*el clima y constelación les ayuda*). Whatever the reason, Toledan Spanish was held to be best at least to the end of the sixteenth century.

BIBLIOGRAPHY

BUCETA, ERASMO. "La tendencia a identificar el español con el latín," in *Homenaje a Menéndez Pidal*, I, 85–108.

———. "El juicio de Carlos V acerca del español," in *Revista de filología española*, XXIV (1937), 11–23.

CASTRO, AMÉRICO. *Lengua, enseñanza y literatura*, pp. 140–155.

———. *El pensamiento de Cervantes*, Madrid, 1925 (*Revista de filología española*, Anejo VI), pp. 190–204.

GAUTHIER, MARCEL (= R. FOULCHÉ-DELBOSC). "Diálogos de antaño," in *Revue Hispanique*, XLV (1919), 34–238.

KNAPP, WILLIAM I. *Concise Bibliography of Spanish Grammars and Dictionaries . . . 1490–1780*, Boston, 1884 (Boston Public Library: *Bibliographies of Special Subjects . . . no. 2*).

KUKENHEIM, L. *Contributions à l'histoire de la grammaire italienne, espagnole et française à l'époque de la renaissance*, Amsterdam, 1932, pp. 198–213.

LYNN, CARO. *A College Professor of the Renaissance: Lucio Marineo Sículo among the Spanish Humanists*, The University of Chicago Press, 1937.

MENÉNDEZ Y PELAYO, M. *La ciencia española*, vol. 3, tercera edición, Madrid, 1888, pp. 250 ff., especially pp. 273–279.

———. *Orígenes de la novela*, II, Madrid, 1907, lxvi (*Nueva biblioteca de autores españoles*, VII).

MOREL-FATIO, A. *Ambrosio de Salazar et l'étude de l'espagnol en France sous Louis XIII*, Paris-Toulouse, 1901, pp. 176–184.

———. *Etudes sur l'Espagne*, quatrième série, Paris, E. Champion, 1925, pp. 189–219, or in *Bulletin Hispanique*, XV (1913), 207–225.

PASTOR, JOSÉ F. *Las apologías de la lengua castellana en el siglo de oro*, Madrid, 1929 (*Los clásicos olvidados*, VIII).

ROMERA-NAVARRO, M. "La defensa de la lengua española en el siglo XVI," in *Bulletin Hispanique*, XXXI (1929), 204–255.

VIÑAZA, CIPRIANO MUÑOZ Y MANZANO, CONDE DE LA. *Biblioteca histórica de la filología castellana*, Madrid, 1893.

Style and Vocabulary

On the wellborn Iñigo López de Mendoza (1398–1458), King Juan II conferred the title of Marquis of Santillana in recognition of his possessing *claras virtudes,* and being worthy of dignity. This *omne agudo e discreto* devoted himself solely to military achievements and the pleasures of study, for, to quote the words of the fifteenth-century biographer Fernando del Pulgar (*Claros varones,* Título IV), *tenía grand copia de libros.* To this learned noble is due one of the first pieces of Spanish literary criticism, the *Proemio e carta al condestable de Portugal* (1448 or 1449), written to serve as a preface to a collection of his poems. The short summary (*proemio* = prologue) of contemporary literature, containing some account of verse forms, does not directly touch on language. It is plain, however, from its very form, that Santillana considered it good style to place the verb at the end of its clause (*devedes estimar que aquellas dueñas que en torno de la fuente de Elicón inçessantemente dançan, en tan nueva edat non inméritamente a la su compañía vos ayan reçebido*). He anticipates the fault of juxtaposition of words of like meaning (*formadas e artiçadas, alegres e jocosas, adórnanlas e compónenlas, dulçes voçes e fermosos sones*). Even *cançion* and *deçir* are regularly found in company (*cançiones e deçires, deçires e cançiones*). The plentiful Latinisms of the *Corbacho* (*ca.* 1438) and of Alfonso de la Torre's *Visión deleitable de la filosofía y de las otras ciençias* (*ca.* 1440) continue in Santillana's *bucólico, elegíaco, fructífero, ínfimo* (notice the *esdrújulo* termination), and the many nouns in *-ion* (*comendaçion, perffetion, restituy-*

çion, vexaçion, etc.). As befits one who ranks the poets of Provence (*la provincia de Equitania*) among the first, there is an occasional Provençal word or form (*obreta*).

In *El laberinto de Fortuna* (printed 1489) of Juan de Mena (1411–1456), one of the first professional literary men in Spain, may be seen the results of a painful striving for perfection of form. The work is dark of thought and expression and employs a Latinized word order, yet it introduced some new Latin terms to Spanish, and was edited with flattering commentary by the humanist, Francisco Sánchez de las Brozas (1582). Studies of Spanish vocabulary have not progressed to the point where one can put his finger on specific words (if any) owed to Juan de Mena, but a stanza (169) from the *Laberinto* shows what he was aiming at:

> *Aun si yo viera la mestrua luna*
> *con cuernos obtusos mostrarse fuscada,*
> *muy rubicunda o muy colorada,*
> *creyera que vientos nos diera Fortuna;*
> *si Febo, dexada la delia cuna,*
> *ígneo viéramos o turbulento,*
> *temiera yo pluvia con fuerça de viento;*
> *en otra manera, non sé que repuna.*

Mestrua [= *menstrua*], *obtuso, fuscada, rubicunda, delia, ígneo, turbulento, pluvia, repuna* [= *repugna*] are sufficient sign of Juan de Mena's Latinisms and his strained style, which provided Nebrija with illustrations for the classical figures of speech treated in the *Gramática*.

This preoccupation with diction crops up in the following century in the sonnets, elegies, and *canciones* of Fernando de Herrera (died 1597), who combed the classical poets and the Bible in his quest for lofty words. The invocation in the first stanza of his heroic *Canción por la victoria de Lepanto* is probably Vergilian; *abisso* is Latinized Greek, and the whole is in imitation of Exodus 15:1-7:

> *Cantemos al Señor, que en la llanura*
> *venció del mar al enemigo fiero:*
> *Tú, Dios de las batallas, tú eres diestra,*
> *salud y gloria nuestra:*
> *Tú rompiste las fuerças y la dura*
> *frente de Faraón, feroz guerrero;*
> *sus escogidos príncipes cubrieron*
> *los abissos del mar, y decendieron*
> *cual piedra en el profundo, y tu ira luego*
> *los tragó como arista seca el fuego.*

In Herrera's commentary on the works of Garcilaso (1580), which stirred up heated discussions among literary folk, are stated his ideas for the improvement of the language as the vehicle of poetry. Praising Spanish, whose attribute of *grave* the poet mentions in prominent place, he points out the necessity of perfection in the sonnet, compares his own tongue favorably with Italian, and presents the contemporary arguments (of classical origin) with respect to the introduction of foreign and new words. In the course of his criticism the double gender of *mar* is observed, not altogether with satisfaction, *tamaño* is rejected on the grounds that it is no longer used by good writers and is poorly formed, ill-sounding, and superfluous since other words sufficiently render its meaning. *Tornados* is an "ancient word," *y que no tiene buen lugar en versos elegantes y suaves.* On the other hand, *natura, ayuda,* and *lindo* are worthy of poetic diction. Of *lindo* he says: *ninguna lengua hay que pueda alabarse de otra palabra mejor que ella.*

Herrera's orthographical reforms included the omission of Latin initial *h* (*aver, ombre, orrible*), the writing of *cual, cuanto, cuatro* (not *qual, quanto, quatro*), etc., the use of the apostrophe (*l'aspereza*), the acute accent mark in *palabras esdrújulas* and in certain monosyllables (p. 207), the circumflex in the preposition *o*, the grave in *e, a < haber*, small letters at the beginning of verses, a dot over vowels to show hiatus (*là òtra*) and the omission of the dot in writing *i* and *j*. In pronunciation he advocated standardization of *afeto < afecto*, etc., *dino < digno, ineto < inepto, ecelente < excelente, deçendençia < desçendençia*, and of *s* in inchoative verb forms (*paresca*, etc.). It may be seen that his preference was for the popular pronunciation (cf. p. 238) as against the learned, which, however, has succeeded in restoring the *c* of *ct*, *g* of *gn*, and etymological *x* and *sc*. In his treatment of *h* and in spelling *cual, cuanto, cuatro*, Herrera was only following the lead of Nebrija.

Among prose writers Latinisms of vocabulary or word order are frequent in the Archpriest of Talavera and in the *Celestina,* of which Valdés complains (*Diálogo,* p. 255) that the author *pone algunos vocablos tan latinos que no se entienden en el castellano, y en partes adonde podría poner propios castellanos.* A favorite rhetorical device, which was to reach its high point in Antonio de Guevara (1480?–1545), was the ending of successive clauses with parallel forms: *Contraer matrimonio con una mujer es cosa muy fácil, mas sustentarlo hasta el fin téngolo por muy difícil: y de aquí es que todos los que se casan por amores viven después con dolores* (*Epístolas familiares*).

Naturalness of expression was soon to be even more violently abused, and the difficulty of simplicity for the rhetoric-loving Spanish was lamented in 1569 by the Neapolitan Massimo Triano; he complained of the abuse of metaphors and of exclamations and rhetorical questions, the heaping up of epithets (*el amontonar de vocablos*), and the larding of conversation with proverbs. For no Spaniard, according to him, could anything be simply black or white; it must be at least blacker than tar or whiter than snow.

Overabundance of rhetorical question and exclamation is a fault especially of the *Celestina: Pero ¿qué digo? ¿Con quién hablo? ¿Estoy en mi seso? ¿Qué es esto, Calisto? ¿Soñabas, duermes o velas? ¿Estás en pie o acostado? Cata que estás en la cámara. ¿No ves que el ofendedor no está presente? ¿Con quién lo has? Torna en ti ...* (XIV, 1514 edition).

Only too familiar is the use *seriatim* of synonymous terms: *en mal punto y en hora menguada, del coraje y brío que enciende y anima a los valientes pechos (Don Quixote, I, 35 and 38), esta concavidad y espacio vi yo a tiempo cuando ya iba cansado y mohíno de verme, pendiente y colgado (ibid., II, 23).*[5]

The Spaniard's pomposity of speech with accompanying gestures in the seventeenth century was noticed by all foreigners. The French in particular ridiculed this apparent bluster in their "Spanish rodomontades."

The role of Herrera fell to Luis de Argote y Góngora (1561–1627), who used his mother's family name, contrary to custom, since (in the opinion of Pfandl) he wished to be different from the multitude. Góngora was a Cordovan

---

[5] There are several instances of this repetition in the famous passage on the Golden Age (*ibid.*, I, 11).

(Córdoba seems to have been a fertile breeding ground for rhetorical bombast) and in his anxiety to set new ideals for perfection of poetic style, he heaped on more and more Latin and Greek words (which to be sure were, for the most part, already in use, if less profusely), strained still further the arrangement of his terms (*cuantas la Libia engendra fieras*), employed classical constructions (omission of the definite article, use of the "Greek accusative"),[6] overloaded his verses with classical references and figures of speech (especially, violent antitheses), abused the ablative absolute, and amplified the meaning of *ser* to *servir* or *causar*. This plague, which appeared in most European literatures at the time, goes in Spain under the various names of *gongorismo, culteranismo, cultismo, estilo culto*. Many of Góngora's theories for lifting poetry out of the reach of the prosaic herd are already found in the *Libro de la erudición póetica* of Luis Carrillo y Sotomayor (1583?–1610). Góngora puts his theories into practice in the *Soledades,* where flashingly expressive, if now shopworn, lines occur, like the famous *En dehesas azules* (or *campos de zafiro*) *pace estrellas; las aves, esquilas dulces de sonora pluma; Entre espinas crepúsculos pisando,* and in the *Fábula de Polifemo y Galatea.* The reader may observe them for himself in the following stanzas (1 and 24) from the *Fábula:*

> Estas que me dictó rimas sonoras,
> culta sí, aunque bucólica Talía,
> ¡oh, excelso conde!, en las purpúreas horas
> que es rosa el alba y rosicler el día,
> agora, que de luz su niebla doras,

---

[6] E.g., *Desnuda el pecho anda ella* (*Angélica y Medoro*).

escucha al son de la zampoña mía,
si ya los muros no te ven de Huelva
peinar el viento o fatigar la selva.

. . .

Salamandra del sol vestido estrellas,
latiendo el can del cielo estaba, cuando
polvo el cabello, húmidas centellas,
si no ardiendo, aljófares sudando,
llegó Acis, y de ambas luces bellas
dulce occidente viendo el sueño blando,
su boca dió y sus ojos cuanto pudo
al sonoro cristal, al cristal mudo.[7]

Another vice of the literature of this period, though a
more ancient fault and one native to the country, was the
partiality to *conceptos* (= conceits), the subtle, unexpected,
ingenious expression of a thought. Decadence has set in
when the absence of ideas must be concealed by the manner
of their formulation, and, although they cannot be accused
of barrenness of thought, the two principal exponents of
conceptismo, Francisco de Quevedo (1580–1645) and Baltasar Gracián (1601–1658) belong to the declining splendor
of the seventeenth century.

Gracián influenced La Rochefoucauld and La Bruyère,
and the maxims of his *Oráculo manual* were translated
by Schopenhauer. The artificialities of Gracián, who, curi-
ously, praised the *Conde Lucanor,* recall Bouterwek's remark that he would have been an excellent writer, if he
hadn't wanted to be an extraordinary one. With the ellipses
of Quevedo and Gracián there passed that ample style of

---

[7] For Gongorism in prose cf. L. Pfandl, *Historia de la literatura nacional española en el siglo de oro,* pp. 355–356, for examples from Castillo Solórzano; and
one must not forget the faults of the romances of chivalry which had poor Don
Quixote beside himself (*Don Quixote,* I, 1).

prose, characteristic of the sixteenth century but never out of date in Spain, in which predominate long sentences of loosely linked clauses (*el cual* was most useful!), generously adorned out of Rhetoric's copious supply.[8]

¡Que en tan poco tiempo tal lengua entre cristianos haya! marvels Lope de Vega in the sonnet beginning *Boscán, tarde llegamos. ¿Hay posada?* And a *nueva lengua* there was. *Latinista* and *vocablista* were the epithets applied to the partisans of Góngora, because of the constantly repeated words with which they furbished up the language, and many are the references made by opponents (Jáuregui, Lope de Vega, Quevedo) to the obscure "Prince of Darkness." The opponents of Góngora, however, often fell ill of the disease they scorned. Even in the sixteenth century there had been ridicule of obscurity of style and extravagant Latinisms by Baltasar del Alcázar in the sonnet beginning *Haz un soneto que no levante el vuelo,* by Barahona del Soto in *Contra los malos poetas afectados y oscuros* and elsewhere, and by Juan de la Cueva in the *Exemplar poético,* III. In Rojas' *Entre bobos anda el juego* (beginning), Doña Isabel complains that her lover is bad to look at and worse to listen to. Her maid inquires if he speaks *culto,* and the mistress answers that his language is not nonsensical (*disparatado*), but that he is trying to win her with *vocablos de estrado* like *crédito, fineza, recato, halago,* and *atención,* which she couldn't digest even if she loved him.

In *El diablo cojuelo* (Tranco X), where some of these same words are listed, poets are further ordered, under

---

[8] In their length the sentences of Tirso de Molina's *Los tres maridos burlados* are indicative of the decay of the rotundity of the sixteenth-century manner.

threat of treason, not to use *fulgor, libar, numen, purpurear, meta, trámite, afectar, pompa, trémula, amago, idilio*. Similarly, in Lope de Vega's *Amar sin saber a quién* the servant Limón derides those *lindísimos mancebos* who say *acción, en substancia, reducción, y todo vocablo nuevo* (I, 13). Again, in *La filomena* (epístola II) the *fénix* condemns *boato, asunto, activo, recalcitrar, morigerar, seleta, terso, culto, embrión, correlativo, recíproco, concreto, abstracto, diablo, épico, garipundio* [?] *y positivo*. Elsewhere Lope gives another list of these *estupendos vocablos, "a quien llama la ironía cultos, por mal cultivados"*: *riesgo, superior, inexcusable, valimiento, acción, despejo, ruidoso, activo, desaire, lucimiento, carabanas* (*El desprecio agradecido*, I, 2). The satirist Quevedo often attacked these new terms, writing essays entitled *Aguja de navegar cultos*, 1631 (*Compass for Navigating Cultos*), *Culta latiniparla*, 1629, and a *Receta* (*Prescription*) for making *Soledades* in one day. At the same time he burlesques the jumbled arrangement of words which the Gongorists were addicted to:

> Quien quisiere ser culto en sólo un día
> la geri (aprenderá) gonza siguiente:
> *fulgores, arrogar, joven, presiente,*
> *candor, construye, métrica armonía,*
> poco mucho, *si no, purpuracía,*
> *neutralidad, conculca, exige, mente,*
> *pulsa, ostenta, librar, adolescente,*
> *señas, traslada, pira, frustra, arpía,*
> *cede, impide, cisuras, petulante,*
> *palestra, liba, meta, argento, alterna,*
> *si bien, disuelve, émulo, canoro.*
> Use mucho de *líquido* y de *errante:*
> su poco de *nocturno* y de *caverna,*
> anden listos *livor, adunco* y *poro* ...

In his *Culta latiniparla* Quevedo adds *ansí, de buen aire, descrédito, desaseado, aplaudir,* and *anhelar* to the list of unwelcome upstarts. He objects also to excessive use of *galante, fino, sazón, emular, lo cierto es, esfuerzos, ejemplo, aunque.* Most of the innovations ridiculed, or legitimate words too frequently used, are now accepted as an integral part of the language, especially nouns in *-ción,* which Valdés (*Diálogo,* pp. 194 ff.) would have liked to nationalize (*ambición, excepción, superstición*), along with *asesinar, aspirar, cómodo* and *incómodo, comodidad, decoro, diseñar* and *diseño, dignar, discurrir* and *discurso, entretener, estilo, facilitar, fantasía, ingeniar, insolencia, jubilar, manejar* and *manejo, martelo, novela* and *novelar, objeto, obnoxio, observar* and *observación, pedante, persuadir* and *persuasión, servitud, solacio, temeridad,* and the Greek words *idiota, ortografía, paradoja, paréntesis,* and *tiranizar* (*Diálogo,* p. 193). Many of these words, however, had already been used by Spanish authors (see the edition of the *Diálogo de la lengua* of José F. Montesinos in the *Clásicos castellanos,* volume 86, Madrid, 1940, p. lii).

It was not by thumbing the *Calepino* (a Latin dictionary) as Lope de Vega once maintained of the Latinizing *cultistas,* that Italian words were discovered for Spanish, because the compelling force of the Italian Renaissance swept Italianisms over all Europe: terms from literature like *esdrújulo, novela, soneto;* military words such as *alerta, bisoño* (since, according to Covarrubias, raw recruits must always be naming their wants: *bisogno* = I need), *cartucho, centinela, coronel, escolta, escuadra, soldado;* expressions drawn from the arts and industry, *balcón, banca, brújula, capitán, carena, esbozo, fachada, galera, lancha, piloto;* and the word *millón,* which displaced *cuento.* Also Italian are *boletín, capricho, facha, fachenda, fracaso* (?). There are a few verbs, also, from Italian, like *atacar, charlar,* and *estropear,* and Spaniards carried home from Italy an occasional term (*mojicón < moccicone, forajido < fuoruscito*) which was not exported to other countries. Of the several words which Valdés proposes (*Diálogo,* p. 196) to adopt into Spanish from Italian, most have been accepted. It does not follow, however, that all were introduced by Valdés, or even in his day, as has been said (p. 150).

At this time the New World began to add its exotic contributions to the Spanish word list. From the Antilles and the adjacent coast of Spanish America came *batata* (which Navagero tasted in Seville in 1526, finding it to savor of chestnuts) and its variant *patata,* and *butaca, cacique, caimán, canoa, caoba, carey, cayo, (e)naguas, hamaca, huracán* (originally from Yucatan), *iguana, maguey, maíz, mico, sabana, tabaco, tiburón, tuna.* The *náhuatl* language of Mexico yielded *cacahuete, cacao, chicle, chile, chocolate, hule, jícara, nopal, petaca, petate, pinole, tamal, tiza, tomate,* but *jitomate* is rare or nonexistent in Spain. From the *quechua* language of South America are *alpaca, cancha, cóndor, china* (native woman), *llama, mate, pampa, papa, puma, quina, tanda, vicuña.* Somewhat later *biombo* traveled the long way from Japan, possibly chaperoned by the Portuguese.

Evolution of Sounds

SOURCES OF INFORMATION

Before 1500, except for the assistance rendered by the grammar of the great Nebrija, the nature of any given sound of Spanish must ordinarily be deduced, by a comparative method, from the direction of progress of the several tongues that developed out of colloquial Latin or from the later history of Spanish itself. With the multiplication of Spanish grammars and orthographies in Spain and the principal countries of Europe after the beginning of the sixteenth century, the task becomes less a matter of inference. After 1500 the statements of contemporary grammarians are a principal source of information. Comparison of Spanish with other languages (French, Italian, English, Portuguese, and, rarely, German) provides further data.

Especially valuable is the testimony of the Sephardim, the Spanish Jews. Upon their expulsion from the Peninsula (1492 and later), they spread around the shore line of the Mediterranean; the Turkish coasts in particular, where colonies grew up at Adrianopolis, Constantinople, and Salonika, became a new homeland. Later there were settlements, often via Portugal, and of less consequence linguistically, at Hamburg, at Amsterdam, and in England. Wherever the *sefardíes* fled, with them went the Spanish of their day, and, living apart as has been their destiny and cut off from the growing stalk of Castilian, they have preserved many of the archaic traits of the Spanish language, as also much of its early popular literature, ballads, proverbs, and folk tales.

The zealous padres who traveled to the New World to

spread the faith among the Indians found that their labors would be lessened by knowledge of the native languages, and numerous grammars of the Indian tongues grew out of this need. In the equation of the sounds of Indian with those of Spanish, information is yielded indirectly to the philologist.

The representation of Spanish in the Arabic or Hebrew alphabet (or vice versa) often throws light on the nature of a sound, the more often since *aljamiado* texts, that is, documents in which Spanish is written with Arabic characters, are fairly numerous.

Finally, there is the study of rhyme words, and for this study there is fortunately an abundance of poetical works in sixteenth- and seventeenth-century Spanish.

CONSONANTS

Of the consonants in Spanish only the sounds represented by *b* and *v*, *ç* and *z, s* and *ss, j* (*ge, gi*), and *x* call for discussion, although the changes undergone were fundamental. (The vowels had long since assumed definitive form.)

B and V.—The writers on grammatical subjects in the period from 1500 to 1700 were often actuated by the desire to fit Spanish into the framework of Latin, and they are not free from the universal error of confusing sound and symbol. Since *b* and *v* are different characters they should stand (so runs the reasoning) for different sounds. And this time the grammarians may have been right. *B* and *v* stand for distinct sounds in Jewish-Spanish, and in the Spanish words anciently adopted by the Indians of Chile. The evidence of the Mexican languages is inconclusive, but in Spain the careful separation in writing of *b* < *p* (*lobo* < *lupum*) and *u* < *b, v* (*cauallo* < *caballum, mouer* < *movere*) must, if the texts are trustworthy, mean a difference in sound, at least in the intervocalic position. Yet after the middle of the sixteenth century even this distinction of occlusive (*b*) and fricative (*u*) disappears, and there is no rule in the writing of *b* and *v* until the adoption of the modern system, based mostly on etymology, but favoring *b* for the initial position, at the beginning of the eighteenth century.[9]

Of the similarity of these two consonants one illustration is sufficient. In *La infanta desesperada,* II, of Lope de Vega, during a game consisting in naming all the attributes of one's beloved which begin with the same letter, Prince Doristán includes *vida* with *bella* and *beldad.* Lavinia, who apparently thought the distinction a quibble, says in defense of the prince ¿*Por eso te habían de dar penitencia? No ha lugar. Vaya el juego.*

Ç and Z.—Ancient evidence of the pronunciation of *ç* is scarce and must be sought in such slips of spelling as those committed by Per Abbat, the copyist of the MS of the *Poema de Mio Cid,* who writes *çeruiçio* (69, 1535) for *servicio,* and *San Çaluador* (2924) for *San Salvador.* In the *Corbacho* one finds *çusio* for *sucio, çusia* for *sucia, çofrir* for *sofrir* (edition of L. B. Simpson, pp. 12, 71, 106, respectively). Similarly in the *Celestina* (XVII, 1514 edition) there is *çufre* for *sufre.* These ancient approximate equivalences,

---

[9] Labiodental *v,* the existence of which in Classic Latin and Vulgar Latin is more than dubious, is now native only to Valencia and parts of southern Catalonia; elsewhere the bilabial occlusive of absolute initial position (or following *m* or *n*) is represented by both *b* and *v,* as is the bilabial fricative of position between vowels, this being the tendency almost from the earliest stages of the language.

some of which have survived as the standard spellings, as *cerrar < serare, cedazo < saetaceum, centinela < sentinella,* show the sibilant element of *ç,* whose exact value of *ts* [ŝ] is almost certain. The statements of foreign contemporary writers on the subject, if vague and unscientific, are always valuable. Italian grammarians almost without exception compare *ç* with the *z* of their own language, although the French make the comparison with *ç* or *s*.[10] For example, "Ledit *c* seul se prononce a guise du siflet de l'oye" (like the hiss of a goose), Gabriel Meurier, 1568;[11] "C before a, o, u like k, as Cabo, Cobrar, save that if the nature of the word require any other pronunciation, it is noted with a little taile, as *ç,* and is called *Cerilla,* sounding almost as the Italian *z* in Senza, Anzi, ... as our *ts* in English, but not altogether so strong upon the *t* ... ," Richard Percyuall, 1591; etc.

Less convincing is the information about the sound represented by *z,* but it is fairly certain that it was a voiced sound about equivalent to *dz* [ẑ]. More than one contemporary writer declares it to differ from *ç con alguna manera de zumbido* (= buzzing), and one in particular (Doergank, *Institutiones in linguam hispanican,* Cologne, 1614) says: Z effertur germanico more et quasi *ds* ... ut alteza, dulceza, vecino, quasi *altedsa,* etc. Other grammarians (D'Urbino, 1560; Miranda, 1595) specifically note that Castilian *z* is like Tuscan *zz.* It was moreover a convention of orthography to write *z,* not *ç,* at the end of a word or syllable, irrespective (presumably) of the theoretical difference of sound:

[10] Only a few can be quoted in the limits of these pages. For amplification of the quotations from grammarians see the works of Cuervo, Ford, and Canfield in the *Bibliography* to this section.

[11] Caroline B. Bourland, "Algo sobre Gabriel Meurier," in *Hispanic Review,* VI (1938), 139–152.

pez < *piscem*, but *peçes*. By the middle of the sixteenth century ç and z stood for one and the same sound and were constantly confused in writing, rhyme tests thus becoming futile. Z had become unvoiced, for a reason as yet not satisfactorily explained, and then the common sound of ç and z was articulated with the tip of the tongue dropped to position between the teeth.[12] Grammarians bemoan the people's inability to make a distinction, but at least they make it clear that the tendency of ç and z was, in Castile, León, Aragon, Murcia, and Extremadura, toward an interdental sound: *la lengua puesta entre los dientes* (1574), *la lengua casi mordida de los dientes* (1582), *abriendo algo los dientes y metiendo la punta de la lengua entre ellos, que salga la lengua un poco fuera* (1589), etc.[13] In Andalusia, however, ç and z were confused with, and later became equal to, (predorsal) *s*. The details of the establishment of the modern *theta* sound are not yet completely known. There would, however, be justification for considering it in its relation to the Andalusian *ceceo*,[14] which is now believed to represent one of the several varieties of the consonant *s* (p. 231). That is to say, *theta*, the sibilant quality of which is noticed by several authorities (see R. J. Cuervo in *Revue Hispanique*, II [1894], 46; R. Lenz, *El español en Chile*, p. 123), is only one of the forms of *ese*. It is likely that *theta* became general in Castile during the first half of the seventeenth century. In 1620 Juan Pablo Bonet, a teacher of deaf-mutes, gives the

---

[12] The disappearance of the dental element is paralleled by the reduction of [ŝ] to [s] in French in the thirteenth century (*cerf*). At the same time in France [č] passed to [š] (*chambre*), a change which is in progress in modern Tuscan (between vowels only).

[13] Cf. note, p. 156.   [14] Cf. p. 231.

following direction for its articulation: *Para que pronuncie esta letra* [i.e., *z*] *ha de poner el mudo la punta de la lengua entre los dientes, y expeler la respiración que salga sin que la lengua se aparte de aquel lugar*.[15] The sound of *theta* finally won for itself, as a consequence of the earlier similarity in sound of *c* and *z*, certain words formerly spelled with *ç* as the equivalent of *s: zurcir* < *sarcire, zahondar* < *suffundare, zafiro* < *sapphirum, lezna* < *alisna* (Gothic), *avizor* < *avisor, quizá* < *qui(te)sapit, Velázquez* < *Velásquez;* the first person singular (and derived forms) of inceptive verbs: *parezco* (< Old Spanish *paresco*) is due to the influence of the remaining persons and numbers: *pareces, parece,* etc. *Ç* was officially abandoned as a character of the Spanish alphabet in 1741.

S and SS.—The English grammarian of Spanish, Richard Percyuall, says of *s* in 1591: "*S,* if he be single in the midst of a word . . . is pronounced with a milde sound between *s* and *z,* as the French do in *chose, maison,* or we in English in pleasure, desire, so in Spanish *cosa, uso.*" Judging again by the metrical test, intervocalic *s* began to lose its voicing around 1550, for from that time forward *s* and *ss* rhyme together more and more freely. The treatise on poetics of Rengifo (1592) makes no distinction. Not until 1763 was the use of *ss*[16] abolished in writing, although it had been superfluous for a century or more. The *z* sound which *s* between vowels has today in parts of Aragon and Extremadura may or may not be a survival of the ancient practice.

[15] In the time of Pedro de Alcalá (*ca.* 1505) the sound of Arabic *tha* [= Eng. *th* as in *think*] was native only to the *ceceosos* in Spain. Cf. Menéndez Pidal, *Cantar de Mio Cid,* I, 212 note; Canfield, *Spanish Literature,* p. 159.

[16] The phonetic value of *ss,* and *s* when initial or final, is treated above (p. 94).

X, J (Ge, Gi), and also S.—In the *bable,* the dialect of
Asturias, and also in Catalan, *x* still has its ancient value of
sh [š]. Anciently there are sporadic spellings like *Carcaxona*
for *Carcassonne* (*Conde Lucanor,* XL), *Xirafontayna* for
Sérifontaine (*El victorial,* p. 131 of the edition of R. Iglesia).
X is still used in Mexico with the sound of *s,* in the Spanish
form of some words originally Indian: *Xochimilco,* pronounced *Sochimilco; Xochicalco = Sochicalco; Xicoténcatl = Sicoténcatl.* The presence formerly of the unvoiced
palatal fricative, that is, *sh,* is sufficiently indicated by its
equivalence with Arabic *shin* and by loan words like *Qui-
chotte* (French) and *Chisciotte* (Italian) < *Quixote, Chi-
mène* < *Ximena, sherry* < *Xerez* (which was considered
a plural form), and by the remarks of those who lived at the
time: for example, the Englishman Miles Phillips, who was
in Mexico from 1568 to 1582, writes *Washaca* for *Oaxaca,*
and *Shalapa* for *Xalapa* (now spelled *Jalapa*); James Howell
in his *Familiar Letters* (October 17, 1634) speaks of the
drink called *Alosha* (modern Spanish *aloja,* formerly spelled
aloxa); Cristóbal de las Casas says (1570): "La *x* con qual-
quier vocal vale como en toscano *sc* con *e, i;* como *caxa,
enxuto* suenan como alla *fascia, asciuto*"; Gabriel Meurier,
who must have been a successful teacher, says: "*X.* Est dite
par les espagnols *equiz* laquelle a telle proprieté que me-
diante l'aide d'vn *o,* fait arrester et demeurer les asnes, mais
en France et en Flandres il fait enuoler les poulailles,"[17]
and in the table of corresponding sounds which follows *x*
is equated with *ch* of French.

---

[17] "*X.* It is called by Spaniards *equis,* which has the property, when followed
by an *o,* of making donkeys stop and stand still, but in France and Flanders, it
makes fowls take wing."

The sound of *j* and *ge, gi* is compared by the grammarians of the sixteenth century both to that in French *jour* [ž] and in Italian *giorno* [ŷ]. It may be presumed that in the beginning the sound was more nearly that of the Italian:

> Se si nomina l'aglio in lingua nostra,
> Et l'ode lo spagnuol, dice a lui trovo ...
> Se sente nomar l'aglio a lo spagnuolo
> Il nostro, parli udir comodo e agio.[18]

Losing its dental element, and becoming unvoiced, as did *z*, for reasons yet unclear, *j, ge, gi* came to have the same sound as *x* from 1550 on, and in writing the two were soon used interchangeably.[19]

Just as Lope wrote *haçer* and *hazer*, etc., without distinction (e.g., *La batalla del honor*, vv. 1781, 1786), so did his contemporaries write *tixeras, tigeras, tijeras*, and the etymological *tiseras* (cf. p. 162). And Covarrubias (1611, and also in the 1674 edition) defends himself for entering the same word under both *x* and *j, ge, gi* by invoking his great predecessor: *yo seguí al Antonio Nebrisense, y por esso no soy tanto de culpar* (cf. the *Tesoro* at the end of *x*). In printing, however, a certain amount of regularity was introduced, as Suárez de Figueroa implies (*Quanto a la ortografía castellana ... comúnmente se sigue la de las Imprentas de Madrid*, cited by Cuervo in *Romania*, XXIV [1895], 104).

---

[18] "If *aglio* [= garlic, *ajo* in Spanish] is named in our language, and the Spaniard hears it, to him it says *trovo* [= *hallo*, I find] . . . If by one of us *aglio* is heard named in the Spanish manner (*ajo* pronounced *aŷo*), he seems to hear 'convenience' and 'ease' (*agio*)." The quotation is from the first half of the sixteenth century. Cf. Cuervo, *Revue Hispanique*, II, 1 ff., or *Disquisiciones filológicas*, I, 131 ff.

[19] Cf. Cuervo, *Revue Hispanique*, II, 56 ff.; Ford, "The Old Spanish Sibilants," pp. 155 ff.; also Canfield, *Spanish Literature*, pp. 201 ff. The disappearance of the dental element occurred in French in the thirteenth century (*général*) and is taking place in Modern Tuscan (between vowels only).

Xomburg is Castillejo's spelling of the name of a lady to whom he addressed some poems, *Anna von Schaumburg.* But in the reign of Charles II, a century later, *Chambergo* is the form Marshal *Schomberg*'s name takes, showing that the sound of *x* had changed and was no longer the equivalent of German *sch* or French *ch*. The former "convertible" quality of *x* and *j, ge, gi* survives in *Texas, México* and *mexicano* (the latter being the only spellings which have the sanction of the Mexican government), *Oaxaca,* and *Xavier, Ximénez* against *Javier, Jiménez* or *Giménez*. In the same way *Ximénes, Quiñónez,* etc., recall the occasional similarity of *s* and *z*. To employ *x* in writing for the *jota* sound of modern Spanish was finally condemned by the Spanish Academy in 1815.

The nature of Castilian *s* (usual except in the south), pronounced with the tip of the tongue against the sockets of the upper teeth and with the fore part of the tongue lying slightly concave, makes it sound somewhat like English *sh* or like *ch* in French. Formerly, the articulation being more often made higher in the roof of the mouth, this quality of *s* must have been general throughout Spain. The stock Moor of the Spanish stage of the Golden Age is represented as always mistaking Castilian *s* for his *shîn,* the *sh* sound formerly written *x* in Spanish, as stated above: *No hay qui perdonanxax, amego; exta la perxona lo que complimox, y voxotrox, voxtra merxe agora en extorballe un palabra no max, baxer [= va a hacer] que perdemox cuanto ex trabaxado* (Lope de Rueda, *Comedia Armelina,* IV; the date is 1567).[20] Thus the approximate equivalence of *s* with *x,* and

[20] Cf. José F. Montesinos, "La lengua morisca," in *Teatro antiguo español,* VII (Madrid, 1929), 218–226.

later with *j, ge, gi,*[21] led to the occasional substitution of *x* (now *j*), for an original *s:* Old Spanish *páxaro* (M.S. *pájaro*) < *passerem;* Old Spanish *roxo* (M.S. *rojo*) < *russum;* Old Spanish *baxo* (M.S. *bajo*) < *bassum;* Old Spanish *tixera* (M.S. *tijera*[*s*]) < *tonsoria* (by telescoping with *cisellum*); Old Spanish *frisol* (M.S. *frijol* or *frejol*) < *phaseolum* (the older dictionaries give only the plural *frisoles;* but *en algunas partes los llaman frixoles,* says the *Autoridades*); Old Spanish *xabón* (M.S. *jabón*) < *saponem;* Old Spanish *Xenil* (M.S. *Genil*) < *Singilis.* A few doublet forms have continued to the present time: *simio* and *jimio* < *simium, sarga* and *jerga* < *sericam, jeme* and *semi-* < *semis, cesar* and *cejar* < *cessare, jilguero* and *silguero* < *sericarium.* The permanent passage of Old Spanish *x, j, ge, gi* to Modern Spanish *s,* as in *cogecha* > *cosecha,* is rare.

Toward the end of the sixteenth century, [š] (spelled *x, j, ge, gi*) began to be pronounced as an aspirate *h* or as *jota* [x], probably through the emphasis of the aspiration or velar frication which completed its articulation. Although some students of the subject do not think the same phenomenon to be involved, one recalls that almost wherever Spanish is spoken, *s,* whether initial or final of syllable, tends to become a mere aspiration or frication: *nosotros* > *nohotros* (orthographically *nojotros*), *siempre* > *hiempre* (orthographically *jiempre*), *pastas* > *pahta*(*h*) (Espinosa, *Estudios,* pp. 186–187, note). The frequent contemporary references to Arabic sounds articulated in the throat and

---

[21] Hence forms like *desencasadamente* (Cervantes, *El celoso extremeño*) = *desencajadamente,* and *desencasados* (Cervantes, *Coloquio de los perros*) = *desencajados.* Both *desencajar* and *desencasar* are listed in the Academy Dictionary. Similar is *quiso* > *quijo,* as in the rhyming by Tirso of *quijo, hijo* (*La villana de Vallecas,* III, 8).

the fact that the sound is first noticed in Andalusia, where it was characteristic of the *bravos* and *jaques* of the day, have long been adduced in confirmation of an Arabic origin, but unconvincingly, since the ancient references do not connect the Moorish guttural articulation specifically with *x, j, ge, gi.*[22]

At first *h* is frequently used, in recollection of its traditional aspirate value, to represent the new sound: *Pahería, mohar, habalí, harro,* writes Quevedo in the last chapter of the *Buscón* (composed *ca.* 1608; first edition, 1626) in imitation of the speech of the braggarts of Seville. *Mohadas* (= knife thrusts), says Doña María, talking "tough," in Lope's *Moza de cántaro,* III, 2 (first edition, 1646?). *Sevilla, centro común ... de la rufianería (a quien ellos llaman hermanía* [= *germanía*], explains Lugo y Dávila, in his *Teatro popular, Novela cuarta,* first edition, 1622). *Hente, huguemos, muher,* etc., anachronistically say the *bravos* of Vélez de Guevara's *La serrana de la Vera, passim* (written not before 1613?). Presumably the old pronunciation as š was gone by 1650, yet one would like to find, for the seventeenth century, such good evidence as is presented a hundred years later by Ramón de la Cruz's Frenchman, whose pronunciation of *mejor* is written *micor, trabajamos* written *trabacamos, mujeres* written *moqueres, jefe* written *quefe,* etc.,

---

[22] Cf. Valdés *Diálogo,* p. 75; Ford, "The Old Spanish Sibilants," pp. 156–157; Cuervo in the *Notas* to Bello's *Grámatica,* p. 21, or in *Revue Hispanique,* II (1895), 59 ff.; A. Castro in his edition of *El buscón* of Quevedo, Madrid, 1927 (*Clásicos castellanos,* vol. 5), p. 281, note; B. Croce, *La lingua spagnuola in Italia,* p. 23; Vélez de Guevara, *El diablo cojuelo,* Tranco X (*gárgaras de algarabía en el gútur*); Canfield, *op. cit.,* pp. 175, 189, 207–208. In the *Familiar Letters* (August 1, 1622), James Howell speaks of a rhyme of "certain hard throaty words" (that is, *abeja, oveja, rabeja, oreja, igreja, vieja*). The saying is in Correas' *Vocabulario de refranes.*

showing plainly the velar value of the sound.[28] The aspiration of *x* and *j* is observed also by Casanova who, in relating his adventures in Spain (1767–1768), says "j'arrivai à Guadalaxara ... ou Guadalajara que les espagnols prononcent Goudalàgara, en aspirant fortement le *g* de *ga* (cf. Jean Sarrailh in *Revista de filología española*, XXII [1935], 285)." In another passage the chevalier again uses *g* to represent the sound of *jota,* writing *parego-ga* for *parejo-ja* (chap. xxx of the Modern Library edition). In the nineteenth century the velar fricative continued to trouble foreigners like Théophile Gautier ("il nous fallut ... écorcher le gosier à râler l'abominable jota," *Voyage en Espagne,* chap. iv), and the Italian ambassador for whose instruction Juan Bautista Arriaza (1770–1837) wrote the verses entitled *Julepe entre un gitano y un jaque.*

---

[28] Cf. Ramón de la Cruz, *Ocho sainetes inéditos,* editados ... por Charles Emil Kany, Berkeley, the University of California Press [1925], p. 204. See further examples in *Revue Hispanique,* LXXVI (1929), 97.

BIBLIOGRAPHY

CANFIELD, DELOS L. *Spanish Literature in Mexican Languages as a Source for the Study of Spanish Pronunciation*, New York, Instituto de las Españas, 1934.

CUERVO, RUFINO J. "Disquisiciones sobre antigua ortografía y pronunciación caste-llanas, I," in *Revue Hispanique*, II (1895), 1 ff.; II, *ibid.*, V (1898), 273 ff., or in *Disquisiciones filológicas*, tomo I, Bogotá, Editorial Centro, 1939, pp. 131 ff. (The first part of this important study appears in very brief summary in the *Notas*, pp. 17–24 of Bello's *Gramática*.)

ESPINOSA, AURELIO M., hijo. *Arcaísmos dialectales: La conservación de s y z sonoras*, Madrid, 1935 (*Revista de filología española, Anejo XIX*).

FORD, J. D. M. "The Old Spanish Sibilants" (*Harvard Studies and Notes in Philology and Literature*, VII).

GAVEL, HENRI. *Essai sur l'évolution de la prononciation du castillan depuis le XIVme siècle*, Paris, E. Champion, 1920.

HANSSEN. *Gramática histórica*, §§ 34–38.

LURIA, MAX A. *A Study of the Monastir Dialect of Judeo-Spanish*, New York, Instituto de las Españas, 1930.

MENÉNDEZ PIDAL. *Manual*, §§ 35 *bis*; 37, 2, *b*; 72, 2.

———. *El lenguaje del siglo XVI*, in *Cruz y raya*, Madrid, I (1933), 9–63; also in *Los romances de América y otros estudios*, Espasa-Calpe Argentina, Buenos Aires [1939], 137–187 (*Colección austral, no. 55*).

NAVARRO TOMÁS. *Manual*, § 106.

WAGNER, M. L. *Caracteres generales del judeo-español de oriente*, Madrid, 1930 (*Revista de filología española, Anejo XII*).

EVOLUTION OF FORMS

Continuing in use in the period between 1500 and 1700 were certain verbal forms already discussed (pp. 108–117): the analytical future and conditional, the infinitive with final *r* assimilated to the *l* of a personal pronoun object, and palatalized (*hablalle, comello, decillas,* etc.), the imperative plural form plus pronoun object of the third person with metathesis of *d* and *l* (*hablalde, comeldo, escribildes,* etc.), the omission of the *d* of the same verb form (*hablá, aprendé, decí,* etc.), and the retention of *-des* in endings whose vowel was unstressed (*hablábades, aprenderíades, viviéssedes,* etc.). In the second person plural of the preterit *-tes* was the customary termination even in seventeenth century texts, although the rare *-teis,* which owes its *i* to the numerous other second person plurals, appears as early as 1555 in a Spanish grammar printed in Louvain, the *Util y breve institution para aprender ... la lengua Hespañola,* by an unnamed author.

Outside the domain of the verb, *el* is still current as the form of the definite article used before unstressed *a: el Alhambra,* etc. (cf. p. 101). In combination with *de,* the normal elision of speech was carried into writing regularly as late as the seventeenth century, and *de + él, ella,* etc. > *del, della,* etc. Likewise, *de + ese, este,* etc. > *dese, deste,* etc.

Somewhat grudgingly allowed by Ximénez Patón in 1614, condemned as late as 1622 as inelegant by Ambrosio de Salazar and only granted to be *propio, más no tan usado* by Correas in 1626 (*Arte grande de la lengua castellana,* edition of Viñaza, p. 72), *quienes* as the plural of *quien* is first found in texts of the early 1500's.[24] The use of *quien* as a plural, both relatively and interrogatively, has lasted into the present, and is not scorned by purists like Juan Valera: *el tendero y su mujer, únicas personas a quien interesaba* (*Juanita la larga,* XXXVI); *¿quién son esas señoras?* (Benavente, *La gobernadora,* I, 10).

Of greater interest to the society of the *Siglo de oro* was the evolution of the pronouns of address. Toward 1600, by the development, through frequency of use, of *vuestra merced* and *vuesa merced,* there were in existence some twenty transformations, varying from the hardly altered *Vuesa erced* to the almost unrecognizable *Océ. Usted* has not been observed in any text before 1620 (Hurtado de Mendoza, *El examinador Miser Palomo*); its second appearance is in Tirso de Molina's *Don Gil de las calzas verdes,* printed in 1635. Of the five ways of addressing an individual (*tú; vos; vuesa merced,* or any of its variants; *él* or *ella,* especially favored by dramatists of the seventeenth century for dialogues between serving people; the third person verb form with no expressed subject), *vos* was originally the choice of polite address, but the touchy Spaniards, ever conscious of a point of honor (witness the discussions over the use of *don!*), soon demanded something more. Already Lazarillo de Tormes' master (*Tratado III*) was offended at the greeting of *Mantenga Dios a vuestra merced,* wanting the minimum of *Bésoos, señor, las manos,* in the courtly style of polished men. Later *vos* came to sound "like a slap on the cheek," being reserved for "people of minor estate" (Am-

[24] Cf. J. Gillet in *Publications of the Modern Language Association of America,* Menasha, Wisconsin, XLVII (1932), 974.

brosio de Salazar) and for "servants or vassals" (Juan de Luna). Cervantes tells of some one who, *con una no vista arrogancia, llamaba de vos a sus iguales y a los mismos que le conocían* (*Don Quixote*, I, 51), and the *pícaro* Estebanillo González, whose *Vida* was printed in 1646, expects no better than a *vos* from the lordly and condescending (*op. cit.*, chaps. iii and xi). In 1666 Jean Muret's guide was *furieusement choqué* at being addressed in the *vos* form, which was deemed a sign of French "brutality " In many parts of Spanish America *vos* has continued in popular usage to be the ordinary form of address to one person, to the extinction of *tú*, whose plural, as so commonly in Andalusia, is not *vosotros* (which has disappeared), but *ustedes*: *¡Ay, niña, qué pena me da de verte … Tu madre también trabaja mucho. ¿Y qué ganan ustedes con esto?* (Valera, *Juanita la larga*, XLI). In Chile the use of *tú* has a certain savor of contempt (according to Lenz), unsuitable to a democratic country. The schools have everywhere tended to regulate the use of the subject pronouns, but in Spain, too, confusion of *tú, vos, vosotros,* and *usted*(*es*) may be observed in the Andalusian writings of Fernán Caballero, and, excepting *vos,* of the Quinteros and Muñoz Seca (cf. p. 234). In the Leonese dialect *él* and *vos* are still used as forms of polite address to one person, though the latter has become very rare.

BIBLIOGRAPHY

(See the works listed on p. 173 below.)

Evolution of Constructions

With diminishing frequency throughout the period *ser* retains its function as auxiliary for intransitive verbs: *ser venido, son idos,* etc. (cf. p. 126). The *-ra* form continues to develop its use in conditional sentences as a simple tense rather than a perfect (p. 125), but as a past perfect indicative it is looked upon with disfavor by Valdés (*Diálogo,* p. 245), becomes rare in the course of his century, and practically nonexistent in the next (cf. p. 124). Not until the last quarter of the 1500's does the *-ra* form encroach noticeably upon the true subjunctive in dependent clauses (except *si* clauses), formerly the domain solely of the legitimately subjunctive in *-se,* which was still in the nineteenth century the favorite of Valera, Pardo Bazán, and Palacio Valdés. Somewhat conspicuous in the seventeenth century is the use of the indicative with impersonal phrases like *es posible* and *es necesario: ¿Es posible, señor Montesinos, que los encantados principales padecen necesidad?* (*Don Quixote,* II, 23), *¿Es posible—dije yo—que hay matemática en eso?* (Quevedo, *El buscón,* VIII). In *doquier que vamos, que quiera que digamos* (*El corbacho,* p. 276 of the edition of L. B. Simpson), and *será bien que vamos un poco adelante* (*Don Quixote,* I, 20), *vamos* is a now obsolete form of the subjunctive (< *vadamus*) still current in the Golden Age but now used only as a so-called first personal plural imperative. *Vais* < *vadatis* was also in frequent use.

In the matter of modal use *jurar, prometer,* etc., continue to function as verbs of willing: *yo vos juro que ... sus mujeres tomen acá venganza dellos* (Guevara, *Letra para don*

Enrique Enríquez); *que yo le prometo que no me falte a mí habilidad para gobernarle* (*Don Quixote*, I, 50).

The use of a redundant *no* with a governing expression of fear or prevention is more frequent at this time than nowadays: *Conjuraba los ratones, de miedo de que no le royesen algunos mendrugos* (Quevedo, *El buscón*, III); *qué grande ocasión pudo impedirme que la noche antes no la hubiera visitado* (Alemán, *Guzmán de Alfarache*, II, 1, 5); *le estorbaba que a su amo no ayudase* (*Don Quixote*, I, 52).

In obedience at least to the ancient rule that an unstressed pronoun form may not begin a sense group, personal pronoun objects continue to stand occasionally before infinitives: *para nos despertar* (Luis de León, *La perfecta casada*, VII); *en que os lo pagar* (*La Celestina*, IX of 1501 edition); *por no me ocurrir* (Hernán Cortes, *Carta dirigida al emperador Carlos V*, 1520); *por nunca se la cortar* (Quevedo, *El buscón*, III); *no sabía qué se decir* (Tirso de Molina, *Los tres maridos burlados*). In 1626 Correas finds it "intolerable" that people should say *¿Te vas?—Me voy* (*Arte grande de la lengua castellana*, edition of Viñaza, p. 94). Preposition is still used in the north of Spain, as in Asturias, León, Zamora, and Galicia (*Con me ceder el señorito las tierras*, Pardo Bazán, *El tesoro de Gastón*, VIII; *Pa non las recordar*, Espina, *La esfinge maragata*, XXIII). In accordance also with the basic principle Cervantes writes *no lo siendo* (*Don Quixote*, II, 1; II, 6), *no me siendo* (*ibid.*, I, 50), *no lo estando* (*El celoso extremeño*), and Quevedo uses *no lo haciendo, no lo siendo*, and *no lo viendo* in the *Premáticas y aranceles generales*.

Not yet fixed, or differing from modern practice, is the

usage of prepositions: *determinó de escrivirme* (Montemayor, *La Diana,* II); *comencé de imaginar* (*ibid.*); the *Lazarillo* usually has *comenzar a,* whereas the *Cid* uses both *de* and *a* with *compeçar* (705, 1114, etc.; 2585, 2735); *prometiendo de satisfacerles* (*Don Quixote,* I, 35); but *ir* never fails now to introduce its infinitive by *a,* in contrast to usage of the preceding period (*exien lo uer, vo meter la uuestra seña; Poema de Mio Cid,* 16 and 707, etc.).

Lastly, some words or uses of words of the preceding period either maintain their dominating position or withstand competition, like the demonstratives *aquese* and *aqueste, tener de* vs. *haber de, porque* against *para que* in clauses of purpose, *mas* against *pero,* which in the sixteenth century has not lost its ancient meaning of "nevertheless" (e.g., *Los caualleros ... fueron todos y allegados, mas pero nunqua se trabaiaron que pudiessen dar en somo de las tablas* (*Crónica general,* chap. 736); *non digas pero que está ferido* (*El corbacho,* III, 8).

Mas que is not yet vulgar in the meaning of "although," and is often used in the *comedia* with the value of *a que* = what do you wager that?[26] The semantic development of *no bien* scarcely, hardly, is clear from the logical order of *no hubo bien oído don Quixote nombrar libro de caballerías cuando dijo,* etc. (*Don Quixote,* I, 24); *No lo hube bien llevado a la boca, cuando ... me lo quitó el mozo* (Quevedo, *El buscón,* III). *Puesto que* regularly has the force of concession (although), but *aunque,* formerly meaning "even (that)" now emerges as the principal concessive conjunc-

[26] Cf. John Brooks, "Más que, mas que *and* mas ¡qué!," in *Hispania,* XVI (1933), 23–34, with references to the numerous previous studies.

tion. *Antes que* becomes *antes de que* through association with clauses of the type *es tiempo de que,* etc., but *después de que* is not yet current.

Qué often means *por qué:* *¿qué buscas otro que a ti mismo?* (Gracián, *El criticón,* I, 11).

A verbal formula which writers favored is illustrated by the *al volver que vuelva* = *al volver* of Cervantes' *La ilustre fregona* and the *Yendo que yuamos* = *Yendo* of *Lazarillo de Tormes,* I.

It appears, then, that except for the retention of a small number of phenomena from the period of Old Spanish, the syntax of Golden Age Spanish is characterized principally by its freedom, its failure to achieve a one hundred per cent observance of grammatical rules. Thus subjunctive and indicative may be used with a liberty approaching interchangeableness, apocopation of adjectives like *primero* is not always practiced, *a* is frequently missing before personal direct objects, the placing of negatives is not rigid. In short, it has not yet felt the disciplining it was to receive in the eighteenth and nineteenth centuries.

BIBLIOGRAPHY

BOURCIEZ. *Eléments*, §§ 377–394.

CUERVO, RUFINO J. *Apuntaciones críticas sobre el lenguaje bogotano*, séptima edición, Bogotá, 1939, §§ 332–334.

HANSSEN. *Gramática histórica*, §§ 453–738.

HAYNES, R. A. *Negation in "Don Quijote,"* Austin, Texas, 1933 (private edition).

HENRÍOUEZ, UREÑA, P. "Observaciones sobre el español en América, I," in *Revista de filología española*, VIII (1921), 357–390.

KENISTON, HAYWARD. *The Syntax of Castilian Prose, passim.*

LENZ. *La oración y sus partes*, pp. 241 ff.

MOREL-FATIO, A. *Ambrosio de Salazar, et l'étude de l'espagnol en France sous Louis XIII*, pp. 63 ff.

PFANDL, L. *Introducción al estudio del siglo de oro*, traducida directamente del alemán, con prólogo del P. Félix García, Barcelona, Casa Editorial Araluce, n.d., pp. 284 ff.

PLA CÁRCELES, J. "La evolución del tratamiento 'vuestra merced,' " in *Revista de filología española*, X (1923), 245 ff., 310 ff., 402 ff.

ROMERA-NAVARRO, M. "Apuntaciones sobre viejas fórmulas castellanas de saludo," in *Romanic Review*, XXI (1930), 218–223.

WEIGERT, L. *Untersuchungen zur spanischen Syntax auf Grund der Werke des Cervantes*, Berlin, Mayer und Müller, 1907.

THE POSITION OF SPANISH IN EUROPE

ENGLAND

However spineless a remark it may have been and however vexing to English historians, when James I in 1617 said to Count Gondomar, the Spanish ambassador, "Of course I know that, so far as greatness is concerned, the King of Spain is greater than all the rest of us Christian kings put together," he was giving expression to a feeling general in the principal European countries even into the declining age of Philip IV. The preëminence of all things Spanish is reflected by Ben Jonson in *The Alchemist* (IV, 4):

> Your Spanish gennet is the best horse; your Spanish
> Stoup [= stooping posture] is the best garb [= fashion];
>   your Spanish beard
> Is the best cut; your Spanish ruffs are the best
> Wear; your Spanish pavin the best dance;
> Your Spanish titillation in a glove
> The best perfume: and for your Spanish pike
> And Spanish blade . . .

In the *Diary,* Samuel Pepys, who several times mentions purchases of Spanish books, who used Spanish words a little more often than French in recording delicate subjects, and who of course ordered his black suit to follow the English Court into mourning at the death of Philip IV (*Diary,* Feb. 11, 1665), does not say who his Spanish teacher was, nor name his textbook, but there had long been a number of both instructors and manuals.[20]

A native of Seville, the Protestant Antonio del Corro

---

[20] Stephen Gaselee, "Samuel Pepys's Spanish Books," in *The Library,* fourth series, II (1922), 1–11.

(died 1591) came to England in 1568. At Oxford in 1586 appeared his *Reglas gramaticales para aprender la lengua española y francesa*. His *Spanish Grammer with certeine Rules teaching both the Spanish and French tongues* was printed in London in 1590 with the addition of a dictionary by John Thorius. A year later William Stepney's *Spanish Schoole Master,* based largely on Noël de Berlaimont's Flemish-Spanish *Vocabulare,*[27] appeared, and, also in that year, the *Bibliotheca Hispanica, Containing a Grammar, with a Dictionarie in Spanish, English, and Latine,* London, the dictionary being based on Nebrija and Las Casas (cf. p. 184), of Richard Percivale, Gent. (the surname is also spelled Perciuall). His *Grammar* and *Dictionary* were "augmented," by John Minsheu (or Minshew) and printed in 1599 with Minsheu's *Pleasant and Delightful Dialogues in Spanish and English, Profitable to the Learner and Not Unpleasant to Any Other Reader*. W. Somerset Maugham was so charmed by Minsheu's dialogues that he recently reprinted one (the fourth) in *Don Fernando* (vii). Maugham tells us that John Minsheu found subscribers at Cambridge, but not at Oxford, for his *Most Copious Spanish Dictionarie,* printed at London in 1617. This industrious "Professor of Languages" is responsible also for a *Ductor in Linguas ... The Guide into the Tongues* (London, 1617). There is also the *Key of the Spanish Tongue* by Lewis Owen (London, 1605). These and other grammatical writings are of the utmost value for the history of Spanish pronunciation, but only one more may be mentioned, the *Arte breve y compen-*

---

[27] See C. B. Bourland, "The Spanish School-master and the Polyglot Derivatives of Noël de Berlaimont's Vocabulare," in *Revue Hispanique*, LXXXI (1933), 283–318.

diosa, composed in France, but printed in London (1623), at the instance of some of his pupils and friends, by Juan de Luna, of whom more will shortly be recounted (p. 180). Dictionary-making is a contribution of James Howell, whose *Lexicon Tetraglotton* (one of the four languages is Spanish) came off the London press in 1659–1660. His *Grammar of the Spanish or Castilian Toung* appeared in 1662. With lessening frequency, lexicographical works (by Captain John Stevens, Pedro Pineda, Delpino, Baretti) or translations (by the same, by Roger L'Estrange, etc.) continued to concern English amateurs of letters in the remainder of the seventeenth century and in the century following, when Quevedo was a favorite author.

The principal English words, exclusive of proper names, which were taken from Spanish during the Elizabethan age (or before) are bilbo < *Bilbao,* booby < *bobo,* cannibal < a form of the name of natives of the *Caribbean* area, cargo, cordovan < *Córdoba,* cork, disembogue < *desembocar,* desperado, flotilla, jennet < *jineta,* guitar, indigo, jade < (*piedra de*) *ijada,* mosquito, negro, parade < *parada,* peccadillo, renegade, sherry < Old Spanish *Xerez,* whose final *s* sound caused it to be taken for a plural. Spanish, too, are bonanza, castanet, cigar, cinch, cockroach < *cucaracha,* comrade, farthingale, silo, spade (in cards), and stevedore. Later, from the Southwest of the United States or from areas adjacent have come alligator < *el lagarto,* bronco, canyon, "chaps" < *chaparejos,* chaparral, lariat < *la reata,* lasso < *lazo,* mustang < *mestengo + mostrenco,* quirt < *cuarta,* ranch, sombrero, stampede < *estampida,* tornado < *tronada* influenced by *tornar,* sambo < *zambo,* etc. A few Spanish words are only local: buckaroo, huarache, mesa, patio, etc. Certain modern slang terms are Spanish in origin: calaboose < *calabozo,* dago < *Diego,* hoosegow < *juzgado,* savvy < *sabe,* wop < *guapo.* Contributions from the Indies, which usually traveled across the Atlantic and then returned to the new English-speaking settlements, have been specified previously in these pages (alpaca, canoe, cocoa, chocolate, hurricane, potato, tobacco, tomato, vanilla). I conclude by making mention only of that "purgative tuberous root of a Mexican convolvulaceous plant, or the abstract, extract, or powder prepared from it," known to pharmacists as "jalap," after the city of *Jalapa,* near Vera Cruz.[28]

---

[28] There are in Chaucer many words of Arabic origin (alembic, almanac, azimuth, hazard, realgar, sugar, etc.), but it can not be said that they came necessarily from Spain (by way, of course, of France). Also Arabic are admiral, albatross < *alcatraz,* alcove < *alcoba,* apricot, arsenal, artichoke, candy, elixir, jessamine, julep, lackey, lilac, mattress, sherbet, syrup, talc, tare, tariff, etc. There is no point here in rehearsing the scientific terms, from astronomy, chemistry, and mathematics, of Arabic origin: nadir, zenith; alcohol, borax, camphor; algebra, cipher, zero; etc.

BIBLIOGRAPHY

BENTLEY, HAROLD E. *A Dictionary of Spanish Terms in English, with Special Reference to the American Southwest,* New York, Columbia University Press, 1932.

CARDIM, LUIS. *Gramaticas Anglo-Castelhanas e Castelhano-Anglicas* (1586–1828), Coimbra, Imprensa da Universidade, 1931.

GILLET, JOSEPH E. "Lexicographical Notes: 'Lagniappe,' 'Bozo,' 'Bull,'" in *American Speech,* XIV (1939), 93–97.

SERJEANTSON, MARY. *A History of Foreign Words in English,* Dutton, New York, 1935, chap. viii.

SKEAT, WALTER W. *Principles of Etymology,* second series, Vol. II, Oxford, Clarendon Press, 1891, chap xv. (The etymologies in this work must always be verified in more modern authorities.)

France.—The original plan of Philip II was to marry his son Don Carlos to Isabel of Valois, daughter of Henry II and Marie dei Medici; instead Isabel became his own wife (1560) upon the death of Mary Tudor. Another Isabel, of the House of Bourbon, was the first wife (1615) of Philip the Prudent's grandson, Philip IV. The first choice of Charles II was the niece of Louis XIV, Marie Louise of Orléans. But the traditional delivery on the banks of the Bidasoa was not invariably of a French princess. The marriage of Philip IV and Isabel de Borbón had been only one part of a double match agreed upon; the other was the betrothal in 1612 of Louis XIII and Ana de Austria, daughter of the third Philip. In 1660 the daughter of Philip IV, María Teresa, was married to Louis XIV. It was not only reasons of state, that is, the desire to isolate England, which turned French eyes toward Spain. The unwillingness of the Spanish hidalgos to labor had brought in great numbers of Frenchmen (70,000 by 1680, according to the estimate of the Marquis of Villars, French ambassador at that time), who principally performed the necessary tasks of agriculture and of the humbler occupations but whose ranks included merchants, from the wealthiest to the most lowly. Nor was it only treaties and profits that princess, peddler, reaper, and shepherd carried back across the Pyrenees.[29]

In *Persiles y Sigismunda* (1617) Cervantes says (III, 13): *En Francia ni varón ni mujer deja de aprender la lengua castellana,* and other writers attest, less positively, however, to the knowledge of Spanish in France. Granting a certain

[29] Cf. Quevedo's *La hora de todos y la fortuna con seso,* XXXI: *Los tres franceses y el español;* M. Herrero García, *Ideas de los españoles del siglo XVII,* Madrid, n.d., II, 14.

amount of exaggeration, Castilian was certainly far from unknown in the neighboring country, especially in the first two decades of the 1600's; interest reawakened with the second Spanish marriage in 1660. As might be expected, the first linguistic works emanated from the French-speaking portion of the Netherlands, where, as has already been noted (p. 137), treatises appeared shortly after the middle of the sixteenth century and where editions of Spanish literary works, like the early *Cancioneros de romances* of Antwerp (1550) and *Lazarillo de Tormes* (Antwerp, 1554), were frequently published. As early as 1520 a phrase book for the use of those born to French had been printed in Antwerp.[30] In France it was only in 1596 that the first of a series of grammars and vocabularies was printed, the *Parfaite méthode* of one Charpentier, later to be executed for political intriguing against the new government of Henry IV, who had no love for Spain. More numerous are the books of the Murcian-born Ambrosio de Salazar. I mention by title only his *Miroir général de la grammaire en dialogues,* Rouen, 1614, in which, recalling his *patria chica,* he declares that the speech of Andalusia pleases him rather more than any other, not even Castilian approaching it.[31] The shocking heresy probably passed unnoticed by the French. When Henry IV was merely a king of Navarre, César Oudin was already in his service, and he so continued, in a more lofty position, after his master's accession to the throne of France. He celebrated his appointment as secretary-interpreter in

---

[30] See Morel-Fatio, *Ambrosio de Salazar,* pp. 87–88; Schevill-Bonilla, *Persiles y Sigismunda,* tomo II, Madrid, 1914, p. 311.

[31] *La langue d'Andalousie me plaist bien plus qu'aucune autre, ny mesme la castillane ne s'approche beaucoup (apud* Morel-Fatio, pp. 17–18).

1597 by the publication of a *Grammaire et observations de la langue espagnolle* of which there were several later editions. The most important of his books, however, is the *Tesoro* or *Thrésor* of the French and Spanish languages, which was printed at Paris in 1607 and which had many later editions. Hierosme Victor's *Tesoro de las tres lenguas francesa, italiana y española,* Genève, 1606, is mainly the material of Oudin. The *Diálogos muy apazibles* (1608) which had already come out in England, in Minsheu's edition (1599) of Percivale's book, were improved in typography, and again printed in Paris (1619) by another Spanish teacher, the Aragonese Juan de Luna, whose *Arte breve y compendiosa* (cf. p. 176) was surely first cast in French. This strict grammarian boasted of having gathered 281 irregular verbs (twice as many as other teachers of Spanish!), and leveled a critical finger at Oudin, as the latter had at Salazar. Luna it was, too, who wrote a "Second Part" to the *Lazarillo de Tormes* (1620), after touching up the original in accordance with his own theories of correctness and clarity. From Paris one might whack at the Spanish clergy with a degree of impunity; Luna did so. Among the earlier bilingual lexicons is the *Diccionario muy copioso de las lenguas española y francesa,* Paris, 1604, of Jean Palet. Oudin's *Thrésor* is the basis of the later dictionaries of Francisco Sobrino, *Diccionario nuevo de las lenguas española y francesa* (1705, etc.), and of Francisco Cormon, *Sobrino aumentado* (1769, etc.).

The language, of literature at least, was invaded during the reign of Philip II by occasional Spanish or Hispanicized words like *alguazil, bizarre* (through Italy), *camarade* (originally Italian?), *fanfaron* > English fanfare, *laquais, quinola*, etc. In the seventeenth century borrowings were more numerous: military terms, *adjudant* < *ayudante, alfanje, escouade;* everyday terms, *cedille, chaconne, guitare, mantille, pavane* (originally Italian?), *alcôve, caramel, disparate, grandesse, hâbler* (cf. *parlar* in Spanish), *parangon* (through Italy?); words for products from America, *cacao, calebasse* < *calabaza, chocolat, cigare, créole, nègre, tabac, tomate, vainille, ouragan,* etc. Many words of Italian origin (e.g., *capitaine*) may have entered France through Spain.

BIBLIOGRAPHY

BRUNOT, F. *Histoire de la langue française,* Tome II, Paris, A. Colin, 1906, pp. 198 ff.

FARINELLI, ARTURO. *Ensayos y discursos de crítica literaria hispano-europea,* Parte segunda [Rome, 1925], pp. 306 ff.

MOREL-FATIO, A. *Ambrosio de Salazar, et l'étude de l'espagnol en France sous Louis XIII, passim.*

———. *Etudes sur l'Espagne,* première série, 2ᵉ édition, Paris, 1895, pp. 1 ff.

NYROP, KR. *Grammaire historique de la langue française,* Tome premier, 3ᵉ édition, Copenhague, 1914, §§ 45, 64–65.

PEETERS-FONTAINAS, J. *Bibliographie des impressions espagnoles des Pays-Bas,* Louvain, 1933.

RUPPERT, R. *Die spanischen Lehn- und Fremdwörten in der französichen Schriftsprache,* Munich, 1915.

SCHMIDT, W. F. *Die spanischen Elemente im franz. Wortschatz,* Halle a.d. Saale, Max Niemeyer, 1914 (*Beihefte zur Zeitschrift für romanische Philologie,* LIV).

Italy.—True that the fame of Don Raimundo's College of Toledan Translators, that group of intellectual workers which in the third and fourth decades of the twelfth century introduced Arabic and Jewish learning into Europe (p. 58), extended to Italy. True that the Catalans (and the term included at least those Spaniards who were subject to the king of Aragon) were widely disliked across the Medi-

terranean for their purposeful and gain-seeking industry,
and that Spaniards in general were popularly regarded as
savages, uncultured, knowing only how to bear arms. It was
not with complete complacency, then, that Italy saw itself
overrun by these crude foreigners in the sixteenth and following centuries. In the astonishment of injury Ariosto
pleadingly asks if Africa, which lies nearer at hand, has not
offended more than his own Italy (*Orlando furioso,* XVII,
76), and if Spain might not turn her attention there.

However, after Pavía there was no help for it. The elec-
tion as Pope Calixto III of Alexander Borgia (of the Borja
family of Játiva, near Valencia) in 1455, the succession to
that high honor of his nephew Roderick as Alexander VI
in 1492, and the ambitions of Alexander's son Caesar, who
died in 1507, filled the Imperial City with compatriots of
the Borgias; from the Lombardy plains to Rome and thence
to Naples, which was really a Spanish province, Italy was
quite thoroughly Hispanicized.[32] Juan de Valdés, need it be
recalled, wrote the *Diálogo de la lengua* at Naples.

The Neapolitan court of Alphonso the Magnanimous
(1416–1458), of Aragon, who was deemed personally a bit
uncouth, was primarily literary (the very portico of the Renaissance in Spain, thought Menéndez y Pelayo). Its chief
production was the *Cancionero* of one Stúñiga, author of
the first two poems in this compilation of poetical work of
the poets, chiefly Aragonese, who surrounded Alphonso.
Yet in matters of the spirit the tables were more often turned
and Spain received more than she gave. Antonio de Nebrija

---

[32] The Spanish impression of Italians and of Italy in the seventeenth century
may be judged from M. Herrero García, *Ideas de los españoles del siglo XVII,*
Madrid, n.d., II, 13.

traveled to Italy, to study (as he himself says) the Latin authors, for so many centuries banished from Spain. In 1369 the Archbishop of Toledo, Gil de Albornoz, had established a college for Spanish students (St. Clement's) at the University of Bologna, where Nebrija remained for seven years. Returning to his own soil he, more than any one else, planted there the new interest in philological studies (cf. p. 136). In Naples Lorenzo Valla, whose ideas were brought home by the great Antonio, in 1444 had become confessor to Ferdinand, Alphonso's son and successor (1458–1494), and many were the Italian savants who went to Spain as tutors to princes or as professors in the universities. Among these were Lucio Marineo Sículo, who, after twelve years of teaching at Salamanca, entered the court of the Catholic Kings, and Pietro Martire d'Anghiera (in Spanish, Pedro Mártir), who preferred, he said, to rank as a great man of letters abroad rather than as a bird among eagles or a dwarf among giants at home. At the court of Ferdinand and Isabel, the position of the admiring chronicler, Pedro Mártir, was high indeed, for there he introduced humanistic studies to the nobility, boasting that he had seen grandees sit at his feet.

One of the active middlemen between Spanish literature and the Italians was Alfonso de Ulloa. His *Introdutione ... a proferir la lingua castigliana* is dated 1553. A long-time resident of Spain was Mario Allesandri d'Urbino, whose contribution was a *Paragone della lingua toscana et castigliana* (Naples, 1560). And Spanish by race was Juan Miranda, whose *Osservationi della lingua castigliana* (Venice, 1566), which influenced most Spanish grammars subsequently printed abroad, was reprinted several times. In Sevilla Cristóbal de las Casas published (1570, 1576, 1583, 1587, 1591, 1618) one of the earliest "dictionaries," the *Vocabulario de las dos lenguas toscana y castellana*. The best known of these grammarians, whose books are a mine for the history of Spanish pronunciatión, was Lorenzo Franciosini, a Florentine. His *Vocabolario italiano e spagnuolo* (Rome, 1620) was printed again and again, and at least as late as 1796. His *Grammatica spagnuola e italiana* (Venice, 1624) likewise saw many, many reprints, and his *Diálogos apazibles* (Venice, 1626 and later) are in reality the now familiar ones of Minsheu, Oudin, and Luna.

Because of Spain's political domination it was natural that Spanish words should be taken up in the daily conversation of the populace, that they should be shouted from the comic stage or in any sort of literary burlesque, and that they should be cordially received into the best of society. *En Italia assí entre damas como entre cavalleros se tiene por gentileza y galanía saber hablar castellano,* says Juan de Valdés (*Diálogo,* p. 33).[33] Castiglione favors accepted foreign terms like *acertar, atildado, criado, primor* as being suitable to proper speech (*Il cortegiano,* I, 34). Castiglione, be it said in passing, spent four years in Spain as ambassador of the pope, and he died in Toledo in 1529. Of the *españolerías* in Italian there have endured *alfiere* < *alférez, azienda, bordo* (?), *borraccia, camarilla, complimento, creanza, disinvoltura, floscio, flotta, giannetta, guerriglia, giunta, lindo* (which Herrera, in his annotations to Garcilaso treasured as a superlatively good word, of which no language had the

---

[33] There are numerous other references in the works of Croce cited below.

equal), *mantiglia, mozzo, rancio. Mucciaccio* did not live, and primarily Neapolitan are *aiuda, attrassare, buglia, cagliare, camerista, caracó, cartiera, cenisa, criato, guappo, lazzaro, papello, perro, soltiero,* and a derivative (*kišare*) of *quejar. Passarica* < Old Spanish *páxaro* is used in the dialect of Calabria. *Chicchera* (< *jícara*) shows by its representation of the *jota* that it was of relatively late importing. It is not registered even in the 1735 or the 1796 edition of Franciosini. Yet, according to Zaccaria, the word appears once in 1606 in Francesco Carletti's account of his travels in the New World. And there are the contributions from America: *caccao, cioccolata, patata, tabacco, uragano, vainiglia,* etc.

BIBLIOGRAPHY

BERTONI, GIULIO. *Italia dialettale,* Milan, U. Hoepli, 1916, § 9.

CROCE, BENEDETTO. *España en la vida italiana durante el Renacimiento, versión española de José Sánchez Rojas,* Madrid, Editorial Mundo Latino, n.d.

FARINELLI, ARTURO. *Italia e Spagna,* Volume II, Torino, Fratelli Bocca, 1929, *passim.*

———. *Divagazioni erudite,* Torino, Fratelli Bocca, 1925, pp. 286 ff.

ZACCARIA, ENRICO. *L'elemento iberico nella lingua toscana,* Bologna, Cappelli, 1927.

ZINNO, D. "A Brief Outline of Foreign Influences on the Neapolitan Dialect," in *Romanic Review,* XXIII (1932), 237–242.

(The relatively slight contribution of the modern German language to Spanish may be contemplated in Arturo Farinelli, *Divagazioni erudite,* Torino, Fratelli Bocca, 1925, pp. 393 ff.; *Les allemands en Espagne et les espagnols en Allemagne, du XVe siècle jusqu' à nos jours,* in Morel-Fatio's *Etudes sur l'Espagne,* quatrième série, Paris, E. Champion, 1925, pp. 131–188; P. Scheid, *Studien zum spanischen Sprachgut im Deutschen,* Greifswald, 1934. For Portuguese compare Menéndez Pidal, *Manual,* § 4, 6; Antenor Nascentes, *Dicionario etimológico da língua portuguesa,* Rio de Janeiro, 1932, pp. xxviii–xxix.)

The Period of French Prestige (1700–1808)

THE PROGRESS OF SCHOLARSHIP A LA FRANCESA

TYPICAL of the eighteenth century was an interest in matters of science, in chemistry, medicine, the branches of the life sciences, geography, etc.[1] This new scientific interest extended to history, where documents now came to be regarded as the only permissible basis for historical knowledge, and to literature, where it brought about the publication, often for the first time, of many texts of linguistic interest. Thus the scholar Gregorio Mayáns y Siscar in the *Orígenes de la lengua* (1737) printed the hitherto unpublished *Diálogo de la lengua* of Valdés, the *Vocabulario de voces de germanía* (1609) of Juan Hidalgo, the *Refranes* attributed to the Marquis of Scantillana, and the works of Enrique de Villena (*Arte de trobar*), etc. He composed also a biography of Nicolás Antonio, the cleric of Seville, whose bibliographical indices (*Bibliotheca hispana vetus* [1696], listing writers to 1500; *Bibliotheca hispana nova* [1672], listing writers from 1500 to 1670) are still standard works of reference. The purpose of Gregorio Garcés' *Fundamento*

---

[1] Here, as illustrative of the erudite works which were composed then, should be recalled the *España sagrada* of Padre Enrique Flórez (died 1773). Useful to students of ecclesiastical history, of literature, and of geography, the 27 volumes published during the lifetime of the author have grown now to 52 plus an Index.

del vigor y elegancia de la lengua castellana (1791, 2 vols.)
is indicated by its title. In the four volumes of his *Colección
de poesías castellanas anteriores al siglo XV* (1779-1790)
Tomás Antonio Sánchez printed, and they had not been
printed before, the *Poema de Mio Cid,* the poems of Berceo,
the *Libro de Alixandre,* and the *Libro de buen amor* of
Juan Ruiz.[2]

In this age of philosophical systems, the polemic element
is predominant in two works which are of interest to students of language: *Los literatos en cuaresma* (1773) of
Tomás de Iriarte (1750-1791), of which more will be said
in a later chapter, and the *Exequias de la lengua castellana,*
which was not printed until the nineteenth century. The
Exequias satirically surveys the decline of literary taste in
Spanish literature, which the author, Juan Pablo Forner
(1756-1797), attributes to the neglect of the Spanish classics,
and to imitation of foreign (French) models: Forner fought
mighty battles with the pen against the tribe of Iriarte and
other literary opponents.

Concrete evidence of the interest in the systematic accu-
mulation of accepted knowledge appears in the foundation,
on French models, of learned societies like the Real Academia de la Historia (1738), and that of Medicina (1734),
the Academia de Nobles Artes de San Fernando (1752),
the establishment of botanical gardens (Jardín Botánico,
Madrid, 1775), and even of astronomical observatories (San

---

[2] For the rare references to some of these by earlier scholars see J. Fitzmaurice-
Kelly, *Historia de la literatura española,* cuarta edición, Madrid, Ruiz Hermanos,
1926, p. 23 (chap. iii, beginning). The *Alixandre* and *El libro del Archypreste
de Hita* are mentioned by Santillana in his *Proemio,* as is also the *Rimos* of Pero
López de Ayala, *el viejo.* The Archipreste de Hita is mentioned twice in the
Corbacho (I, 4 and III, 8).

Fernando, at Cádiz, which had replaced Seville as the gateway to the New World, 1753). Closer to our subject are the National Library, founded as such in 1711 by Philip V, and the Real Academia de la Lengua (1713). The first dictionary of the Academia de la Lengua, since called the *Diccionario de autoridades* (1726–1739, six volumes), was a credit to the young organization. Subsequent editions of the *Diccionario,* in one volume, appeared in 1780, 1783, 1791, 1803, 1817, 1822, 1832, 1837, 1843, 1852, 1869, 1884, 1899, 1914, 1925, and 1936. Only lately (1933) has the Academy again made such extensive use of quotation and statement of source, in its *Diccionario histórico de la lengua española,* tomo I-A; tomo II-B-C (*cevilla*), Madrid, 1936. Not until 1771 did the Academy print a *Gramática.* Whatever influence, if any, the grammar, in its successive editions (second edition, 1772; third, 1781; fourth, 1796; reprinted until *circa* 1821; latest edition 1931), may have had on the solution of minor problems of morphology and syntax has not been discussed, but the *Ortografía* promulgated several reforms, as will be noticed (p. 207). It will be well to record them. In the first edition (1741) the use of *ç* was rejected in accordance with the dicta of the *Discurso proemial* of the *Diccionario* (1726), and the bounds of *c* and *z* were more definitely fixed; in the third (1763) *ss* was abolished without exception; in the eighth (1815) *qua-, qüe-,* etc., were replaced by *cua-, cue-,* as had long before been suggested by Nebrija, *x* with the value of *jota* was proscribed, the functions of *y* and *i* delimited (cf. p. 77). In the fourth edition of the *Diccionario* (1803) the disappearance of *ch = c, ph = f,* and *th = t* was decreed. At the same time it recommended as

A LANGUAGE GALLICIZED

There were not many French words, and no constructions, introduced in the sixteenth and seventeenth centuries. However, there were a few French terms brought in at this time, especially from military administration, *banquete, bonete* (possibly much older), *convoy, furriel, marcha, marchar, sorprender, sorpresa, sumiller, tusón = toisón, ujier, víveres;* but the complaint becomes acute in the century following.

The disorder from which Spanish suffered in the period which is under discussion is diagnosed by Iriarte at the very outset of his *Retrato de golilla:*

> De frase extranjera el mal pegadizo
> hoy a nuestro idioma gravemente aqueja;
> pero habrá quien piense que no habla castizo
> si por lo anticuado lo usado no deja.[3]

The contagion was French, whichever way one turned. *El lenguaje se muda a cada paso como las costumbres,* sighs Gazel to Ben-Beley in Cadalso's *Cartas marruecas* (*Carta* XXXV) and he must go from door to door, he says, to beg assistance in deciphering this note of his sister:

Hoy no ha sido día en mi apartamento hasta medio día y medio. Tomé dos tazas de te; púseme un deshabillé y bonete de noche; hice un tour en mi jardín; leí cerca de ocho versos del segundo acto de la *Zaira.* Vino Mr. Labanda; empecé mi toeleta; no estuvo el abate. Mandé pagar mi modista. Pasé a la sala de compañía. Me sequé toda sola. Entró un poco de mundo; jugué una partida de mediator; tiré las cartas. Jugué al piquete. El maitre d'hotel avisó. Mi nuevo jefe de cocina es divino; él viene de arribar de París. La crapaudina, mi plato favorito, estaba deliciosa. Tomé cafe y licor. Otra partida de

---

[3] The significance of the fondness for archaisms manifested by a few authors will be dealt with later (p. 195, note).

quince; perdí mi todo. Fuí al espectáculo; la pieza que han dado
es execrable; la pequeña pieza que han anunciado para el lunes
que viene es muy galante; pero los actores son pitoyables; los vesti-
dos, horribles; las decoraciones, tristes. La Mayorita cantó una cava-
tina pasablemente bien. El actor que hace los criados es un poquito
extremado; sin eso sería pasable. El que hace los amorosos no juga-
ría mal; pero su figura no es preveniente. Es menester tomar pacien-
cia, porque es preciso matar el tiempo. Salí al tercer acto, y me volví
de allí a casa. Tomé de la limonada; entré en mi gabinete para
escribirte ésta, porque soy tu veritable amiga. Mi hermano no aban-
dona su humor de misántropo; él siente todavía furiosamente el siglo
pasado, y no le pondré jamás en estado de brillar; ahora quiere irse
a su provincia. Mi primo ha dejado a la joven persona que él entre-
tenía. Mi tío ha dado en la devoción; ha sido en vano que yo he
pretendido hacerle entender la razón. Adiós, mi querida amiga,
hasta otra posta; y ceso, porque me traen un dominó nuevo para
ensayar.

Admittedly, the colors are laid on too thickly, but Cadalso is not the sole objector to Gallicization: witness Iriarte
in *Los literatos en cuaresma:*

Verdad es, señores, verdad es, que sermones y comedias (o trage-
dias) he oído yo demasiado a la francesa; quiero decir escritos en
una lengua parecida a la castellana; pero que usa ciertas voces como
verbi gracia . . . Son tantas que no sé por cuál empezar. *Transportes,*
por extremos, ímpetus, raptos o enajenamientos; *conocimientos,* por
luces, especies o noticias; *detalle,* en vez de pormenor; y *relación
detallada,* por circunstanciada o individual; *rango,* por clase, esfera,
jerarquía, condición, calidad, estado; *el fondo del corazón,* por lo
íntimo del corazón; celo *por* el bien público, amor *por* la patria, en
vez de celo *del* bien público, amor *a* la patria; *golpe de ojo,* por
mirada; *golpe de teatro,* por lance de teatro; *entradas,* por los platos
que llamamos principios; *interesante,* por importante o digno de
atención; *producciones,* por obras, composiciones o partos del ingenio; *pequeño libro, pequeña ventana,* por librito, ventanita, y a
este tenor los demás diminutivos; *tiempo dulce,* por tiempo suave,
blando, benigno, apacible, sereno, templado, etc.; *resorte,* por muelle,
o por móvil y agente; *hacer ver,* por mostrar, demostrar, manifestar,

dar a conocer, hacer evidente o patente; *remarcable,* por notable, reparable, señalado, digno de advertencia; *montar diamantes,* por engastarlos; *montar un sombrero,* por armarle o apuntarle; *intriga,* ya por trama, o manejo secreto, ya por amorío, trato o comercio amoroso; *cubrir de horror,* por horrorizar; *hacer temblar,* por estremecer o conmover; *alarmar,* por asustar, sobrecoger, sobresaltar, inquietar; alcanzar victoria *sobre* el enemigo, por alcanzar victoria *del* enemigo; *importar granos,* por introducirlos; e *importación,* por introducción de ellos; *útiles,* por herramientas; *gaje,* por prenda; *contractar,* por contraer; *estar en boga,* por estar o andar valido, privar, tener aplauso, aceptacion, crédito o fama; y qué sé yo qué otros vocablos y frases ... que me degüellan.[4]

Iriarte does not object to foreign words like *coqueta* and *ambigú* which have no equivalent in Spanish, or no ready one, but he rightly laments that poverty of individual style should be attributed to one's native tongue. It was in the eighteenth century, too, by the way, that *mamá* and *papá,* stylishly French, supplanted to a degree *madre* and *padre* and completely replaced the native *mama* and *papa,* now reduced to provincial rustication. Compare Larra, *Casarse pronto y mal* (1832): *padre y madre eran cosa de brutos, y(que)a papá y mamá se les debía tratar de tú.*

The form taken in Spanish by French adoptions is conditioned in some respects by the date of their introduction. In words borrowed before the sixteenth century[5] *ge, gi* (French) $>$ *j, ge, gi* (Spanish): *geôle* $>$ *jaula, léger* $>$ *ligero, gelée* $>$ *jalea;* in such Spanish words *j, ge, gi* = [ŷ] or [ž]. Less exact equivalences of sound appear in *chef* $>$ *jefe, huissier* $>$ Old Spanish *usier, ugier* $>$ *ujier,* introduced

[4] Other French "vocables and phrases" may be found in Isla's *Fray Gerundio,* II, 4, 8, and in Ramón de la Cruz's *El hospital de moda. Jefe* and *equipaje* are listed in the *Autoridades; corsé* appears in a poem of Meléndez Valdés; *bagaje* is even as old at least as *Don Quixote* (II, 24).

[5] Cf. p. 160.

presumably after *j* had become unvoiced (cf. p. 160).[6] By the eighteenth century, since the sound represented by *j, ge, gi* of Spanish had changed, French *j, ge, gi* > *ch: jaquette* > *chaqueta* (also *chaquet, saqué*), *argent* > *archant* (in Ramón de la Cruz, *El cocinero,* 154), *jarretière* > *charretera, pigeon* > *pichón.* Occasionally *j* of French now > *s* of Spanish: *néglige* > *neglisé, Folies Bergère* > *Foli Bersé;* compare *saqué* above. And at times the spelling is retained, the pronunciation modified accordingly: *jaquette* > *jaquet, jarretière* > *jarretera, concierge* > *conserje.*

Relentlessly pursued by grammarians, not many phenomena of French syntax have become a part of Spanish. Yet *amor por* has lived, and the phrase *embajador cerca de un rey, una corte,* etc., is standard now, though even Larra pretended not to understand it (in his brief essay entitled *Filología*). Never welcome has been the use of *que* in sentences like *Fué Napoleón* que *lo dijo* (properly *quien* or *el que* lo dijo), *Era allí* que *solía hallarla* (properly *donde,* etc.). The *gerundio* continues to increase its domain, but *Leía un libro* tratando *del mismo asunto* is felt to be incorrect, grammarians allowing the gerund only when the notion of picturing is involved: *Napoleón* pasando *los Alpes, Un cartel representaba varios perros* lanzándose *sobre un oso* (cf. Bello-Cuervo, *Nota* 72; the *Gramática* of the Spanish Academy, 1931 edition, § 456, 2). Also non-Spanish is the abuse of the possessive adjectives. *Los franceses todo lo hacen suyo,* slyly says Toro y Gisbert, *se ponen su sombrero en su cabeza, se meten sus manos en sus bolsillos. Nosotros*

---

[6] I do not know how, at a slightly later date *Chénier* > *Genieiy* (Larra, *La fonda nueva*), since *ch* of French usually > *s* in Spanish in modern times: *cliché* > *clisé.*

somos menos tacaños y no creemos necesario reivindicar la propiedad de cosas que nadie piensa en disputarnos. Clearly it is not only the French who live in glass houses, but in any case the last sentence well expresses the spirit of Spanish in respect to the possessives. Into the vocabulary, however, many of the terms stigmatized in the eighteenth century have now penetrated, and have lost any taint of foreign origin. In spite of all the *castizo* synonyms presented by Cadalso (and limiting ourselves to his list), the Gallicisms he criticizes are largely a part of Spanish, as also will be in time many of those that have continued since his age to flood the language.[7]

---

[7] In the latter half of the eighteenth century there becomes apparent in the best prose of the period, that of Jovellanos, an artistic device which was to make its name later, namely, the use of regional vocabulary. In his letters particularly Jovellanos introduces a number of his native Asturian words (*escazabellar, peñerar, solmenar*), thus anticipating Fernán Caballero, Valera, Pereda, and the other great novelists of the nineteenth century.

BIBLIOGRAPHY

Castro, Américo. *Lengua, enseñanza y literatura,* pp. 102–139.

Kany, Charles E. *Life and Manners in Madrid, 1750–1800,* University of California Press, Berkeley, California, 1932, *passim.*

Menéndez Pidal. *Manual,* § 4, 5.

Rubio, Antonio. *La crítica del galicismo en España (1726–1832),* Ediciones de la Universidad Nacional de México, 1937.

⟆ 9 ⟆

The Modern Period (1808–   )

SOME INFLUENTIAL GRAMMATICAL CONTRIBUTIONS

El amor a las cosas patrias se aviva además mucho con la distancia, y llega casi a delirio la predilección al propio idioma, cuando se ve el hombre rodeado de los que no lo hablan. Thus in its preface does Vicente Salvá, after lamenting the lack of grammars of the Spanish language, account for the conception, during six years (1824–1830) of exile in England, of his *Gramática de la lengua castellana según ahora se habla,* first printed in Paris in 1830. Based on authors who flourished after 1750 (cf. p. xxvi of the preface), and bulwarked by its author's acquaintance with the older Spanish classics, this estimable work has attained at least fourteen editions. Its fame has, however, been overshadowed by the *Gramática de la lengua castellana destinada al uso de los americanos* (first edition, Santiago, 1847; nineteenth edition, 1918) of the Chilean scholar Andrés Bello. In its *Prólogo,* the author highly praises Salvá, and avows that he does not presume to instruct Castilians. His efforts, he says, are directed to the inhabitants of Spanish America, for the "preservation of the common tongue in its possible purity" will be a "bond of fraternity among the various nations of Spanish origin" (*ibid.,* p. vii). Don Andrés' work has become the standard reference grammar of Spanish, and deservedly, although some details of his theory, especially

in his conception of the verb, are not completely satisfying
The well-known *Textbook of Modern Spanish* (New York,
Henry Holt and Company [1894]), of Marathon Montrose
Ramsey draws freely on the text of Bello, as comparison will
readily show.[1] I have not observed the extent of Ramsey's
indebtedness (if any) to Salvá for illustrations, though the
latter is cited in the *Textbook* (pp. 439, 586).

A large share of the fame of Bello's *Gramática* should
accrue to the *Notas* prepared by Rufino José Cuervo (1844–
1911), and appended to it after 1874. This Colombian-born
scholar lived in Paris after 1882, where in hermitlike isola-
tion he produced most of the basic journal articles which
have been the object of frequent reference herein. His
Apuntaciones críticas sobre el lenguaje bogotano (1867;
seventh edition, 1939) is by no means limited to the language of Bogotá, but treats philological problems of general
interest to Spanish. Of the detailed *Diccionario de construc-
ción y régimen de la lengua castellana,* only two volumes
(922 and 1348 pages respectively of two columns in each,
carrying through the letter *d*) have been printed (1886–
1893), the author growing aware of the lack of authenticity
of the texts from which he extracted his illustrations. The
remainder of the manuscript is in Bogotá, and its early publication has been announced.[2]

Friedrich Hanssen (1857–1919), the Chilean professor of
German birth, produced several monographs on early Spanish metrics and the conjugations. His *Spanischer Gram-*

---

[1] In the following, the paragraph number first given is from Ramsey, that after
the sign of equality is from Bello: 305 Remark = 283, 436 = 1165, 452 = 1164,
700 = 805 and 812, 702 = 802 ff., 1223 = 1106, 1468 = 844, etc., etc.

[2] Cf. E. C. Hills, "The Cuervo Dictionary," in *Hispania,* XI (1928), 215.

matik auf historischer Grundlage (Halle, 1910) received attention from several reviewers. Revised in the light of their criticisms, enlarged, and this time written in Spanish, the *Gramática histórica de la lengua castellana,* as it was now entitled, appeared (at Halle) in 1913. This highly meritorious work, which, unlike Menéndez Pidal's *Manual,* treats syntax as well as the evolution of sounds and forms, has the advantage of representing the author's most mature judgment.[3]

Ramón Menéndez Pidal (1869–), who ranks as the leading scholar of Spain (and surely he stands among the first anywhere), was, and is, interested primarily not in language but in medieval Spanish literature. This interest is appropriate to a student of the literary critic and historian Marcelino Menéndez y Pelayo (1856–1912), who in his youth sat to the teachings of the Catalan Manuel Milá y Fontanals (1818–1884), a specialist in the origins of epic and ballad. Yet Don Ramón is also a major philologist, and it is only the philological aspect of his work that concerns us here. His enormous abilities, and his industry, appear together in the two volumes of commentary forming part of his edition and study of the *Poema de Mio Cid (Cantar de Mio Cid, texto, gramática y vocabulario,* 3 volumes, Madrid, 1908–1911). His *Manual de gramática histórica española* (1904; sixth edition, 1941), the collection of texts comprising the *Documentos lingüísticos de España* (1919), and the study of preliterary Spanish in the *Orígenes del español* (1926; second edition, [1929]) are vade mecums of the student of Spanish philology. Director, until his retirement, of the *Centro de estudios históricos* in Madrid, Menéndez Pidal has inspired to methods of scientific scholarship a large group of disciples who have carried their training out of Spain and whose investigations are embodied in the quarterly *Revista de filología* (1914–   ).[4] At the University of Buenos Aires, the Instituto de Filología continues the work. The several volumes of the *Biblioteca de dialectología hispanoamericana,* directed by Amado Alonso, contain material of the greatest utility.

[4] A bibliography of his writings to 1925 is in the *Homenaje a Menéndez Pidal,* Madrid, 1925, III, 655-674.

EVOLUTION OF SOUNDS, FORMS, AND CONSTRUCTIONS

Since the language crystallized in the sixteenth century, and had two centuries of hardening, changes in its structure in the course of the nineteenth and twentieth centuries are not sweeping.

A tendency to pronounce *e* with a marked openness ("abriendo mucho la *e* de *pueblos,* como era moda entonces"; Palacio Valdés, *Riverita,* XIX, end) is characteristic of the south of Spain primarily. Frequent everywhere is the inclination of final *o* to pass to the closer position of *ų* upon the complete suppression of intervocalic *d: soldado > soldau, hablado > hablau.* Whether these phenomena are ephemeral or will effect a permanent change in the sound system of Spanish must be determined by the passing of time. The disappearance of final *d* has been a matter of record for five centuries (cf. fifteenth-century forms like *hablá > hablad,* etc.), but that of the consonant in *-ado* is only now becoming so widespread as to be accepted as correct.

In the course of the nineteenth century, discussion of the proper use of *le* and *lo* as direct object forms reached the point where one's usage classified him as *leísta* or *loísta.* Discussion had been in progress since the sixteenth century. The use of *le,* referring to persons or things, belongs mainly to Castilla la vieja and León and was already dominant in Madrid in the seventeenth century; the preference for the older *lo* is southern and eastern. Confusion, however, is ancient, appearing even in the *Poema de Mio Cid: nol coge nadi en casa* (59), *que Dios le curie de mal* (364), *moros le Reciben* (712), *en la Red le metio* (2301); *al cuello lo tomo* (2300), *bien lo acorren* (745), *violo Myo Cid* (748), *por acogello acabo de tres semanas* (883). The later distinction of *le* for persons and *lo* for things is a compromise approximating to written use, formerly favored by the Academy, and first proposed as a definite rule by Salvá, in his grammar. The use of *le* as direct object perhaps arose from the analogy of *me, te,* and even *se,* but the competition of dative and accusative may also be involved (see p. 118).

The use of *la* as an indirect object form for the feminine gender has not had comparable official acceptance, in spite of its frequency, but influential early sponsors (*laístas*) seem to be responsible for its introduction into sentences of the type *se la ve, se las trata.* That is to say, *la* and *las* in this impersonal reflexive substitute for the passive voice were originally dative forms, however they may be classified today.

The use of the convenient participial adjective in *-ante,* observable in many contemporary writers, is to an extent limited to literary Spanish: *bailante, emocionante, espumante, exultante, rezumante, temblante,* etc. Substantives termininating in *ante* and *ente* began generally in the eighteenth century to have a feminine form in *a: confidente, confidenta;* compare the more modern *debutanta* (Arniches, *El chico de las Peñuelas,* II, 4), but the process is not yet complete, and *estudianta* meets with resistance, though *comedianta* and *giganta* are listed without any comment in the dictionaries. *Parienta* is already in the *Corbacho,* II, 4, and *sirvienta* is in Timoneda's *Paso de la razón y la fama y el tiempo.*

Syntactically, the most impressive phenomenon is the return from the garret of disuse of the *-ra* indicative form in the Romantic Age (e.g., *¿No fueras antes conmigo que con Dios perjura?*, García Gutiérrez, *El trovador*, III, 5; *Estas voces favoritas han solido siempre desaparecer con las circunstancias que las produjeran,* Larra, *En este país; las mismas armas que ésta les confiara para su defensa,* Martínez de la Rosa, *La conjuración de Venecia,* V, 1). Conventionally held to be one of the archaisms which the Romantics plundered from the Middle Ages, the *-ra* indicative crops up in the eighteenth-century poetry of Meléndez Valdés, who employed it indiscriminately as a past tense (cf. Bello, *Gramática,* § 720, note), and in the work of the Asturian-born Jovellanos. To employ the *-ra* form as an indicative in independent clauses is characteristic of modern writers from northern Spain (Galicia, Asturias): *El caballero legitimista los convocara secretamente* (Valle-Inclán, *Los cruzados de la Causa,* XXXI). Compare p. 124.

Just as the form in *-ra* passed from the result clause of conditional sentences to the if clause (p. 125), so, toward the beginning of the nineteenth century, the form·in *-se* began to be used in the result clause. This usage, the extent of which was "incredible" to Cuervo (*Notas a la Gramática ... de Bello,* no. 99), is now so frequent even in careful writers as to cause no comment: *soy tan débil y tan tonta, que no hubiese atinado a decírselo* (Valera, *El comendador Mendoza,* X); *hubiese querido prolongar aquella visita* (Pardo Bazán, *El tesoro de Gastón,* IX); *aun cuando no hubiese aceptado el sacrificio, se hubiese afligido mucho* (Valera, *Juanita la larga,* XXVI).

Another development in the realm of construction is the gradual usurpation by *estar* of territory once belonging to *ser*: *Buen par de tarabillas estáis tu primo y tú* (Alvarez Quintero, *El genio alegre*, II) ; *La escena en el foro estuvo muy bien representada* (Baroja, *La ciudad de la niebla*, II, 13). On the other hand, such an archaism as *ser lleno* is used (unconsciously ?) by Benavente and (consciously ?) by Valle-Inclán in this twentieth century (e.g., *Aquella carta ... era llena de afán, Sonata de otoño*, beginning).[5]

Modern, too, appears to be the encroachment of *el* (*la*, etc.) *que* upon the simple relative pronouns *que* and *quien* (in the sense of "he who"), especially after *a, con, de,* and *en: Las condujo a este sitio, en el que se perdió a sus pies* (Fernán Caballero, *La familia de Alvareda*, I, 6) ; *Existen numerosas cuestiones políticas en las que España está profundamente interesada* (Ganivet, *Idearium español*, B); *limpiaban aquel mostrador en el que gastaba sus codos todo el pueblo* (Blasco Ibáñez, *Cañas y barro*, III) ; *Esa es una enfermedad de la que debía curarse* (Baroja, *El mundo es ansí*, III, 14).

In some writers of the contemporary period (Blasco Ibáñez, Azorín, Valle-Inclán) much is gained by diverting the adjective from its normal place or function. The descriptions of the Valencian novelist are enhanced by the unusual position of the adjectives of color: *la pequeña iglesia se le aparecía como un palacio encantado, con su luz crepuscular filtrándose por las* verdes *ventanas, sus paredes enjalbegadas de cal y el pavimento de* rojos *ladrillos respirando la humedad del suelo pantanoso* (*Cañas y barro,* III). In *La barraca,*

---

[5] Cf. also *Ellos serán muy contentos de conocer a usted* (Benavente, *Las cigarras hormigas*, III, 2).

IX, there is intentional adornment in the adjectives of *Las brillantes hoces iban tonsurando los campos, echando abajo las rubias cabelleras de trigo, las gruesas espigas que apoplécticas de vida buscaban el suelo doblando las débiles cañas.* The nicety of the play of adjectives illustrated in the lines following, although in accordance with the rules of Bello (*Gramática,* §§ 47–48) and Salvá (*Gramática,* ed. cit., pp. 117 ff.), goes far beyond these rules in its conscious artistry and so reveals a later origin: *en una alquería verde, bajo el añoso emparrado, agitábanse como amalgama de colores faldas floreadas, pañuelos vistosos, y sonaban las guitarras con dormilona cadencia, arrullando al cornetín que se desgañitaba, lanzando a todos los extremos de la vega dormida bajo el sol los morunos sones de la jota valenciana* (*La barraca,* IX). The quest of cadenced harmony has led Ramón del Valle-Inclán, and also Azorín, into the mannerism of a trio of adjectives, especially to finish a sentence: *La capilla era húmeda, tenebrosa, resonante* (*El miedo*); *Era nudoso, seco y fuerte, como el tronco de una vid patriarcal* (*Un cabecilla*); *Rodó la vieja con ruido mortecino, y a su lado la alcuza iba saltando hueca, metálica y clueca* (*Gerifaltes de antaño,* XIV, end). That an adjective perform the function of an adverb of manner is ordinarily permissible: *el fuelle sopla y resopla ronco* (*Los pueblos, Una elegía*), but the process is unwisely extended by Azorín in his avoidance of the suffix *-mente: sobre los anchos barrotes destacan áureos en la penumbra* (*La voluntad,* I, 25), *las manchas pálidas de los ventanos se disuelven lechosas* (*ibid.,* I, 3).

THE ORTHOGRAPHIC ACCENT

The discussion of Nebrija (*Gramática,* libro II, cap. ii) deals
with the terms *agudo, grave,* and *circunflexo* as matters of
pitch. In his illustrations, however, only the acute accent
mark is used. In his text the infrequent orthographic accent
serves mainly to distinguish between words of like spelling
but different meaning according to the stress: *hállo* vs. *halló.*
Recognizing the three symbols, Herrera (cf. p. 144) used
the circumflex sign for the interjection *o,* the grave for *e, a*
(< *haber*) and the acute for the preposition *a* and most
esdrújulos. Up to the middle of the eighteenth century the
use of a written accent mark is inconsistent (when used at
all) and within the covers of one volume the three traditional signs may be employed interchangeably: *habló, ha-
blò, habló.* But the acute accent mark is the only one to
receive official recognition, though the circumflex is proposed to indicate that a preceding *ch* = *k* (e.g., *chîroman-
cía*), *x* = *cs* (e.g., *exîmio*), as early as the third impression
(1763) of the *Ortografía* of the Academy. Other rules, still
in force, such as the distinction of the function of monosyllables (*dé* vs. *de, sí* vs. *si,* etc.), date from the early orthographies of the Academy. As late as 1876 the Academy did
not use the graphic accent in the imperfect indicative of the
-er and *-ir* conjugations (except in the first person plural),
nor in the conditional, nor did it use the accent to destroy
the diphthong in infinitives like *oír, reír,* or in their participles (*oído, reído*). The superlative ending *ísimo* is ex-
pressly excused at this time (*no hay necesidad de poner
acentos, pues esta terminación indica por sí sola que son*

esdrújulos). Until 1885 (when the Academy issued new rulings) words ending in *n* and *s* were treated like others whose final letter was a consonant. That is to say, the stress of all such words was on the final syllable unless the contrary was indicated by the graphic accent: *miéntras, órden, ambicion*. A further step was taken in 1911 when it was decreed that the preposition *a* and the conjunctions *e, o,* and *u* and some monosyllabic verb forms (*di, vi, ve*) might dispense with the accent mark (except that *o* should retain it when standing between Arabic figures, lest it be taken for zero).

Vocabulary

In the first half of the century a curious amount of attention was given to the subject of Spanish synonyms. Salvá (in the preface to his *Gramática*, p. xx) declares that he has been preparing a *Diccionario de sinónimos castellanos* "for years." Bretón de los Herreros prepared 526 articles on the subject. Mariano de Larra left incomplete a synonym dictionary (this fragment was not printed until 1886).

Maguerista is the epithet which the *erudito* Gómez Hermosilla applies to Meléndez Valdés for the poet's use of archaic words like *maguer = aunque, empero,* and *ora = ahora.* True that the Romantic attitude encouraged the use of old and picturesque language, and that Hartzenbusch composed *cuentos* in imitation medieval Spanish. But the *pronunciamiento* of the literary revolutionists, the *Prólogo* of Antonio Alcalá Galiano (already forty-five and cautious) for the *Moro expósito* (1834) of the Duque de Rivas, hardly needed to mention the question of language (it just does), because of the similarity of the new drama to that of the *Siglo de oro* in which colloquial speech freely entered. The use of obsolete speech in the Romantic theater is superficial, like the introduction of *vos, usía,* etc., and an occasional archaism. On the other hand, López Soler laments, in the *Prólogo* to *Los bandos de Castilla,* Valencia, 1830, *que aun no se ha fijado en nuestro idioma el modo de expresar ciertas ideas que gozan en el día de singular aplauso.*

The case against the *galicismo* was now recognized to the extent of formal condemnation, in the *Diccionario de galicismos* (Madrid, 1855) of the Venezuelan poet Rafael

María Baralt. Baralt was often, however, too severe, as Hartzenbusch observed in the prologue, since he criticized phrases of long standing in Spanish. Still, from the *sortú* (*surtout*)[6] of Larra (*Empeños y desempeños*) or the same author's *echarpe* (*La diligencia*) and the *canezú* (= *cane-zou*) of Bretón (*Marcela,* I, 3), French words continued and continue to become a part of Spanish; this applies especially to terms of fashion and of cooking; dress: *blusa batista,* batiste blouse, *pandantif(e)*, pendant, *riviere,* necklace; cookery: *bechamela* or *besamel,* cream sauce, *chateaubriand,* steak, *consomé, filete, flan, merengue, potaje* (which is already in the *Diálogo de la lengua,* ed. cit., p. 173), *puré,* etc. Even in its latest edition (1931) the *Grammar* of the Academy still bravely lists (§ 477, 3, *c*) some of these "poisonous" vocables: *acaparar, accidentado, afeccionado, aliaje, aprovisionar, avalancha, banalidad, bisutería, confeccionar, debutar, etiqueta, finanzas, pretencioso, rango, remarcable, revancha,* and "others innumerable." Later arrivals are *bidé, bulevar, buró, carnet, chantaje* (the native designation of blackmail is *la forzosa*), *cuplé, entrenar, matinée, menú, reclamo, soirée, varieté* (as in *teatro de varietés*).

In the splendorous days of the 1600's Spain had provided English with a few words like sherry, jade < *ijada* (the stone being believed to relieve pain in the side), jennet < *jineta* (cf. p. 176). English more slowly reciprocated with words such as *dandi* or *dandí; monís* or *monises,* money, supposedly introduced by soldiers of the Peninsular Wars; *spleen* or *esplín,* boredom, gloomy temper (the *Pequeño Larousse* quaintly illustrates this last: *El esplín es enferme-*

---

[6] *Surtú* is already in *Fray Gerundio* (II, 4, 8).

dad muy común entre los ingleses). We may leave aside contributions like *rosbif*, roastbeef; *bar; bisté* or *biftec*, beefsteak; *cheque*, check; *coctel*, cocktail; *comité*, committee; *detective; hall* (meaning "large room" or "hotel lobby"); *interviú*, interview; *líder*, leader; *mitin*, meeting; *ponche*, punch; *repórter; revólver; trole*, trolley. The greater part of the language of sport is, not unnaturally, of English origin: *besbol, futbol, tenis, gol, box* or *boxeo, sport, batir el record*, etc., etc.; a glance at any sporting sheet will show how lacking are Spanish words for athletic entertainment.

Such respectable English institutions as *club, whiskey, smoking* (jacket) in the sense of "tuxedo," *sandwich, miss* with the meaning of señorita, *cakewalk* (and the more modern dances), and *water closet* have now received citizenship in Spain, in spite of recurring protests.

The profound changes in society effected by the advances of the nineteenth century were reflected by Spanish in political or financial newcomers like *cotización, cupón, emancipación, fraternizar, fusión, oposición, opresión, polémica, prima* = premium. The philosophies of the preceding age yielded a number of abstract words like *capacidad, doctrinario, notabilidad, refractario*. Against *filantropía, fraternidad, ilustración*, and other favorites of the "freethinkers" Fernán Caballero and others repeatedly railed. (These usually came to Spain via France; compare *La nueva nomenclatura galo-hispana* of the poet Eugenio de Tapia.) The rapid political changes within the country which saw 118 prime ministers between 1833 and 1923, produced now forgotten words like *servil* in the sense of "absolutist"; *cristino*, adhering to the party of María Cristina, opposed by the carlistas; *doceañista,* favoring the constitution of 1812; *maurista,* partisan to the policies of the minister Maura; *polaco,* equivalent to "tyrant," applied by the opposing side to the party of the Conde de San Luis, Luis José Sartorius.

Possibly the establishment of stagecoach service (Madrid to Irún, 1821; Madrid to Seville, 1824; etc.) increased to some degree the use of carriages of different types; called *birlocho, bombé, calesa, calesín, cabriolé, coche de colleras, landó, milord, tilburi, volante,* etc.

The list of dances (and songs), already long in the Golden Age,[7] continued in the 1700's with the *vito, villano, zapateado, fandango* (which fascinated Casanova; the word is probably of African [?] Negro origin), *bolero, cachucha, guaracha, zorongo, mollares, tirana, ole,* and the more aristocratic *gavota, mazurca, minué, vals.* These were in due time followed by the *polka, chotis, maxixe,* etc., etc. Somewhat less changeable are the *bailes regionales: prima asturiana, muñeira gallega, zortzico vasco, jota aragonesa* and *valenciana, seguidillas manchegas, sevillanas, tango andaluz* (*tango* is probably of African [?] Negro origin).

With the adoption of the metrical system in 1859, *gramo, litro, metro,* and their fractions or multiples, the former with Latin prefixes (e.g., *centímetro, decímetro, milímetro*), the latter with Greek (e.g., *decagramo, kilogramo, miriagramo*), took precedence over, but did not displace, the native *arroba, fanega, libra,* and *quintal*—all but *libra* of Arabic provenance. The installation in 1868 of the decimal system of coinage can not be said to have propagated many

---

[7] Compare F. Rodríguez Marín, *El Loaysa de* El celoso extremeño, pp. 257–273; Mérimée-Morley, *History of Spanish Literature,* p. 350 and note; also Estébanez Calderón, *Un baile en Triana.*

new terms. The engraving of the lion was crudely enough done to warrant the copper coins of five and ten *céntimos* issued in 1870 being since called *perros-as chicos-as,* and *perros-as grandes* (or *gordos-as*) respectively, but *duro, peseta,* and *real* were carried on from the system of coinage as revised by Charles III *circa* 1770. His coinage included the copper *maravedí, ochavo,* and *cuarto,* the silver *real* and *peseta,* the *duro* in silver and gold, and, in gold only, the *doblón* and *onza.*[8]

The establishment of railroads (Barcelona to Mataró, 1848; Madrid to Aranjuez, 1851; Madrid to the French border, 1860) yielded new words: *balasto, camino de hierro, exprés, rail, ténder, túnel, vagón,* as did other material progress, the applications of steam and electricity, the growth of industry and trade, of the day. Thus did language adjust itself to the needs of society.

Among the members of the Generation of '98, the literary style, especially of the novelist Valle-Inclán and of the essayist Azorín, pseudonym of José Martínez Ruiz, is a bit *précieux.* It is marked by the revival of obsolete words, unusual use (incorrect use, say the grammarians) of those current, and the invention of new terms.

The misuse of language hardly knows chronological limits and the "mistakes" of modern writers need no extended discussion here. Their occurrence in high quarters is no

---

[8] The names and values of these and of more ancient coins are treated in Liciniano Sáez, *Demostración histórica del verdadero valor de todas las monedas,* etc., Madrid, 1796 and 1805; also in N. Sentenach, *El maravedí. Su grandeza y decadencia,* in *Revista de archivos, bibliotecas y museos,* XII (1905), 195–220; *idem, Monedas de plata y vellón castellanas, ibid.,* XIV (1906), 329–345; M. de Rivero, "Escrutinio de monedas matritenses," in *Revista de biblioteca, archivo, museo,* V (1928), 28–34, and 381–402.

novelty, for even Bretón de los Herreros, who in his time was a member of the Royal Spanish Academy (*de la lengua!*), director of government printing, and librarian of the national library, thought *sendos* meant "large" (see P. Juan Mir, *Prontuario,* II, 757; the passage is in *Los españoles pintados por sí mismos,* p. 34). *Algido,* cold, has long been misused as "serious," "violent," "hot," "critical" (cf. Pereda, *El buey suelto,* III). Another frequent *barbarismo* is the employment of *lívido* in the meaning of "pale." Within the twentieth century all Madrid laughs at a slip which, wanting to say "waxlike hands" (*manos de cera*), says *manos cerúleas*—*cerúleo* means "azure blue."[9]

The number of *arcaísmos* briefly revivified by contemporary writers is neither large nor consequential: *anacalo* for *criado de la hornera, desdeño* for *desdén, disanto* for *día de fiesta, desplacer* for *disgustar, descontentar, los que han hambre y sed de felicidad* for *los que tienen,* etc. The question of new coinages (*neologismos*) requires lengthier discussion, however.

Already in the golden days of the 1600's, the invention of words was something of a specialty among certain authors, for example Cervantes, who made comic effect of *argamasillesco, pollinesco, tobosesco,* etc. Tirso de Molina also was facile in the art, coining *bigotismo, casildar, gilada, duquenceo-a, jabonatriz, fregatrizar, melindrizar, pastelizar, olear = decir hola,* etc.; to the criticisms leveled at him, he gave a ready retort in the *Prólogo* to the *Parte quinta* (1636) of his plays. The use of terminations counts for a good share of these modern formations: *agonioso, alcurnioso, patoso,*

---

[9] Cf. J. Casares, *Crítica efímera,* vol. 2, pp. 159 ff.

sanguinoso, sombrajoso < French *ombrageux* + *sombra,*
telarañoso; canallesco, cursilesco, notariesco, porcelanesco,
simiesco; numerous nouns in *-eo, campanilleo, cascabeleo,*
mariposeo, tamborileo, in *-ismo, didactismo, localismo, pi-*
carismo, snobismo; nouns or adjectives in *-ista, alcoholista,*
intelectualista, tenista; and obvious modern formations,
often on foreign models, like *autoretrato, emocional, en-*
soñador, guardés < *guardesa, ideofobia, mayestático* <
German *majestätisch* following the vogué of Krausism, *oca-*
cidad = *oquedad, reposorio* = *pausa* or *descanso, sugestivo,*
vagabundez, etc., etc. Latinisms like *anfractuosidad, coer-*
ción, conqueridor, fulgir, nítido, urbe, vespertillo represent
a minor aspect of this present-day genesis (cf. Casares, *Crí-*
tica profana).

More worthy of praise is the anxiety of some contemporary authors (Azorín, Ricardo León) to diffuse words of
Arabic source (*alcacel* = *cebada verde, alcor* = *colina, alha-*
quín = *tejedor* and also *médico, alizar* = *friso de azulejos,*
almazara = *molino de aceite, almocrebe* = *arriero de mulos,*
almona = *jabonería, anacalo* = *criado de la hornera, azaga-*
dor = *vereda* or *paso del ganado, azarbe* = *canal para el*
riego) and to preserve picturesque names of trades (*arca-*
dor=wool beater, *chicarrero*=*el que hace o vende zapatillas,*
pegujalero = *labrador* or *ganadero pobre, peltrero* = pew-
terer, *peraile* = *cardador de paños,* etc.). Only as a concession to science may the excessive and improper use of
technical names like *cetonio, evónimo, glomerido, metiló-*
filo, etc., be excused.

Slang

By dictionary definition slang was originally the cant of thieves, gypsies, beggars, etc. This definition closely fits the *germanía* so frequently met with in the writings of Cervantes (e.g., in *Rinconete y Cortadillo*), Quevedo (e.g., in the *Buscón*, the *romances de jácaras*), and other fanciers of the picaresque. Juan Hidalgo made his *Vocabulario* of it in 1609 (cf. p. 139). Emanating from the jargon of low life, then, are *banco*, jail; *calandria*, public crier; *cantar*, to confess (under torture); *cica*, purse; *finibusterre*, gallows; *gura*, justice; *gurapas*, galleys; *gurullada*, patrol of constables and bailiffs; *guzpátaro*, hole; *respe(c)to*, lover, or sword; *trena*, jail; *viuda*, gallows; and others, now mostly obsolete. Not necessarily of such provenance are classic expressions like *busilis*, point, difficulty; *gabacho*, originally applied to Frenchman from the Pyrenean slopes (Fr. *gave* = torrential stream), then extended to any native of France; *gato*, sneak thief; *la sin hueso*, tongue; *oíslo*, wife; *pichelingue*, pirate (e.g., Tirso de Molina, *Marta la piadosa*, II, 2); *rendibúy*, rendezvous (*La vida de Estebanillo González*, VII). The spirit of the eighteenth century was not at all sympathetic to the introduction of slang terms, but since then numerous words, most of them still of the *caló* (talk of gypsies) have become familiar: *achares*, jealousy; *beata*, peseta, *chalarse*, go, or be madly in love; *canguelo*, fear; *chaval* or *chavó*, youth; *(de)mistó, de órdago*, first-rate; *diquelar*, look at, see; *gachí*, woman; *gachó*, man; *garlochí*, heart; *gilí (jilí)*, simple, silly; *paripé*, deception; *por mor de*, because of; *tasca*, saloon. Living in a better neighborhood are *achan-*

tarse, "stick it out"; *arrimar candela,* beat; *cúrsil* as a variant of *cursi; chinche,* pest; *chuleta,* slap; *chuleta de la huerta,* potato; *darla con queso,* deceive, "take in"; *guindilla,* policeman; *impepinable,* superlatively good *or* bad; *inglés,* creditor; *lacha,* sense of shame; *la mar* (*de*), a great deal (of); *media naranja,* wife; *maremagno,* confusion; *pajolero,* good-for-nothing; *panoli,* simple; *patatús,* fainting fit; *pinré,* foot; *primo* and *blanco,* simple, innocent; (*s*)*infundio,* trick, cheat; *si se quiere,* rather; *tobillera,* "flapper"; *tomar el pelo,* "kid"; *tupé,* "nerve," "cheek," and a countless host of expressions, some consecrated by usage, others being added daily, and all now, purism being in disfavor, deserving only the stigma of "popular," "colloquial," "familiar." As in most languages, a few concepts are particularly liable to slang expression. Thus for drunkenness (*borrachera*) there are *canóniga, cogorza, curda, chispa, filoxera, humera* (with aspirate *h*), *lobo, merluza, mona, mordaga, papalina, pea, pítima, tablón, tajada, toquilla, turca, zorra.* To be "crazy" is *estar chiflado, estar mochales, estar viruta* or *guillarse.* To depart (more or less hastily) runs from the classical *tomar las·de Villadiego* and *poner pies en polvorosa* through the less colorful *afufar*(*se*), *hacer la del humo, largarse* and *salir por pies* to *ahuecar el ala, guillarse, pirárselas, coger el dos.* Money is *parné, guita,* or *jayeres.* Like all fashions, many of these words or phrases are transient. The dude has been a *lindo* (*don Diego*) in the 1600's, a *petimetre* (Fr. *petit-maître*), *pisaverde, currutaco, tónico, señorito de ciento en boca, pirraca, paquete* (the last three according to Navarrete, *El elegante,* in *Los españoles pintados por sí mismos,* p. 157), in the later 1700's and the earlier

1800's, a *lechuguino* in the 1830's and 1840's, a *gomoso, pollo líqui(do)* in more modern times, and *elegante* has long been used to describe his sort.

Pápiro = bank note, which derives from *papiro* = papyrus, recalls that a tendency among not fully literate people is the accentuation of the antepenultimate syllable: *intérvalo, kilógramo, méndigo, périto, telégrama, váyamos,* etc. Transference of the stress is probably to be explained by association with words of frequent use like *código, estómago, Málaga, ánimo, próximo, último, pálido, rápido,* etc., the *esdrújulo* termination responding to the desire to be "correct."[10]

---

[10] See A. Espinosa, *Estudios sobre el español de Nuevo Méjico,* pp. 345 ff.

BIBLIOGRAPHY

BEINHAUER, WERNER. *Spanischer Sprachhumor,* Bonn-Köln, L. Rohrscheid, 1932.

BESSES, LUIS. *Diccionario de argot español,* Barcelona, n.d. (*Manuales Gallach,* no. 65).

BOURCIEZ. *Eléments,* § 343*b.*

MAYO, F. DE S. *El gitanismo ... ,* Madrid, V. Suárez, 1870 (the author uses the pseudonym of Francisco Quindalé).

PASTOR Y MOLINA, R. "Vocabulario de madrileñismos," in *Revue Hispanique,* XVIII (1908), 51 ff.

REBOLLEDO, TINEO. *Gitanos y castellanos; diccionario gitano-español y español-gitano,* Barcelona, Maucci, 1909.

RUIZ MORCUENDE, F. "Algunas notas de lenguaje popular madrileño," in *Homenaje a Menéndez Pidal,* Madrid, 1925, II, 205–212.

SALILLAS, R. *El delincuente español: El lenguaje,* Madrid, V. Suárez, 1896.

WAGNER, M. L. *Notes linguistiques sur l'argot barcelonais,* Barcelona, 1924 (Institut d'estudis catalans, Barcelona. Institut de la llengua catalana. *Biblioteca filologica,* XVI).

———. "Sobre algunas palabras gitano-españolas y otras jergales," in *Revista de filología española,* XXV (1941), 161–181.

LEONESE

Leonese is the most direct heir of the vernacular as it was spoken at court in the Visigothic period and the most faithful preserver of the ancient traits.[11] It is perhaps significant of the archaic features of Leonese that the phrase *estar en babia* (= to be completely alien to what is going on) takes the name *Babia* from an isolated region on the southern slope of the *Cordillera cantábrica.* The boundaries of Leonese, roughly those of the ancient kingdom of León, include the modern provinces of Oviedo (the old kingdom of Asturias), León, Zamora, Salamanca, Santander, most of Palencia, a good share of Valladolid and the western portion of Cáceres and Badajoz.

Leonese has three subdivisions. To the east, where it has been greatly contaminated by Castilian, lies the dialect of the Montaña, the province of Santandar, beloved of the novelist José María de Pereda, who introduced into his books much of the talk of its natives.[12] Possibly richest in dialectal traits is the *bable* of Asturias, as heard from its coastline to the south side of the Cantabrian mountains, where a leveling of linguistic peculiarities begins, the result of immigration from all parts of Spain during the Reconquest and of the area's political bond with Toledo. Western Leonese (west of the River Navia) contains a heavy infiltration of Galician features.

One manuscript of the *Libro de Alixandre,* shows, in the

---

[11] Compare Menéndez Pidal, *Orígenes,* p. 474, or *Idioma español,* p. 91.

[12] To *Sotileza* is appended a vocabulary of some of the technical and local terms used throughout the novel. Compare also E. de Huidobro, *Palabras, giros y belle-zas del lenguaje popular, elevado por Pereda ...* , Santander, 1907.

opinion of some scholars, the hand of a Leonese copyist or author in certain forms (*leyte, muller;* see the discussion below, plurals in *-es,* preference for infinitives in *-er: dizer, morrer, viver,* etc.). The extensive ballad literature of Asturias has received attention from scholars of the nineteenth century (for example, Juan Menéndez Pidal).

Modern formal literature has not often availed itself of the medium or the resources of Leonese, but in the *Coplas de Mingo Revulgo* and in the early theater of Juan del Encina and Lucas Fernández the peasant speech of the region of Salamanca and of Alba de Tormes, seat of Fadrique Alvarez de Toledo, Duke of Alba, is used as a rustic dialect. Often called *sayagués* (after the area of Sayago in the province of Zamora), this became the conventional speech for stage countrymen in the sixteenth and seventeenth centuries. To what degree the "father of the Spanish theater" and his successors are linguistically accurate in their imitation of rural speech, no study has yet ascertained. The traditional stage use of this speech is continued in the eighteenth century in P. Isla's *Fray Gerundio.* Some modern regional poets, such as José Caveda, Luis Chamizo (*El miajón de los castúos,* 1921), Teodoro Cuesta, etc., have sung in the language of their province.

As the Leonese dialect is not the language of instruction, of the law courts, or of literature, it is not subject to their standardizing influence, and therefore may vary widely from village to village, or even from door to door within a settlement. Among the phonological features which can be considered characteristic of it are:

The stressing of either element of the diphthongs *ie* and

uo and the presence of later stages, *ua, ue,* of the latter. See p. 82.

The retention of *ie* before *ll* (*siella*). See p. 83.

The passage of *ia* to *ie* and vice versa (*tenía > tenie, tenié,* see p. 113; *diez > díaz*) and of final *a* to *e* (*a estes hores, les sardines*).

The diphthongization of *e* (chiefly in verbs) and *o* in spite of *yod* (*teneo > tiengo; foliam > fuolla, fuella, fueya*).

The retention of the intermediate diphthongs *ei* and *ou* (*basium > beiso, causam > cousa*) and the preservation of *-oiro -a* < Vulgar Latin *-orium -aṁ* (*Dorium > Doiro, tractoria > treitoira*).

The tendency of final *o* to pass to *u* (*cristianu, malu;* compare the *osu* of *Peñas arriba,* XIX–XX) and of final *e* to pass to *i* (*nochi, tocanti, cuantu antis*); the more general loss of final *e* after *l, r, n, s, z* (*quier, vien, paez < parece*).

The continuance of initial *f* in Western Leonese and in the *bable* of Asturias (*fierru, facer*). Santander, a small part of Salamanca, and Extremadura use the later aspirate *h*.

The palatalization in Asturias of initial *l* (*llobu, lleña*). At times *elle* is replaced by a sound which may be described as *ts* [ŝ] (*tsobu < llobu < lobo*).

The development of initial *j, ge, gi* to [ž] or [ŷ], which has become [š] (written *x*) in Asturias (*gelum > xelu*).

The development of initial *pl, cl, fl* to [ĉ] or [ŝ] approximately (in the western subdivision): *pluviam > chuvia* or *tsuvia.* In some parts *pl, bl, cl, fl > pr, br, cr, fr* (*plomo > promo, pueblo > puebro, clavel > cravel, flor > fror*).

The retention of *x* as [š]: *axem > eixe* (compare *Juanín = Xuanín* and *xelu* above).

The development of *li, c'l,* to *ll, y* (*mulierem* > Old Leonese *muller,* Modern Leonese *muyer, veculum* > Old Leonese *viello,* Modern Leonese *vieyo*). See p. 97.

The retention of *ct* at the stage of *it,* particularly in the west (*strictum* > *estreito*). See p. 96.

The retention of *mb* (*lombo, palombar*).

The partiality to antihiatic *y* (*veyer*).

In the precincts of morphology the chief characteristics are the preservation of the masculine definite article *lo;* the masculine subject personal pronoun *elli;* the survival, in Asturias, of the dative *i(s),* anciently *lli(s)*; the assimilation to the definite article of *con, en, por* (*con el palo* > *col palu, con la otra* > *conna otra*); the frequency of the termination *ino, in* (*angelín, padrín* < *padrino, paisanino, palombina*) and of *-uco* in Santander (*hombruco, tierruca*). The possessive adjectives continue a number of archaic forms like *to, so; túa, súa; míe, túe, súe.* Strangely, the form *mio* is sometimes feminine: *mio vida* (e.g., Pérez de Ayala, *La pata de la raposa,* p. 129 of the 1923 edition). There is a strong tendency to insert *i* in nonverbal terminations (*acaso* > *atasio, melena* > *melenia*) especially.

Among verbs there is the use of stressed forms of *ser* (*es* > *yes, est* > *ye, era* > *yera*), of terminations in *e* < *a* (*cante* < *canta, cantabemus* < *cantabamus,* etc.), of *-este, -emos, -esteis* in the preterit indicative of *-ar* verbs (*canteste, cantemos, cantesteis*) and of *-oron* or *-oren* as the ending of the third person plural of the same tense in all conjugations (*temioron, temioren*).

In syntax Modern Leonese clings to the use of the definite article before possessive adjectives (*el nuestru puebru, la mia muyer*). The loyalty of Galician and Leonese to the indicative function of the *-ra* form has been discussed earlier (p. 203). In some portions of Asturias the perfect tense form (*he hablado*) is not known, the preterit serving in its stead, thus recalling the dual function of the perfect tense form in Latin. Postposition of the object pronouns is still usual in Asturias, León, and Zamora. Cf. pp. 119, 170.

BIBLIOGRAPHY

ACEVEDO Y HUELVES, B. and FERNÁNDEZ, M. *Vocabulario del bable de occidente*, Madrid, P. Aguirre, 1932.

ALONSO GARROTE, S. *El dialecto vulgar leonés hablado en Maragatería y Tierra de Astorga*, segunda edición, Madrid, 1947.

ENTWISTLE. *The Spanish Language*. pp. 134–141, 224–228.

FINK, OSKAR. *Studien über die Mundarten der Sierra de Gata (Hamburger Studien zum Volkstum und Kultur der Romanen)*, Hamburg, 1929.

GARCÍA LOMAS, G. *Estudio del dialecto popular montañés*, San Sebastián, 1922.

GARCÍA REY, V. *Vocabulario del Bierzo*, Madrid, Archivo de tradiciones populares, IV, Madrid, 1934.

GILLET, JOSEPH E. "Notes on the language of the rustics in the drama of the sixteenth century," in *Homenaje a Menéndez Pidal*, Madrid, 1925, I, 443–453.

HANSSEN. *Gramática histórica*, § 17 and *passim* (§§ 49, 53, 71, 106–108, 123, 128, 131–134, etc.).

KRÜGER, F. *Studien zur Lautgeschichte westspanischer Mundarten*, Hamburg, 1914 (7. *Beihefte zum Jahrbuch der Hamburgischen Wissenschaftlichen Anstalt*, XXXI, 1913).

———. *El dialecto de San Ciprián de Sanabria, monografía leonesa*, Madrid, 1923 (*Revista de filología española, Anejo IV*).

LAMANO Y BENEITE, J. DE. *El dialecto vulgar salmantino*, Salamanca, Imprenta de "El salmantino," 1915.

LEITE DE VASCONCELLOS, J. *Opusculos, IV, Filologia* (Parte II), Coimbra, Imprensa da Universidade, 1929.

———. *Estudos de Philologia mirandesa*, 2 vols., Lisboa, Imprensa Nacional, 1900–1901.

MENÉNDEZ PIDAL, R. "El dialecto leonés," in *Revista de archivos, bibliotecas y museos*, XIV (1906), 128–172, 294–311.

———. *Orígenes*, pp. 461–485 or *Idioma español*, pp. 69–108.

RÍO, A. DEL. "Los estudios de Jovellanos sobre el dialecto asturiano," in *Revista de filología hispánica*, V (1943), 209–243.

ZAMORA VICENTE, A. *El habla de Mérida y sus cercanías*, Madrid, 1943.

ARAGONESE

Thanks to the individuality of the Aragonese peasants (*baturros*), obstinate (*aragonés tozudo, mete el clavo en la peña por la cabeza, y dale en la punta con el puño y jura que ha de entrar,* already says Correas in his *Vocabulario de refranes*), shrewd, and benevolent withal, the Aragonese dialect is more widely familiar than the Leonese, in spite of the number of Leonese folk songs and folk tales. The *Cuentos* of Eusebio Blasco (1844–1903) and the appearance on the stage of Aragonese rustics (as in *Solico en el mundo* of the Quinteros), whose somewhat conventional speech is there high-lighted by the use of the diminutive termination *-ico,* the ejaculation *maño, maña,* and *hi < he,* have obtained for it a certain popularity. The fault charged by Cervantes to the false *Quixote* of Avellaneda (*el lenguaje es aragonés, porque tal vez escribe sin artículos, Don Quixote,* II, 59) is not reported by modern students of the dialect.

Originating in the ancient kingdom of Aragon (or the modern provinces of Zaragoza, Huesca, and Teruel), Aragonese extends westward into Navarre, where, especially in the north, it comes into contact with Basque, and extends toward the Mediterranean as far as the hills of Ribagorza in the province of Huesca.

To the southwest in Navarre is the fertile region of the river Oja (*La Rioja*), whose western half (*Rioja Alta*) has, definitely since 1176, been associated politically and ecclesiastically with Castile. And on the very Castilian border is the monastery of San Millán de la Cogolla. Looking toward Catalonia, we see in the northeast the mountainous *condado* (county) of Ribagorza, in the eastern portion of which Catalan is spoken. North of Huesca is the *país de Sobrarbe,* in the valleys and on the southern slopes of the "green ash" of the Pyrenees. In the remote confines of this extreme Upper Aragon (*Alto Aragón*) there are found some very peculiar linguistic traits which are also in evidence across the border in the departments of the Basses- and Hautes-Pyrénées.

Aragon was joined to Catalonia in 1137, upon the marriage of Ramón Berenguer IV, Count of Barcelona, to the daughter of Ramiro el Monje, and for several centuries thereafter the Mediterranean area was to feel the force of the energetic kingdom. Although designated as Aragon, it was the commercial abilities of the industrious Catalans (which term included all the Spanish subjects of the king of Aragon) that made the Spanish house known, if not loved, on *mare nostrum* in the fourteenth and fifteenth centuries. In spite of all her stubborn fighting later against Philip II and Philip V, too, Aragon was subordinated to Castile after the marriage of Ferdinand and Isabel in 1469.

In its sound system Aragonese shares with Leonese, or some subgroup thereof, the variable diphthongs *ie, ia, uo, ua, ue;* diphthongization in the face of *yod* (*lectum* > *lieito, podium* > *pueyo*); the frequency of *y* to avoid hiatus (*trayer*);[13] the retention of initial *f* (*feno, faba*), of *ct* at *it* (*noctem* > *nueite*) and of *li̯, c'l* at *ll* (*fuella, ovella*); in the north and east of the sound of [š], orthographically *x* (*coixo*); and the tendency to palatalize initial, and even intervocalic, *l. Ie* is retained before *ll* (*portiello*).

[13] This trait is prominent in the sole MS of the *Libro de Apolonio.*

In its own right it offers the loss of final *e* and sometimes, after *l*, *n*, *r*, of *o* (*pastors* < *pastores*, *gorriñóns* < *gorriñones*, *chen* < *gente*, *chirmán* < *germanum*), the preservation of initial *pl*, *cl*, *fl* except in Ribagorza, where the *l* is palatalized (*pll*, etc., orthographically), and, in the Sobrarbe, of the unvoiced intervocalic consonant sounds *p*, *k*, *t* (*napo* = Castilian *nabo*, *taleca* = *talega*, *tenito* = *tenido*). Further, *j*, *ge*, *gi* evolve through [ž] or [ŷ] to [ĉ] (orthographically *ch*: *jenuarium* > *jenero* > *chinero*, *gemiqueo* >*chemequeo*). Like Castilian, *mb* > *m* and, at least in the ancient dialect, *nd* > *n* (*quando* > *quan*).

Morphologically, there appears again in Aragonese the use of the masculine definite article *lo*, of forms (*yes*, *ye*, *yera*, etc.) deriving from *es*, *est*, *era*, etc., when stressed, and of *-oron* as the preterit ending in the third person plural. As a possessive of the third person, *lur* (pl. *lures*) < *illorum* is still current in Upper Aragon. The relative *qui* is likewise living, though there is little sign of the dative *li*(*s*), so frequent in Berceo (*Todos li dauan algo, qui media, qui çatico; Vida de Santo Domingo de Silos*, 105*d*).

A preference for *-o, -a* as an adjectival ending is sometimes held characteristic of the region, but it is found in Asturian and in the *género chico* pieces generally (*cualo* in Arniches, *El puñao de rosas*, I; *El santo de la Isidra*, I, 13; *cuálas* in *La pena negra*, I, 5; López Silva-Fernández Shaw, *La revoltosa*, V and IX). In fact, many of the phenomena usually ascribed to a single region are likely to belong to the language of the people, in whatever part of Spain it be spoken.

BIBLIOGRAPHY

ARNAL CAVERO, P. *Vocabulario del alto aragonés (De Alquézar y pueblos próximos)*, Madrid, Consejo Superior de Investigaciones Científicas, 1944.

BORAO, J. *Diccionario de voces aragonesas*, Zaragoza, 1859 (second enlarged edition, 1908; this contains the vocabularies printed in the *Diccionario aragonés* mentioned below).

El diccionario aragonés, Zaragoza, Imprenta del Hospicio Provincial, 1902 (this contains *Colecciones* of Aragonese terms by B. Coll, L. V. López Puyoles, and J. Valenzuela La Rosa).

ELCOCK, W. D. *De quelques affinités entre l'aragonais et le béarnais*, Paris, E. Droz, 1938.

ENTWISTLE. *The Spanish Language*, pp. 141–145, 224–228.

FERRAZ Y CASTÁN, V. *Vocabulario del dialecto que se habla en la Alta Ribagorza*, Madrid, 1934.

GARCÍA DE DIEGO, V. "Caracteres fundamentales del dialecto aragonés," in his *Miscelánea filológica*, Madrid, n.d. [1925], pp. 1–18.

HANSSEN. *Gramática histórica*, § 19 and *passim*.

INDURAIN, F. *Contribución al estudio del dialecto navarro-aragonés antiguo*, Zaragoza, Archivo de Filología Aragonesa, Serie A, Anejo I, Zaragoza, 1945.

KUHN, ALWIN. "Der hocharagonesische Dialekt," in *Revue de linguistique romane*, XI (1935), 1–312.

MENÉNDEZ PIDAL. *Orígenes*, pp. 485–497; or *Idioma español*, pp. 109–132.

UMPHREY, G. W. "The Aragonese Dialect," in *Revue Hispanique*, XXIV (1911), 5–45.

ANDALUSIAN

Anciently desired by Phoenicians, Carthaginians, Greeks, Romans, and Berbers successively, the Land of the Blessed Virgin (*la tierra de María Santísima,* the Spaniard says) is now portioned into eight provinces. Within her bounds are the four Moorish kingdoms (*"los cuatro reinos"*) of Córdoba, Granada, Jaén, and Sevilla. But linguistic peculiarities do not necessarily coincide with political groupings, and the characteristics of Andalusian speech extend into Extremadura and include also the realm of Murcia northward on the Mediterranean.

After Columbus the chief city became Seville, through which men went to and metal returned from the *Nuevo Mundo.* As the center of colonial trade, the "gran Babilonia de España," the "escala del Nuevo Mundo," attracted those who for their existence must depend on their wits (*Bellaco me ha parecido,* says someone of Limón, who explains, *Soy de Sevilla, señor,* as if that accounted for everything; Lope de Vega, *Amar sin saber a quién,* I, 10). *Pícaros* like Guzmán de Alfarache, Estebanillo González, Pablos el Buscón were born in Seville or went there; there Monipodio kept school for thieves. The speech of its underworld was soon remarked for its peculiarities (compare p. 163): *Denota bravosidad quitar letras a las palabras, como* Erez, arro, *por* jarro *y* Jerez (Suárez de Figueroa, *El pasajero,* VIII).

Among the dialects, *andaluz* does not rank with Aragonese and Leonese,[14] but is classed rather as a slovenly articu-

---

[14] Galician is more properly an offshoot of Portuguese. There is a good summary in Entwistle, *The Spanish Language,* pp. 304 ff.

lated Castilian. We become conscious of the low regard in which it is held by those dwelling on the central plateau north of the dividing *Sierra Morena,* in the early sixteenth century, when Valdés repeatedly scorns the authority of the Andalusian Nebrija: *al fin no se puede negar que era andaluz y no castellano, No me aleguéis otra vez para la lengua castellana el autoridad de Librixa andaluz,* etc., *Diálogo de la lengua,* ed. cit., pp. 40, 95. Over ten decades later, commenting on the fact of linguistic change, Gracián mentions that of those who passed in the wheel of time one *ya decía gixo a lo andaluz* (*El criticón,* III, 10). Andalusian had its defenders, however. Ambrosio de Salazar claims that "not even Castilian distantly approaches it," and somewhat ambiguously, that "people spoke quite rudely in Castile not long ago" (cf. p. 179). More recently, the folk-loving Fernán Caballero, the fad of *andalucismo* in the theater, as represented by the Quintero brothers and by Pedro Muñoz Seca, the bull fight and *flamenquismo,* have focused attention on the soft talk of the expressive, lively, and not always stable *andaluces.*

In the evolution of sounds, and beginning with the vowels, Andalusian, which inclines generally toward muscular relaxation in the process of articulating, presents the tendency to pronounce the vowels in a more open manner than is held good in Castile.

Among its consonantal traits is the use (but not in Murcia and Extremadura, nor in the northern parts of Huelva and Córdoba, nor the greater part of Jaén and Almería) of *s* for *theta* (orthographically *z, ce, ci*) = *seseo,* as in *dise, serca, corasón, conosco, pasiensia.* There is reason for believing that the replacement of the older *ç* and *z* by *s* began in the second half of the sixteenth century. The *s*-sound is of course the Andalusian coronal or predorsal *s,* in which the tip of the tongue rests to a greater or lesser extent against the inner surface of the lower incisors and the blade of the tongue plays the principal role in the articulation.[15] Along the coast, around Seville as a center, and throughout most of the province of Granada, the practice is to *cecear. Ceceo* is the substitution of *theta,* or some variety thereof, for orthographical *s, z, ce, ci* (*Es máz, quize oponerme a eyo* [= ello] *porque zabía que éza era la hora en que uté* [= usted] *echaba zu parrafiyo;* Palacio Valdés, *La hermana San Sulpicio,* X); it is held to be the result of a local form of Arabic *s* (*sín*), inherited from the Moriscos. Estebanillo González found it most attractive (*Vida y hechos de Estebanillo González,* V) *ca.* 1625. The gypsies' habit of speaking *ceceoso* is not natural to them (*Preciosa ... como gitana, hablaba ceceoso, y esto es artificio en ellas; que no naturaleza,* Cervantes, *La gitanilla*). It is a curious fact, of unlikely relation to the geography of linguistic phenomena, that in the *Claros varones* Fernando del Pulgar records the lisp of at least four of the figures he describes (*Títulos* VIII, XII, XXII, XXIII). The same defect of speech (*hablar çeçeoso, çeçear,* says the fifteenth century biographer) is ascribed to Pedro el Cruel (according to López de Ayala in his *Crónica del rey don Pedro,* chap. viii) and to Charles V.

A vulgarism in the south of Spain is to reduce *s* to a mere

---

[15] In the articulation of Castilian *s* (alveolar or cacuminal *s*), used over most of northern and central Spain, the tongue tip rests against the sockets of the upper teeth. *Seseo* is the rule also in the Basque provinces, Catalonia and Valencia, when Spanish is spoken by the people.

aspiration at the end of a syllable and to omit it entirely at the end of a breath group: *gusta* > *guhta*, often written *guta; usted* > *uhté*, often written *uté; loh médico; acá tene-moh tre*. This practice is not limited to the South. Cf. p. 162.

The passage of *l* to *r* is frequent at the end of a syllable in Andalusian and in Extremaduran: *er toreo, argo, cien mir duros, er agua que cae der sielo*. Especially in Murcia, *r* in this position is replaced by a sound that approximates to *l: tolpe, entendel*. The total disappearance of final *l* and *r* is extremely common: *asú = azul, chavá = chaval, vení = venir, mujé = mujer*. Before a pronoun object beginning with *l, r* of the infinitive may simply be omitted (*hablale, vendelo, escribilo*) over the entire country, or it may be assimilated to the *l* following (*hablalle, vendello*, pronounced *hablal-le, vendel-lo*), as in Andalusia (including Murcia and Extremadura).

As one of its archaic survivals *andaluz* retains the aspiration of *h* < Latin initial *f;* orthographically the aspiration is usually represented by *j: jondo* in *cante jondo, jumo, jasienda, ajogar* (*a* being considered a prefix), *juerza* (also *huerza*), *juéramos, jayo = hallo*. Castilian *jota* often becomes a mere aspiration by relaxing the contact of the back of the tongue with the hard palate. This sound is written *h: trabaho, dihe, monha, hente*, etc.

The pronunciation of *ll* as *y* (*yeísmo*) is general, but not universal, over all Andalusia, and in the provinces of Ciudad Real, Madrid, and Toledo (compare p. 239). This development, which comes about by failure to make a broad contact of tongue and hard palate, makes sporadic appearance in early texts, where *ll* is used to describe the sound of

y: llugero = yuguero (*Libro de buen amor,* 1092*b* of the
Salamanca MS), *alluda* writes Ruiz de Alarcón in 1602 for
ayuda. An occasional error of this sort becomes a part of
the language: *gruam > gruya* (with antihiatic *y*) *> grulla,
Maiorca > Mallorca,* though there is no such danger in
words of frequent use: *Que halla* [i.e., *haya*] *podido esca-
parse, decía, es lo único que deseo* (Benavente, *La propia
estimación,* Teatro, tomo XXI, 5ª edicion, 1929, p. 41). It
serves for mild witticism: *¿Y qué son zanjas?—Hoyas.—
¿Para guisar?* [i.e., *ollas*] (Fernán Caballero, *Un servilón
y un liberalito,* VII) and has given permanent form to the
California place name *Berryessa < Berrelleza,* the family
name of some of the earliest (1776) settlers in San Francisco.
The confusion or even the similarity of *ll* and *y* is not mentioned by grammarians of the sixteenth and seventeenth
centuries. Mistakes in writing *ll* and *y* are relatively rare before the nineteenth century. The inference is therefore that
the *yeísmo* of Andalusia is a modern evolution. It is, however, already indicated as a characteristic trait of the dialect
in Ramón de la Cruz's *Las provincias españolas unidas por
el placer* (1789). The [y] thus produced is subject to the
modification of an original one, so that *caballo* and *llave*
become not only *cabayo* and *yave* but also *cabažo, cabaŷo*
and *žave, ŷave,* or some variation of [ž] and [ŷ], in the
south and in parts of New Castile.

From their vocabulary Leonese and Aragonese have
added little to the common fund, but Andalusian, as the
home of *los toros, gitanismo,* and *sal,* has been more generous. Preserving for itself many obsolete words and phrases
(which caused Rodríguez Marín to see *andalucismo* in the

Popular Spanish

The phenomena of syntax are essentially the same wherever Spanish is spoken over the Peninsula; linguistic geographers have only lately begun work in delimiting the features of regional vocabulary. Common to the use of the little educated, not restricted as a general rule to any portion of the country, is the preservation of archaic words or forms (*ande = donde, ascuchar = escuchar, asín*[*a*] *= así, asperar = esperar, entoavía = todavía, mesmo, mochacho, truje,* etc. *= traje,* etc., *vía,* etc. *= veía,* etc.) and vulgarisms like *ir* (*venir, bajar,* etc.) *a por agua* (*vino,* etc.) and *en ca*(*s*) *de = en casa de;* as is also the evolution of certain sounds, often begun centuries ago; and numerous details of morphology.

In the treatment of vowels colloquial speech carries on the tendency to the diphthongization of successive vowels by closing unstressed *e* to *i, o* to *u,* or by immediate transference of the stress to the more open element: *caen > cain, peor > pior, Joaquín > Juaquín, almohada > almuada, maíz > maiz, boina* is now preferred to *boína, maestro > máestro > maistro > meistro > mestro* (cf. p. 34). This phenomenon does not appear to be frequent in Andalusia or Extremadura.

Muy regularly becomes *mu.*

Ei tends to become *ai: seis > sais,* and, with the suppression of intervocalic *d,* final *o* becomes *u: hablado > hablau, dedo > deu.*

The confusion of *e* and *i, o* and *u* in unstressed syllables likewise continues: *militar > melitar, regular > rigular* or *rigulá, usted > osté, política > pulítica.* Often the vocalic change is aided by the confusion of prefixes (*distrito* > *destrito*), the influence of a *yod* (?) in *siñor* < *señor*, or the forces of assimilation and dissimilation (*cirimonia* < *ceremonia*, *revulución* < *revolución*).

The complete suppression of the vowel of *me, te, se, le* before *a* or *e* similarly continues to be observed (cf. p. 104): *m'acuerdo, s'ha quedao, l'habrá orvidao;* compare also *d'un picador, moso d'estoque, un grano d'arpiste.*

The consonantal history includes the aspiration, especially in Andalusia, the region of Santander, eastern Asturias, the province of Salamanca, and in Extremadura, of initial *h* < *f: jasé* < *hacer.* (See p. 89).

Elimination of intervocalic and final *d* is practically universal: *estampida* > *estampía* (listed in the Academy dictionary), *herida* > *hería, matador* > *mataó, bailadora* > *bailaora, un poquillo de jamón* > *un poquiyo e jamón, puede* > *puée* > *pué, nada* > *náa* > *ná, todo* > *tóo* > *tó;* its dropping in the participial *-ado* is even "correct." The disappearance of intervocalic *d* begins at least as early as the latter half of the eighteenth century: *moa, marío, ganao* (Ramón de la Cruz, *El chasco de los aderezos*).

In the desire to be "correct" *d* is then often wrongly introduced: *tonterida* < *tontería, El Atenedo* < *El Ateneo, bacalado* < *bacalao, vacida* < *vacía.*

Final *d*, ordinarily omitted (*salud* > *salú*) *Madrid* > *Madrí*, becomes a variant of *theta* in parts of Old Castile and in Madrid (*admirable* > *azmirable, salud* > *saluz, Madrid* > *Madriz*). Historically, the latter tendency has yielded *juzgar* < Old Spanish *judgar* < *judicare, -azgo,* < Old Spanish *-adgo* < *-aticum* (cf. p. 132).

The relaxation of intervocalic *g* to disappearance shows in *miaja* < *migaja*, *juar* < *jugar*, *aúja* < *aguja*.

The group *ct* is always difficult, and its evolution is varied: the palatal consonant may be omitted (*rectifique* > *retifique*); it may be vocalized as *i̯* or *u̯* (*directores* > *direitores*, *efecto* > *efeuto*); or a new consonant may develop (*afecto* > *afezto, octubre* > *ortubre*). Compare p. 97.

Cc is most frequently simplified to *c* (*satisfacción* > *satisfación*), but vocalization may occur (*facciones* > *faiciones*), or a new consonant may develop (*accidentes* > *arcidentes;* cf. *reflexión* > *reflersión*).

Mb > *m*: *también* > *tamién*. Compare p. 99.

Gn > *n*: *indigno* > *indino* or *endino, Ignacia* > *Inacia, ignorancia* > *inorancia*. Compare p. 97.

X > *s*: *sexo* > *seso, máximas* > *másimas;* the insistence of the Spanish Academy upon restoring in writing the Latin prefix *ex* has led to the occasional pronunciation of *es* as *ks* (*excucha* in los Quinteros, *Las flores,* II), but the normal sound is ordinarily *s* (cf. p. 190).

Ps, pt > *u̯s, u̯t*: *cápsula* > *cáusula, concepto* > *conceuto*. The vocalization of the occlusive consonant took place long ago in *captivum* > *cautivo, rapidum* > *raudo*, etc.

Emphatic pronunciation of *w* yields a consonantal velar element: *huevo* > *güevo, huerta* > *güerta*.

R is vocalized and omitted in forms of *haber, querer,* and *ser* after *ie, ue,* and in intervocalic position, *e* often disappearing; the stress then passes to the more open vowel: *hubiéramos* > *hubiéamos* > *hubiámos, quiero* > *quió, fueran* > *fuán, mira* > *miá, mire usted* > *miste, parece* > *páece* or *paice;* compare *señora* > *señá, para* > *pa*.

The confusion of *r* and *l* is sufficiently recalled by citing the punning phrase *tener el alma en el almario* (i.e., *armario*).

The passage of [y] to [ž] or [ŷ] is widespread (cf. p. 98). In *Fortunata y Jacinta* (I, 4, 1) Pérez Galdós already speaks of someone who *Daba a la elle el tono arrastrado que la gente baja da a la* y *consonante*.

The simple metathesis of *r* is frequent: *catredal* < *catedral*, *drento* < *dentro*, *treato* < *teatro;* reciprocal exchange occurs in forms like *flaire* < *fraile*, *paderes* < *paredes*.

The equivalence (cf. p. 96) of *b* (*v*) and *g* as voiced occlusives, of *b* and *m* as voiced bilabials, of *n, r*, and *d* approximately in the position of the tongue tip, leads to their improper substitution: *bofes* > *gofes* (Pérez Galdós, *Misericordia*, XXVIII), *abuela* > *agüela, vuelto* > *güerto, aguja* > *abuja, agur* > *abur, ninguno* > *denguno, mejor* > *mejón* (Andalusian only ?).

A peculiarity of a noun terminating in a stressed vowel is the formation of a new plural on the old: *feses,* plural of *fe; maniquises,* plural of *maniquí; sofases,* plural of *sofá;* etc. Doubling the sign of plurality here results from the feeling that pluralization of noun or adjective not ending in unstressed *e, o,* or *a* involves the addition of a syllable; *sofás* and *bajáes* are considered the correct forms, as are *rubíes* and *zaquizamís*. To *-ís* the spoken language prefers *-íes*, which may in the future become standard, though *-ises* (*alelises*) is as old as Tirso and Lope.

Beginning apparently in Andalusia (cf. p. 234) is the replacement of *vosotros* by *ustedes*. Avoidance of *vosotros* extends to *os*, for which *se* is ordinarily substituted: *les voy*

*a enseñá a ustedes una cosa que se vais a queá con la boca
abierta* (Muñoz Seca, *El roble de la Jarosa*, III); *¿Queréis
venirse?* (Alvarez Quintero, *El patio*, I); cf. also *sos, sus =
se + os* (?): *no sus apuréis* (Arniches, *El santo de la Isidra*,
I, 5); *¿Sus habéis mudado?* (Arniches, *La pena negra*, I, 5),
Hombre, podíais haber avisao. Ya sus echábamos de menos
(*ibid.*, I, 14); *¿Ande vais que mejó sos quieran?* (Alvarez
Quintero, *Las buñoleras*). The plural of *me* is analogically
mos: *los poemos vé sin que ellos mos vean* (*El roble de la
Jarosa*, I; cf. *ibid.*, *mos va a salvá*).

The most common verb form currently used by the populace is *haiga* (= *haya*); the use of this word is, like the inability to cope with *h* in spelling, a sign of humble social
status. Although it enjoys the support of the Academy,
whose *Grammar* (§ 89*a* of the 1931 edition) lists it as an
alternative form, *habemos* is infrequently found in the literary form of even conversational style, but it is regular in
the speech of the *pueblo*. *Semos* < *sedemus* replaces *somos*.
Analogic imperfects in *-eba, -iba* are met with in several
parts of Spain: *queriba* (Arniches, *El santo de la Isidra*, III,
1). There is, too, the use of *-emos, -esteis* in the preterit (cf.
p. 109): *hace quince días … averigüemos*, etc. (Arniches, *El
santo de la Isidra*, I, 5). To the same principle of analogy
are assignable gerunds like *hiciendo, supusiendo*, obviously
modeled on the corresponding preterit indicative forms.
The use of *-on* < *-ieron* (*vinon* < *vinieron*) is general except in Andalusia. A common form (Andalusian only ?)
is *vi = voy: Vi a verlo, en esta casa vi yo a hasé un escarmiento*
(*El roble de la Jarosa*, I and *passim*).

Prefixing of *a* has been a feature of word formation since

early times: *afigúrate, ajuntar, aluego* (*El roble de la Jarosa*), *asentar = sentar* (Arniches, *La pena negra*, I, 3), *allego = llego* (Arniches, *El terrible Pérez*, I, 9), *arrecoge = recoge, arrepare = repare* (*El roble de la Jarosa*, II), *arrodeo = rodeo* (Benavente, *Señora ama*, I, 3). *Arr-* is probably an attempt at times to reproduce the multiple trill of an initial *r*. Compare *rancar* (764) and *arrancar* (1142, 2400), *rebata* (468) and *ar[r]ebata* (562) in the *Poema de Mio Cid; arrecoge* in Ramón de la Cruz, *La maja majada*.

Another trait of popular Spanish is the clipping of final syllables: *Bombilla > Bombi, María > Mari, Trinidad > Trini, policía > poli, bicicleta > bici, combinación > combina, delegación > delega, pequeño > peque,* etc.

Very common is the transposition of verbal *n*, when the verb form is followed by an enclitic pronoun, to the end of its phrase (*dígamen < díganme, figúresen < figúrense*) or addition of another *n* (*figúrensen < figúrense*).

Syntactically, misuse of prepositions is the most frequent error: *Esa es una cosa muy ordinarias* [*sic*] *que no sabemos de hasé las señoras, A usté no debo de ocurtárselo* (*El roble de la Jarosa*, II); *¿Qué debo de decir a Monseñor?* (Valle-Inclán, *Sonata de primavera*); *así de que llegó a casa, escribió una carta* (Arniches, *La pena negra*, III, 2); *me hizo de estornudar* (Arniches, *El santo*, I, 5); compare p. 171. Noticeable, too, are the use of the conditional as a past subjunctive (*Si Juan vendría*), errors in the position of the personal pronoun objects (*me se figura*), and errors in the formation of plurals (*cualesquier día*).

THE ACOUSTIC IMPRESSION OF CASTILIAN

Returning at last to the constancy of correct Castilian, we end with a brief analysis of the acoustic features which have acquired for it such universal praise as "upright," "sound and strong," "robust and vigorous," "sweet and harmonious."

The clarity and distinctness of its sounds are the product of several factors of articulation. In Castilian, the speech organs (lips, tongue, larynx, palates hard and soft, teeth and alveoles) function with tensity rather than with muscular relaxation. Play of lips and jaws is quite pronounced. The quantity of air expelled through the mouth is slight, and the unvoiced explosives (*p, t, k*) are not enunciated with the concomitant aspiration of the corresponding English consonants. The beat, the rhythm, of Castilian pronunciation is unhurried; the pitch of Castilian is deep and low (*grave*) rather than shrill and high (*agudo*). So indeed, as Navarro Tomás says, must have spoken the Cid, the counts of Castile, the *conquistadores*. Surprisingly, Pérez de Guzmán and Fernando del Pulgar remark upon the pleasant quality of the speech of more than a few of the great names of the fifteenth century, as described in their biographical sketches.

Phonetically, the character of a language is determined by the pronunciation of its vowels. In Castilian the latter, whose frequency decreases in the order of *a, e, o, i, u,* share equally with the consonants in the makeup of words, and it is the simplicity and the stability of its clear vocalic sounds that gives Castilian its essential phonetic uniformity.

Voiced consonants are of more frequent occurrence than unvoiced, *r, l, n* being noticeably recurrent. The fricative quality of *b, d, g* predominates over the the occlusive. Rarest among the consonantal sounds are *f* and *ch* [ĉ].

The intonation which gives to Castilian its character has the general tendency not to lower the voice until the end of a declarative sentence, whatever the number of breath groups it may contain. Within a breath group the voice rises gradually from the initial syllable to the first stressed syllable, where the normal tone of the group begins. In *Otra de las mesas del comedor solía estar ocupada por los americanos, comedor* is spoken with an ascending inflection; *Al tercer día, a la hora del almuerzo, oí con el corazón alborozado la voz de Iturrioz en la sala,* is spoken with a brief interruption after *día,* then the sentence is continued at the same level, *almuerzo* is pronounced with rising inflection, and the voice finally descends with *sala.*

In sentences, or parts of sentences, consisting of independent and dependent clause (irrespective of their order), or in any whole made up of two parts, the first ends with a rising inflection of the voice. *Si mañana no me trae Vd. el dinero* (spoken with an ascent of the voice), *se lo digo a su padre; Quien canta* (with rising inflection), *sus males espanta.*

If, however, there is an enumeration, a series of parallel words or phrases, at the end of a sentence or constituting the sentence, the voice ordinarily descends on each member of the series but the next to last.[16] In *La capilla era húmeda,*

---

[16] If the last two members of the series are not connected by a conjunction, the voice falls on the final word of each member: *Es bueno, generoso, noble.*

tenebrosa y resonante there is a descent on *húmeda,* a rise on *tenebrosa;* in *Me senté al lado de ellos, aparenté buen humor, estuve jaranero en exceso y procuré por todos los medios que se fijasen en el ligero bastoncillo* the voice falls on *ellos* and *humor,* rises on *exceso.* But if the enumeration is not at the end of the sentence, then the elevation of the voice takes place on the last member of the series: *Mi cuarto era claro, limpio, confortable, con su chimenea de carbón, que algunas veces encendía.* The voice falls on *claro, limpio, confortable,* rises on *carbón.*

And for some of these traits, then, does Spanish deserve commendation like that of the divine Herrera: *ni corta ni añade silabas a las diciones, ni trueca ni altera forma; antes toda entera y perpetua muestra su castidad i cultura i admirable grandeza i espiritu, con que ecede sin proporcion a todas las vulgares, y en la facilidad y dulçura de su pronunciacion.*[17] In the words of Aldrete, *por no alargarme, no digo de su pronunciacion quan facil, y suave es, como reparte las letras, que en el hablar no causen fealdad ... i otras muchas cosas.*[18]

[17] In the commentary to his edition of Garcilaso de la Vega; compare José Francisco Pastor, *Las apologías de la lengua castellana en el siglo de oro,* Madrid, 1929 (Los clásicos olvidados, VIII), p. 101.

[18] In *Del origen y principio de la lengua castellana;* compare José Francisco Pastor, *op. cit.,* pp. 171–172.

BIBLIOGRAPHY

NAVARRO TOMÁS. *Compendio, passim* (pp. 41, 46, 47, etc.).

———. *Manual, passim* (§§ 70, 132, 181 ff., etc.).

———. "El acento castellano," in *Hispania,* XVIII (1935), 375–380.

Index

a, 118, 207
a (< haber), 207
a (final) > e, 223
abedul, 12
abierto, 117
abolengo, 50
abuja, 96, 239
abur, 239
aceite, 60
aceituna, 60
aceña, 60
acequia, 60
acertar, 184
achacar, 61
achaque, 61
adalid, 59
adarga, 59
adarme, 59
adelfa, 60
-adgo > -azgo, 132,
  237
-ado, 201, 237
adobe, 59
aduana, 59
afecto, 144
afeitar, 97
afeto, 144; afezto, 238
afición, 97
afigúrate, 241
agasajar, 50
agora, 95
agosto, 95
agüela, 239
aguja, 96
ahí, ai, 35
ahorrar, 61
aislar, 93
aiude, 78
ajogar, 232
ajorca, 60
ajuntar, 241
al, 105

alacrán, 60
alambique, 61
alarde, 59
albacea, 59
albahaca, 60
albañal, 59
albañil, 59
albarda, 59
albaricoque, 60
albéitar, 61
alberca, 60
albergue, 50
albóndiga, 61
albricias, 61
alcabala, 59
alcachofa, 60
alcaide, 59
Alcalá, 58
alcalde, 59
alcanfor, 61
alcantarilla, 59
alcatraz, 177
alcázar, 59
alcoba, 59, 177
alcohol, 61
alcuza, 60
aldea, 59
alegre, 34
Alejandría, Alejandria,
  18
alelises, 239
Alemaña, 77
alerta, 150
aleve, 49
alfalfa, 60
alfarero, 59
alfayate, 61
alféizar, 59
alferecía, 61
alférez, 59, 184
alfiler, 60
alfombra, 60

alfombrilla, 61
Alfonso, 50
alforja, 59
álgido, 214
algodón, 60
alguien, 106
alhaja, 60
Alhambra, 98
alhelí, 60
aliso, 49
aljibe, 60
alma, 87
almacén, 59
Almadén, 58
Almanzor, 64
almario, 239
almena, 59
almenaque, 86
almirez, 60
almohada, 60
almoneda, 59
almuada, 236
alnado, 29
aloja, 159
aloxa, 159
aloya, 12
alpaca, 151
alpargata, 60
alquiler, 61
alquimia, 61
a(l)tramuz, 60
aluego, 241
aluen, 83
Alvarez, 93
allego, 241
ama, 30
ambición, 150; ambi-
  cion, 208
ambigú, 193
amenaza, 37
amos, 99
análisis, 87

anbos, 81
anca, 49
anchoa, 31, 94; anchova, 94
andamio, 59
ande, 236
andove, andude, anduve, 114
ángel, 18
-ante, 202
antes (de) que, 172
antiséptico, 19
aprenderíades, 166
a que, 171
aquese, aqueste, 171
arañón, 12
arcador, 215
arcidentes, 238
archant, 194
ardido, 50
ardiment, 131
ardite, 121
arenga, 50
arpa, 50
arr = r, 241
arrabal, 59
arracada, 60
arrancar, 50
arro, 229
arroba, 212
arrojar, 98
arroyo, 8
arroz, 60
arruga, 95
artritis, 19
asa, 112
asconder, 133
ascuchar, 236
asentar, 241
asesinar, 150
asesino, 61
asgo < aso, 112
asín(a), 236
aspa, 50
asperar, 133, 236
aspirar, 150
astronomía, 18

asú, 232
atacar, 151
atalaya, 59
atamor, 59
ataúd, 60, 94
Atenedo, 237
atildado, 184
auer, 36, 81
aúja < aguja, 238
aunque, 171
auto, 97
aver, 144
avetarda > avutarda, 29
avieso, 37
avizor, 158
aya, 49
ayuda, 78, 143
ayudante, 181
azafate, 60
azafrán, 60
azahar, 60
azmirable, 237
azogue, 61
azotea, 59
azúcar, 60, 100
azucena, 60
azul, 61
azumbre, 59

Babia, 220
bable, 159, 220
babucha, 60
bacalado, 237
bahía, 31
bailadora, bailaora, 237
bajáes, 239
bajel, 131
bajo, 162
balcón, 150
balsa, 8
baluz, 8
banca, 150
banco, 50
bandera, 49
bandido, 49
bando, 49

bar, 211
barato, 18
Barcelona, 96
barnax, 131
barón, 50
barrer, 31
barrio, 59
batata, 151
baúl, baul, 35
bautizar, 18
baxo, 162
bazar, 59
beata, 217
becerro, 8
beiso, 222
bellota, 61
beodo, 117
berenjena, 60
Bermudo, 50
Bernal, 96
Berrelleza, 233
berro, 12
beuer, 80
biblia, 18
bici, 241
bigotismo, 214
Bilbao, 176
biombo, 151
bisoño, 150
biuir, 80
bizarro, 8
bl, cl, fl, pl, > br, cr, fr, pr, 222
blanco, 50
blandir, 49
blasón, 49
bledo, 121
bobo, 84, 176
boda, 79, 102
bodega, 17
bogar, 50
boína, boina, 236
bola, 35
bolero, 212
boletín, 151
Bombi, 24
bórax, 61

botánica, 18
botica, 17
botín, 49
bracelete, 86
bragas, 12
bramar, 50
brasa, 50
bravos, 163
brida, 49
briga, 11
brío, 12
brújula, 150
bucólico, 141
buen, 86
buhardilla, 96
buñelo, 96
burgo, 49
burro, 8
buscar, 31
butaca, 151

ca(s), 87, 236
caballo, 12
cabaña, 12, 29
cabayo, cabaýo, cabažo, 233
cabteloso, 80
cacahuete, 151
cacao, 151
cacique, 151
cachorro, 8
cada, 18, 105
cahiz, 59
caigo, 112
caimán, 151
cain, 236
cal (< calcem), 17
cal (< calle), 88
calabaza, 181
calabozo, 177
Calahorra, 95
Calatayud, 58
Cal de Abades, 88
Caldebayona, 88
caló, 217
calor, 101
callar, 31

cama, 29
cambiar, 12
camino, 12; camino
    francés, 65, 131
Camino de la Plata, 24
camisa, 12
canbiar, 81
cancha, 151
candado, 29
canoa, 151
canpo, 80
canto, 29
caoba, 151
capitán, 151
capricho, 151
cara, 18
caráiter, caráter, caráu-
    ter, carázter, 97
cardíaco, 19
carena, 151
carey, 151
Carlos, 102
carpio, 8
carro, 12
carta, 17
cartucho, 150
casildar, 214
Castiella, 83
castigar, 132
catarro, 8
catredal, 239
cauallo, 155
cáusula, 238
cautivo, 238
caya, cayo, 112
cayo, 151
cecear, çeçear, 231
cecco, 157, 231; çeçeo-
    so, 231
cedazo, 156
cedilla, 79
cejar, 162
Celipe, 96
celo por, celo del, 192
cencerro, 8
cenefa, 60
cenit, 61

centinela, 150, 156
Cerilla, 156
cero, 61
cerrar, 156
çeruiçio, 155
cerúleo, 214
cerveza, 12
cesar, 162
cibdad, 80
ciclatón, 60
cieno, 30
cifra, 61
cigarra -o, 8
-ción, 141–142, 148–
    150
cirimonia, 237
ciruela, 30
c'l, evolution of, 98,
    223, 226
clas, 88
clisé, 194
cobre, 101
cofia, 50
çofrir, 155
cogecha, 97, 162
cogombro > cohom-
    bro, 95
Coimbra, 11
cojo, 30
col, 223
colmillo, 30, 86
Colombaira, 68
color, 101
collazo, 30
combina, 241
combré, 115
comé, come, 111
comedes, comés, 109
comedianta, 202
comello, 166
comenzar a + inf.,
    comenzar de + inf.,
    171
comer, 30
comeredes, comerés,
    comeréis, 109
comerides, 116

comés, 109
comiemos, 110
comier, 110
comierdes, 110
comiés, 110
comino, 121
comodidad, 150
cómodo, 150
comulgar, 96
conceuto, 238
conde, 93
cóndor, 151
conejo, 29, 98
conello, 68
confidenta, confidente, 202
congoja, congoxa, 99
conna, 223
conplido, 81
consegar, consego, 78
conserje, 194
convento, conviento, 234
cope, 114
coqueta, 193
coraje, 131
corazón, 30
cordero, 30
Córdoba, 176
corneia, 78
coronel, 150
cosa, 84, 158
coscojo, 8
cosecha, 162
cosiment, 131
cotorra, 8
cousa, 222
crea, 112
creiga, 112
criado, 184
cristal, 17
Cristo, 17
crove, 114
crudo, 94; cruo, 93
ct, evolution of, 96, 144, 223, 226, 238
cual, 144; cuala, cualo, 227

cuanto, 144
cuarta, 176
cuatro, 144
cucaracha, 176
cuento, 151
cueva, 30
çufre, 155
cuidar, 132
cuita, 132
cundir, 49
cupe, 114
çusia, çusio, 155
cuyo, 30

Chambergo, 161
chaparejos, 176
chaquet, chaqueta, 194
charlar, 151
charretera, 194
chavá, 232
chicle, 151
chile, 151
china, 151
chirivía, 60
chirmán, 227
chiromancia, 207
chocolate, 151
chorro, 8
chulo, 31
chuvia, 222

d' < de, 237
dandí, dandy, 210
dardo, 50
dársena, 59
de, introducing agent, 126; wrongly used, 241
dé, de, 207
debda, 80
deber de, 241
debré, 115
debutanta, 202
deçendençia, 144
decillas, 166
decoro, 150
de juro, 234

del = de + él, della = de + ella, etc., 166
delega, 241
deleitar, 97
delgado, 86
denguno, 96, 239
de órdago, 217
de que, 133
derranchar, 131
-des, 166
desdeño, 214
dese, deste, etc. = de ese, este, etc., 166
desembocar, 176
desencajadamente, desencasadamente, desencajados, desencasados; desencajar, desencasar, 162
desmayar, 50
desnudo, 94; desnuyo, 93
desplacer, 214
después (de) que, 171
desque, 132
destrito, 237
determinar de + inf., 171
deu, 236
di, 208
día, 30, 101
diablo, 18
díaz, 222
Díaz, 93
Diego, 177
dignar, 150
dijerdes, 110
dino, 144
dintel, 96
Dios, 102
diré, 115
disanto, 214
discurrir, 150
discurso, 150
disenteria, disentería, 150
diseñar, diseño, 150

diz, 87, 108
dl >ld, 111, 166
do > doi, 111
Doiro, 222
Don, 86
doncel, 131
drama, 19
drento, 239
dubda, 80
duçe > duz, 84; palo
   duz, 88
duquenceo -a, 214
dureta, 29

e (< de), 237
e (< et), 107, 207, 208
e (< haber), 207
e (final) > i, 222
-eba, 240
ecelente, 144
efecto, efeito, efeto,
   efeuto, efezto, 97, 238
el (< ille), 100; el
   (< ela), 100, 166
él, ella = you, 167, 168
elegíaco, 141
el que, 204
Elvira, 50
ell, 78, 101
elli, 106, 223
-emos < -amos, 109,
   223, 240; -este <
   -aste, 110, 223;
   -esteis < -asteis,
   223, 240
empero, 209
(e)naguas, 151
encía, 94
ende, 105
endino, 238
enérjico, 190
enero, 90
Enrico, Enrique, 132
ensayo, 37
-ente, 202
entendredes, 115
entero, 34

entoavía, 236
entregar, 30
entretener, 150
-eo, 215
érades, 109
Erez, 229
esbozo, 151
escanciar, 49
escarlata, 61
escarnio, 50
escatimar, 61
escolta, 150
escrito, 117
escriuia, escriuies, etc.,
   113
escuadra, 150
escucha, 97
escudo, 37
escuerzo, 85
escueto, 31
esdrújulo, 150
ese, 37, 102
esfera, 18
esgrimir, 50
eslabón, 49
esmoquin, 37
espalda, 33
espécimen, 37
esperiencia, 190
espiar, 50
esplín, 37, 210
espuela, 50
Esquilache, 37
esquivar, 50
estaca, 50
estades, 109
estampía, 237;
   estampida, 176, 237
estar, 127, 204; estar en
   babia, 220
este, 50, 102
Esteban, 37
estilo, 150
estó, 111
estofa, 50
estove, 114
estraño, 190

estrecho, 117
estribo, 50
estropear, 151
estude, 114
estudianta, 202
estuve, 114
Etiopia, Etiopía, 18
excepción, 150
excucha, 238
exîmio, 207

f, evolution of initial,
   88 ff., 222, 226, 232,
   237
fablá, fabla, 111
fablades, 108
fablaes, fabláis, 109
fablandos, 111
fablar < fablare, 110
fablaredes, 108
fablár(e)des, 108, 110
fablarés, fablaréis, 109
fablarides, 116
fablás, 110
fabláuades, 108
facilitar, 150
facha, 151
fachada, 151
fachenda, 151
faiciones, 238
falda, 50
falsso, 95
famne, famre, 98
fandango, 212
fanega, 59, 212
fantasía, 150
faraute, 49
fardido, 50, 90
fazer, 93
fecho, feito, feycho, 97
Federico, 50
Felipe, 17, 96
Fernán, 86; Fernando,
   50
feses, 239
fieltro, 50
fiesta, 102

Filipo, 132
filo, 90
filosofía, 19
filtro, 19
fin, 102
física, 19
fiuza, 93
flaco, 92, 93
fleco, 83
flecha, 12
flueco, 83
foja, 97
fol, 131
Foli Bersé, 194
follía, 131
fonógrafo, 18
fonta, 49, 90
forajido, 151
forma, 90
forzosa, 210
fracaso, 151
fraile, 131
frambuesa, 50
Francisco, 50
frase, 19
fregatrizar, 214
freisno, 85
frejol, 162
frente, 83
fresco, 50
frijol, frisol(es),
    frixoles, 162
fructífero, 141
fruente, 83
fruncir, 50
fruta -o, 102
fuán < fueran, 238
fuella, 97
fuent, 83
fuer de, (a), 86
Fuero Juzgo, 47, 102
fuert, 82
fueya, 98
fulano, 61

gabán, 60
galápago, 31

galardón, 50
galera, 151
ganao, 237
ganar, 49
gandul, 61
ganso, 49
García, 8
garduña, 31
garra, 8
gastar, 50
gato, 12, 96, 217
gavilla, 12
ge, 103
ge, gi, evolution of, 91,
    95, 159 ff., 222, 227
Genil, 162
gente, 91
germanía, 163, 217
Gibraltar, 58
giganta, 202
gilada, 214
Giménez, 161
gobernar, 18
godo, 48
gofes, 239
golpe, 17
Gonçaluo, 94; Gon-
    zalo, 50, 94
gordo, 29
gramática, 19
grava, 12
grave, 207
greña, 12
gris, 50
grulla, 233
grupo, 50
gruya, 233
Guadalajara, 59
Guadalquivir, 59
Guadalupe, 59
guadañar, 50
Guadarrama, 59
guante, 50
guañir, 50
guapo, 31, 177
guardar, 50
guardilla, 96

guarecer, 50
guarir, 50
guarismo, 61
guarnecer, 50
guarnir, 50
guerra, 50
güerta -o, 238, 239
güevo, 238
guía, 50
guijarra -o, 8
guiñar, 50
guisa, 50
gulpeja, 96

h, orthographical, 3
    81, 163, 232
habemos, 240
haber, in expression
    time, 127
haber de, 171
hablá, 166, 201
hablábades, 166
hablad, 201
hablado > hablau,
hablalde, 166
hablale, 232; hablal
    116, 166; hablal-
    232
hablar, 30
hablau, 201, 236
hablistán, 234
haçer, 160
hacer mala orilla, 2
hacha, 50
haiga, 112, 240
hamaca, 151
hambre, 98; hambre
    calagurritana, 22
hamelgo, 234
haraute, 90
haré, 115
harina, 88
hasta, 61
he (< habeo), 112
he (as in he aquí), 6
he (< fe), 88
hei, 111

hemos, heis, 115
hente, 163, 232
hereje, 131
hería, 237
hermanía, 163
(h)ermano, 91
hermoso, 30
Hernán, 87
hi (< he), 225
(h)ía, (h)ie, etc. <
  había, etc., 116
hiciendo, 240
hiedra, 81
hielo, 81
hiempre, 162
hierba, 81
higo, 93
hilo, 90
(h)iniesta, 91
(h)inojo, 91
hiperestesia, 19
historia, 18
holgorio, 90
horma, 90
hormazo, 29
horro, 61
hove, 114
hoz (< falcem), 84;
  hoz (< faucem), 84
hube, 114
hubiámos < hubiéa-
  mos, 238
huego, 88
huelga, 90, 234
huera, 88
huerta -o, 102
huerza, 232
(h)uesa, 49
hueso, 81
huéspede, 88
huevo, 81
huguemos, 163
hule, 151
humera, 218, 234
humillar, 37, 97
huracán, 151
Hurdes (Las), 90

-ía (< -ibam), 94, 113
-iba, 240
-ico, 225
idiota, 150
-ie (< ía), 101, 222
iglesia, 18
igreja, 163
iguana, 151
ijada, 176, 210
-ín, -ino, 223
Inacia, 238
incómodo, 150
indino, 238
ineto, 144
ínfimo, 141
ingeniar, 150
inorancia, 238
insolencia, 150
intérvalo, 219
Íñigo, 8
ir + inf., ir a + inf., 171;
  ir a por agua, etc., 236
iredes, 109
i(s), 223
-ísimo, 41, 207
-ismo, 215
issie, 79
-ista, 215
i(y) (< et), 107, 190
i(y) (< hic or ibi), 105
izquierdo, 8

j, evolution of, 91, 95,
  159 ff., 222, 227
jabón, 49, 93, 162
jabonatriz, 214
Jalapa, 159, 177
jalea, 193
jamás, 92
jamelgo, 90, 234
jamón, 131
jamuga, 12
jaqueca, 60
jaques, 163
jaquet, 194
jardín, 131
jarope, 61

jarretera, 194
jarro, 229
jasé, 237
jasienda, 232
jaula, 131, 193
Javier, 8, 161
jayán, 131
jazmín, 60
jefe, 193
jeme, 162
jente, 190
Jerez, 229
jerga, 162
jícara, 151, 185
jiempre, 162
jilguero, 162
Jiménez, 161
jimio, 162
jineta, 176, 210
jitomate, 151
jofaina, 60
jolgorio, 90
jondo, 232
jónico, 92
jota, 92
Juaquín, 236
juar, 238
jubilar, 150
judgar > juzgar, 237
judío, 91
juéramos, 232
juerga, 90, 234
juerza, 232
juete, 95
jueves, 91, 102
juicio, ju(u)izio, 94
jumera, 234
jumo, 232
junio, 91
Junqueira, 68
junta, 92
jurar, 169
Jurdes (Las), 90
juzgado, 177

kilogramo, 19, 212;
  kilógramo, 219

l: evolution of initial, 222, 226; evolution of final, 232
'l, 100
l' < le, 104, 237
la(s), 100, 103, 202
labor, 101
labrar, 31
lacayo, 59
laceria, 18
lacio, 92
ladino, 56
lagarto, 176
lago, 93
laísta, 202
lamer, 99
lancha, 151
lanza, 12
lastar, 49
lauxa, 68
lazo, 176
ld < dl, 111
le(s), 100, 201; le = les, 103
lea, 112
Lebrija, 96
lechuga, 85
legua, 12
leiga, 212
leísta, 201
leite, 68
lejos, 85
lenguage, 131
leña, 102; leño, 97, 102
León, 23
Lérida, 22
lesonja, 131
letra, 86; letra francesa, 69, 79
lezna, 158
lj, evolution of, 97, 223, 226
li(s), 100, 227
libra, 212
librete, 132
lición, 97
lienzo, 85

lieva, 97
ligero, 193
limón, 60
linaje, 132
linde, 102
lindo, 31, 143
lintel, 96
lisonja, 50, 131
listo, 50
lívido, 214
lo(s), 100, 103, 201, 223, 227
lo + adjective or adverb, 127
lobo, 155
loco, 31
loísta, 201
loma, 102; lombo, 223; lomo, 102
lonja, 50
losa, 12
lueo, 95
lunes, 102
lur(es), 227
luto, 97
luva, 50

-ll < -rl, 116
llama (< flammam), 92
llama (< Quechua), 151
llamar, 92
llano, 92
llave, 92, 233
llegar, 31
lleno, 35
lleña, 222
lli(s), 223
llobu, 222
llugero, 233

m' < me, 104, 237
madeja, 18
madre, 193
Madri(z), 237
madrugar, 30

maes, mais, mayes,
maestro, 95
maguer, 209; magu[
rista, 209
maguey, 151
Mahón, 95
maison, 132
maíz, maiz, 151, 2
majestad, 92
majo, 31
mama, mamá, 193
manejar, manejo, 1
manía, 18
maniquises, 239
manjar, 132
mansalva (a), 86
manteca, 8
manto, 29
manzana, manzan[
102
maña, 18
maña, maño, 225
mapa, 12
máquina, 18
mar, 102, 143
maravedí, 53, 58
maravilla, 86
marca, 50
margen, 102
Mari, 87, 241
marío, 237
marroquí, 58
martelo, 150
'martes, 102
más, 31, 95
mas, 171
masà, 17
mas que, 171
mata, 12
matao, 237
matar, 61
mate, 151
Matilde, 50
mayor, 92
mayoradgo > may[
razgo, 132
mazmorra, 59

meaja, 95
Medinaceli, 59
medir, 30
mejón, 239
melindrizar, 214
melitar, 236
membrar, 98
membrillo, 30
méndigo, 219
mensage, mensaie, 78, 132
menudo, 93
merendar, 29
mesmo, 236
mestenco, 176
mestro, 236
Mexicano, México, 161
mezquino, 61
mi, 86; míe, 101, 223; mio, 223
miá < mira, 238
miaja, 238
mico, 151
microparasitología, 19
miedo, 30
miércoles, 102
milgrana, mingrana, minglana, 96
millón, 151
mimbre, 102
minio, 8
mintieron, 85
mirai, 111
miste, 238
mistó (de), 217
moa, 237
mochacho, 236
modorra, 8
mohadas, 163; mohar, 163
mojar, 97
mojicón, 151
momia, 61
mon(t), 88
Moncayo, Monforte, 88
monís, monises, 210
monje, 132

mono, 61
morón, 8
morremos, 115
mos, 240
mostrar, 37
mostrenco, 170
mouer, 155
mozárabe, 56
mu, 236
muchacho, 31
mucho, 97
muert, 83
muga, 8
muher, 163
mui, 190
mujé, 232; mujer, 37
muñuelo, 96
murcigalo, murciélago, 30
murió, 85
muy, 86
muyer, 223

ná (< náa < nada), 237
nada, 106
nadi(e), nadien, naide, naidie(n), 106
nadir, 61
naguas, 151
naipe, 96
napo, 227
naranja, 60
natura, 143
nava, 8
Navarra, 8
nd < dn, 111
Nebrija, 96
necio, 99
neglisé, 194
neuritis, 19
Niebla, 23
niervo, 234
nieta, 37
nimbla, 98, 105
niño gótico, 48
no (redundant), 121, 170

no bien, 171
noch, 87; noche, 85
nohotros, nojotros, 162
nol, 103
nopal, 151
noria, 60
norte, 50
nosotros, 162
novela, novelar, 150
nuca, 61
nuef, 87
Núñez, 93

ñeso, 77
ñeto, 77

o (< aut), 84, 107, 207, 208
o (interjection), 207
o (final) > u, 222
Oaxaca, 159, 161
obispo, 18
objeto, 97, 150
obnoxio, 150
Obra de romanos, 25
obreta, 142
observación, observar, 150
océ, 167
océano, oceano, 35
octubre, 30
odredes, 111
oeste, 50
of(f), 87
oído, 117
oído, oír, 207
oigo, 112
ojalá, 61
ojepto, 239
ojo, 85
ola, 12
Olalla, 97
olear, 214
ombre, 144
omenaje, 132
omne, 106
-on < -ieron, 240

ora, 209
orden, 102
oreja, 98, 163
-oren, 223
orgía, 18
orgullo, 49, 50
-oron, 223, 227
orrible, 144
ortografía, 150
os, disappearance of,
239
oscuro, 190
-oso, 214
osté, 236
ostrogodo, 48
otri(e), otri, otrie(n),
otro, 106
ove, oviera, 114
oya, oyo, 112

pa, 238
Pablos, 102
pachorra, 8
paderes, 239
padre, 193
pácce, 238
pacz, 222
pahería, 163
pahta(h) > pastas, 162
paice, 238
paire, 111
país, pais, 35
pájaro, 101, 162
paje, 132
pajolero, 218
palafré, 132
palanca, 17
palombar, 223
pampa, 151
panarra, 8
pantógrafo, 18
papa, papá, 193
papa (< Quechua),
151
papiro, pápiro, 219
paquete, 218
parada, 176

paradoja, 150
paraíso, 18.
páramo, 9
para que, 171
pardo, 96
parecer, 99
pareces, parece, etc.,
158
paréntesis, 150
paresca, 144; paresco,
158; parezco, 158
parienta, 202
parlar, 181
parra, 31
part, 87
pastelizar, 214
pastors, 227
patata, 151
pauta, 97
páxaro, 162, 185
peçe, 99
peçes, 157
pecho, 85
pedante, 150
peine, 97
Peiro, 111
peje, 99
pelo, 35
pensar de + inf., 133
peón, 93
peque, 241
Per(o), 87
Pérez, 93
perfecto, perfeto, 97
período, periodo, 35
périto, 219
pero, 171
perras chicas, perras
gordas; perros chicos,
perros gordos, 213
perro, 31
persuadir, persuasión,
150
petaca, 151
petate, 151
pez, 85, 99, 157
pichón, 194

(piedra de) ijada, 1
pieira, 111
pienssan, 95
pieza, 12
piloto, 151
pinole, 151
piña, 37
pior, 236
pirraca, 218
pisaverde, 218
pitorro, 8
pizarra, 8
pl, cl, fl, evolution o
92, 222, 227
plantáin, 68
plática, 96
playa, 18
plaz, 108
plogue, 114
plomo, 99
plugue, 114
plus, 40
poco, 84
podenco, 31
podré, 115
poema, 19
polaco, 211
poli, 241
pongo, 112
Ponpeyo, 81
porfía, 30
porque, 171
prebo, 83
predicar, predigar, 9
preguntar, 31
presbítero, 18
preso, 117
priado, 94
priesa, 84
primer, 86; primero
85, 172
primor, 184
prisa, 84
prometer, 169; pro-
meter de + inf.,
171
provecho, 93

pruebo, 83
psicoterapia, 19
psiquiatría, 19
puchero, 30
pué, 237
puée, 237
puente, 93, 102
puesto que, 171
pulítica, 236
puma, 151
puré, 210

qual, 144
quan, 227
quanto, 144
quatro, 144
qué = por qué, 172
quedai, 111
queiso, 85
quejar, 185
quel, 104
querer, 31
queso, 85
qui, 106, 227
quien(es), 106, 166
quier, 222
quijo, 162
quilate, 59
química, 19
quina, 151
quintal, 59, 212
Quiñónez, 161
quió, 238
Quixote, 159
quizá, 158

-ra, verb form in, 123–
    125, 169, 203, 224
rabeja, 163
raja, 98
ralo, 96
rambla, 98
Ramiro, 50
rápido, 86
raudo, 86, 238
rayo, 37
reata, 176

rede, 88
redoma, 31
reflersión, 238
reina, 34
reír, reído, 207
reja, 98
repintrá, 115
res, 61
respeto, 97
ría, 102
Ricardo, 50
rico, 50
rigulá(r), 236
río, 94, 102
ritmo, 17
rl > ll, 116; rl >l,
    227, 232; rl > l-l,
    232
robar, 50
roca, 12
rodio, 19
Rodrigo, 50
rojo, 162
ropa, 50
rostro, 31
roxo, 162
rubíes, 239
rueca, 50
ruido, 95
Ruiz, 93

s' < se, 104, 237
sábana, 86
sabana, 151
sabe, 177
sabré, 115
sahumar, 31
sais, 236
saldrá, 115
salgo, 112
salú(z), 237
salvest, 87
San(t), 86
San Çaluador, 155
Sánchez, 93
sandía, 60
sangne, sangre, 96

Santander, 102
Santiago, 63, 103
Santi Yagüe, 103
sapo, 8
saqué, 194
sarga, 162
sarna, 8
sarro, 8
satisfación, 238
sayagués, 221
sayo, 12, 95
sayón, 49
sé, 112
-se, verb form in, 125–
    126, 169, 203
sefardíes, 153
Segorbe, 11
semejar, 97
-semi, 162
semos, 240
sendos, 214
señá, 238
señorito de ciento en
    boca, 218
sepa, 85
ser, 128, 169, 204
sergente, 132
servitud, 150
seseo, 230
seso, 31
Setúbal, 8
Sevilla, 23
sey, 113
si, sí, 207
sí (< sibi), 94
siella, 222
siempre, 162
silguero, 162
simio, 162
sin < así + me, 105
siñor, 237
sirvienta, 202
so (< sum), 111
so (< suum), 127, 223
sofás(es), 239
soi, 77, 190
sol, 35

solacio, 150
soldado, 20, 150
soneto, 150
sopa, 50
sope, 114
sove, 114
soy, 112
spleen, 210
súa, súe, 223
sucio, 33
supe, 114
superstición, 150
supusiendo, 240
sur, 50
sus, 240

t' < te, 104, 237
tabaco, 151
tábano, 29
tabarra, 8
tabarro, 8
tacaño, 60
tahona, 60
Tajo, 59
taladro, 12
taleca, 227
tamal, 151
tamaño, 143
tambor, 59
tamién, 99, 238
tamiz, 12
tanda, 151
tango, 212
Tarragona, 23
tarro, 8
tascar, 49
-teis, -tes, 166
telegrafía, 18
telégrama, 219
telescopio, 18
temblar, 98
temeridad, 150
templo, 234
tendré, tenrré, terné,
   115
tener de, 171
tengo, 112

tenito, 227
tercer, 87; tercero, 37
termómetro, 19
testerudo, 86
Texas, 161
theta, 157, 230, 231
tiatro, 34
tiburón, 151
tiemplo, 234
tien, 88, 108
tieso, 117
tigeras, tijeras, 160
tilde, 102
tío, 18
tiranizar, 150
tirar, 31
tixera(s), 160, 162
tiza, 151
tizne, 102
to (< tuum), 127, 223
tó (< tóo < todo),
   237
toalla, 50
toca, 8
toldo, 49
tomar, 31
tona, 12
tonterida, 237
tóo, 237
tornados, 143
tornar, 133, 176
toronja, 60
torpe, 31
toto, 68
toveldo, 105
trai, 34
traigo, 112
trasponer, 190
tratar, 97
traya, trayo, 112
treato, 239
trébole, 88
tregua, 50
treitoira, 222
tribu, 87
Trini, 241
tronada, 176

truhán, 12
truje, 236
tú, 167, 168; túa, tú
   223
tuétano, 31
tumba, 17
tuna, 151
tunarra, 8

u, 107, 208
uço, 99
-uco, 223
-udo, 117
uesa, 49
ugier, 193
uhté < usted, 232
ujier, 191, 193
un(o), 40, 86
urraca, 8
usaje, 132
usía, 209
usier, 193
uso, 158
usted, 167, 168, 234
   239
uviesse, 114

vacida, 237
vaho, 31
vaiga, 112
vaina, 34
vais, vamos, 169
val, 87
vala, valo, 112
Valdemoro, 88
Valdepeñas, 88
Valera, 85
valgo, 112
Valverde, 87
varón, 50
vasallo, 12
vaya, 112
váyamos, 219
ve, 208
vea, 112
vega, 8
veiga, 112

velar, 95
Velásquez, Velázquez, 93, 158
vendelo, 232; vendel-lo, 232
vendré, venrré, verné, 98
vendría, 116
venganza catalana, 66
vengo, 112
vení, 232
vergel, 132
vi, 208, 240
vía, 236
vianda, 132
vicuña, 151
vien, 108, 222
viernes, 102
viéspera, 84
víspera, 84
viví, vivi, 111
vivides, 109
viviemos, 110
viviéssedes, 166
viviredes, vivirés, viviréis, 109
vivís, 109
vivredes, 115
vo, 111
volver que vuelva, (al), 172
vos, 167–168, 209
vosotros, 168, 234, 239

vuesa erced, vuesa merced, vuestra merced, 167
vulpeja, 96

x, evolution of, 144, 159 ff., 222, 226, 238
xabón, 162
Xalapa, 159
Xavier, 8, 161
xélu, 222
Xenil, 162
Xerez, 159, 176
Xicoténcatl, 159
Ximena, 159
Ximénes, 161
Xochicalco, 159
Xochimilco, 159
Xomburg, 161
Xuanín, 222

y, antihiatic, 223, 226, 233
y(i) (< et), 107
y(i) (< hic or ibi), 105
ya (< Arabic ?), 133
yace, 91
yamás, 92
ŷave, 233
ye, yera, yes, 223, 227
yedra, 81
yeísmo, 98, 232, 233
yelmo, 50
yelo, 81

yenáir, 68
yendo que yuamos, 172
yent(e), 87, 91
yerbá, 81
Ygnacio, 77
Ynés, 77
yod, effect of, 85, 222, 226, 237
Ysabel, 77
yuguero, 233
yunta, 92

zafiro, 158
zaga, 59
zagal, 61
zaguán, 60
zahondar, 158
zahorí, 58
zalamero, 61
zamarra, 8
zambo, 176
zanahoria, 60
zaquizamí(s), 58, 239
Zaragoza, 23, 59
zaragüelles, 60
žave, 233
Zocodover, 59
zodíaco, 17
zorra, 8
zurcir, 158
zurdo, 31
zutano, 61